SCHOOL OF
ORIENTAL AND AFRICAN STUDIES
UNIVERSITY OF LONDON

Administration and Politics in a Nepalese Town

Administration and Politics in a Nepalese Town

THE STUDY OF A
DISTRICT CAPITAL AND
ITS ENVIRONS

LIONEL CAPLAN

*Reader in Anthropology with reference to South Asia
at the School of Oriental and African Studies,
University of London*

LONDON
OXFORD UNIVERSITY PRESS
BOMBAY   NEW YORK   TORONTO
1975

Oxford University Press, Ely House, London W.1

GLASGOW NEW YORK TORONTO MELBOURNE WELLINGTON
CAPE TOWN IBADAN NAIROBI DAR ES SALAAM LUSAKA ADDIS ABABA
DELHI BOMBAY CALCUTTA MADRAS KARACHI LAHORE DACCA
KUALA LUMPUR SINGAPORE HONG KONG TOKYO

ISBN 0 19 713585 4

© *Lionel Caplan 1975*

*Printed in Great Britain
by W. & J. Mackay Limited, Chatham*

To the memory of my brother,
Sydney Caplan

Contents

Tables

Preface

This is an anthropological study of a small township, which serves as the administrative capital and market centre of a district in the far western hills of Nepal. It traces the effects of currents, both national and international, on certain social institutions and relationships in the town, and on the traditional links between townspeople and villagers in the surrounding countryside.

The data here presented were gathered during the course of a year's fieldtrip in 1969.

In the Nepalese capital, my work was facilitated by the authorities of Tribhuvan University, who approved and encouraged the research project, and arranged for the necessary travel documents to be granted. While preparing for and during breaks from fieldwork I was able to enjoy the delightful surroundings and excellent facilities provided by the Nepal Research Center, and I have to thank its director Professor Dr. W. Hellmich of Munich University, and Mr. G. B. Kalikote, the Center's warden in Kathmandu, for their kind hospitality.

In Belaspur Bazaar, the locus of this study, officials at every level of the district administration were unfailingly helpful. I express my gratitude to them, as well as to the inhabitants of the town itself, who made me welcome in their midst. Equally helpful and cooperative were the many people I met from the surrounding villages who came regularly to work in or visit the town.

I record my gratitude to two young residents of the area, Sri Biswo Bandhu Thapa and Sri Khagendra Bahadur Malla, who acted as my assistants at various stages of the work.

My thanks are also due to Professors Christoph von Furer-Haimendorf, Adrian Mayer and Abner Cohen, and to Dr. David Parkin who were generous enough to read and criticize different versions of the manuscript. I am especially grateful to my wife, Dr. Patricia Caplan, who shared the field experience, and, despite a busy research and writing programme of her own, contributed in manifold ways to the preparation of this book.

I am much beholden to the School of Oriental and African Studies which granted the necessary study leave and financing to enable me to undertake fieldwork in Nepal. I would like, in particular, to acknowledge the many kinds of help and encouragement received from the Secretary, Mr. J. Bracken and Assistant Secretary, Mr. M.

Gatehouse, during an illness which forced me to interrupt my work and return to Kathmandu for treatment and a period of convalescence. Finally, I express my appreciation to the School for meeting the cost of publication of this study.

Lionel Caplan
February, 1975

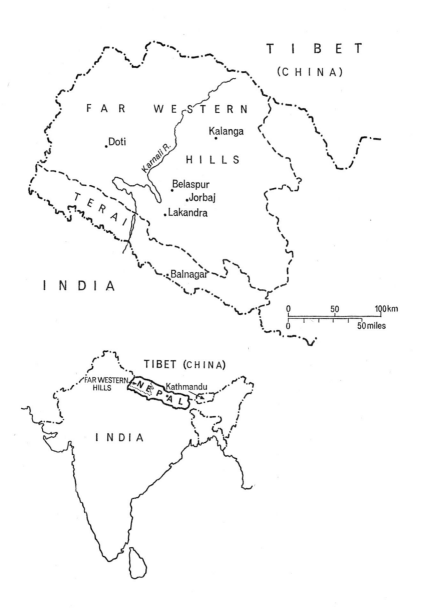

1

Introductory

THIS book, about an administrative centre in the far western hills of Nepal lies, in a manner of speaking, in the vague borderland between rural and urban studies. Belaspur Bazaar, the pseudonym of the settlement, is not quite a village, nor yet, some might argue, a town.

In Nepal, the sole census criterion for an 'urban' designation is size, i.e., a population of 5,000 or more inhabitants. In 1952–4, when the country held its first census using modern enumeration techniques, only ten settlements contained more than this number: half of these were in the Valley of Kathmandu, and the remainder were in the terai, a belt of plains forming the kingdom's southern border with India. By 1961, although the nation's population had increased by approximately one million to a total of some 10 millions, there were still no 'urban' localities in the hills, which contained well over half the country's inhabitants. Officially, then, the vast majority of Nepal's district capitals, including Belaspur Bazaar, because they contain fewer than 5,000 inhabitants, are regarded as 'villages'.

In India, considerably more attention has been devoted to the definition of a town, although after surveying the census history of the last six decades Bose (1964) is not convinced that a satisfactory conclusion has been reached. Whereas in 1901 the primary consideration was the administrative designation of a place, by 1921, census superintendents were asked to examine the 'character' of the population, the relative density of the dwellings, the importance of the place as a centre of trade and its historic associations' (ibid: 86). Three decades later a town was assumed to have a population of 5,000 or more, although superintendents were given discretion to exclude villages which had exceeded that size, and to include localities with less than this number, provided they exhibited some 'urban characteristics'. The 1961 census while retaining this ambiguous condition, applied more rigorous criteria of density and occupation, as well as an already established minimal population.

The result of this attempt to circumscribe the area of individual discretion and render a more uniform definition was a reduction in the number of recorded towns with a population of under 5,000 from 638 in 1951 to 266 in 1961. (Indeed, those with a population of between 5,000 and 10,000 fell by a similar number.)

Sjoberg is no less vague in his characterization of an urban community, although he has written extensively and with great authority on various aspects of the subject (see, for example, Sjoberg 1960). As distinguished from a rural community, he suggests, it 'is characterized by larger size, greater density and heterogeneity, and the presence of a significant number of full-time specialists . . . engaged in a relatively wide range of non-agricultural activities' (1969:220). Rather than a categorical definition we have here an invitation to perceive the town in contrast to the village. Fox endorses this approach in his study of a market centre in north India with a population of some 7,000 persons. He writes: 'The organization of trade and traders, the physical morphology of shop and market area, the ties of commerce and credit to rural localities all demarcate (the market centre) from surrounding population clusters. These institutions have defined and still do define the town as an urban area with a characteristic style of life and social pattern' (1969:viii).

For reasons to do with its administrative and commercial importance, and the economic concerns of its inhabitants, Belaspur Bazaar may similarly be seen to contrast starkly with its rural surroundings. Moreover, it is perceived by those who live there—'bazaariyas'—as well as by villagers, as distinct and opposed to the settlements which surround it. In these senses, then, the bazaar, although it contains a population of just under 1,000 persons, may be regarded as an urban locale.

It is one purpose of this book to contribute to the study of such small townships which, despite their ubiquity and obvious significance, have been almost totally neglected by sociologists working in South Asia. With a few notable exceptions (Karve and Ranadive 1965; Sinha 1968; Fox 1969) they have concentrated their investigations on villages, or, where inclined to problems of urbanization, have tended to focus on the larger cosmopolitan cities of the subcontinent.

One feature of small urban settlements which has been noted is their 'rural' character. Abrahams, in a brief discussion of a district capital in East Africa with a population of 1,500 people, notes how many of the inhabitants still depend on cultivation for a livelihood, and remarks that it is 'not fully developed as a town' (1961:253).[1]

Indeed, the relatively high proportion of population engaged in agricultural pursuits has led some urban geographers in India, who have devoted more effort than any other category of social scientist to the study of small towns, to refer to them as 'rurban' centres (Singh, R. L. and Singh, S. M. 1960). On the basis of a number of studies, the conclusion seems to be that in towns with a population of under 20,000 a higher proportion of inhabitants rely on agriculture than do residents of larger cities (see K. N. Singh 1959; Janaki and Sayed 1962).[2]

But a simple gauge of population size and occupational distribution masks certain important differences in the processes of town formation, and so the manner in which this 'rurban' character may be acquired. Many small townships in India, for example, would appear to have attracted their populations mainly from the immediate hinterlands which would imply the retention by immigrant settlers of at least some interest in land and cultivation (see Karve and Ranadive 1965). Others, however, were founded as strategic centres (see Gillion 1968). District capitals in the mountains of Nepal, if my data on Belaspur Bazaar are at all typical, were formed on this latter basis as well. Their very creation was an outgrowth, not of any 'urbanising' tendencies within the local peasantry, but of the military and administrative needs of an expanding Gorkha empire. The kingdom of Nepal emerged during the last four decades of the eighteenth century as a consequence of the unification by conquest and alliance of all the independent and semi-independent territories within a rectangle bounded roughly by Tibet, the Gangetic plain of India, Sikkim and Kumaon. To secure the new state the ascendant Shah monarch of Gorkha created a series of fortifications at strategic points throughout the kingdom, around which an embryonic administrative structure arose. Belaspur Bazaar was one such emplacement, and by the time of the Rana coup in the mid-nineteenth century, by which this prominent lineage usurped the power of the monarchy, the bazaar had become a district capital and the commercial focus of the area. Moreover, it drew its original inhabitants not from the surrounding countryside but more distant parts. They came either as part of the official or personal entourages of senior administrators sent from the nation's capital, or in the case of certain 'untouchable' groups, to provide specialist services for the military garrison. Many, for a variety of reasons, then remained to settle in the township. They entered commerce, continued to work in the local administration, or, in the case of craftsmen, provide their services to a wider public. The immigration of peasants from the near hinterland began much later, indeed only during the past 50 years or so.

Thus, for well over a century, bazaariyas were almost wholly engaged in non-agricultural occupations, and only in recent years have they become substantial landowners and cultivators. This development, then, alongside the influx of people from surrounding villages who retained their stake in agriculture, has given the town a 'rural character' it did not previously possess.

Fledgling towns have also been viewed by some as mediatory in nature. Karve and Ranadive suggest that they play an important role between the 'extremes' of the metropolitan areas and the rural society (1965:114). Middleton, too, singles out as a special category of African towns ('Type C') the small trading and administrative centres which 'provide the main loci for the dissemination of external influence to the rural areas. . . .' (1966:34). Certainly, Nepalese peasants from the countryside are brought into contact with officials of the district administration in Belaspur Bazaar, who communicate and interpret the central authority's goals and policies; they observe technical 'experts' using typewriters, operating wireless apparatus, or giving smallpox innoculations; they hear the discourses of senior administrators, full of allusions to unfamiliar places and events, see the clothes they wear and the games they play; wonder at the range of imported consumer goods available in the bazaar's shops; scan the magazines, newspapers and books available in its tiny library: in these and other ways local peasants are introduced to a world far beyond their traditional horizons.

But a small urban centre does not simply function as the channel through which national and international currents are disseminated to isolated areas: it is itself affected by these very currents. To understand the nature of social change in this remote township we are compelled to refer to events which have occurred and decisions which have been taken outside the community under examination.

The period of Rana rule which began in 1846 imposed on the country almost total isolation from the outside world, the outcome of which was technological standstill and a stagnant, if stable, society. The overthrow of the regime in 1950–1, therefore, marks a critical watershed in the nation's history (see Chapter 8 for details of events at this time). Nepal was exposed for the first time to non-traditional influences which swept like a tidal wave over the tiny Himalayan kingdom.

This book describes and analyses the process by which they have impinged on institutions and social relationships within a small town, and affected the links between townspeople and villagers.

The changing nature of bazaariya-peasant interaction can be summarized briefly. In the years of Rana rule relations were essentially organic, inasmuch as their economic and political interests were, on the whole, distinct and complementary. Villagers relied almost totally on subsistence agriculture for their livelihood, while residents of the district capital (save for a number of untouchable craftsmen) depended on employment in the lower ranks of the district administration, which were the only levels accessible to inhabitants of the area, and monopolised the bazaar's incipient commercial life; their association with cultivation activities was, as I have noted, tentative. Politically, as well, there were no contexts in which these two categories of the population competed with one another.

Since 1951, a major programme of economic development, much of it financed by foreign aid, has resulted, among other things, in a proliferation of educational facilities, improvements in transport and communications, better health care, the effective eradication of malaria, and a host of other technical innovations which have, in varying degree and magnitude, touched most small-scale communities throughout Nepal. To implement such a programme has necessitated a considerable expansion and comprehensive reform of the country's administrative system. From the small, highly personalistic Rana administration concerned primarily with the maintenance of law and order and the collection of land revenues, the Nepalese civil service has grown into a large organization following bureaucratic procedures and dealing with the myriad problems of a changing society. For residents of the district capital and its environs this has created unprecedented economic opportunities of two main kinds. First of all, the increase of administrative activities, by channelling relatively large sums of money into the region, has contributed directly to the growth of opportunities for commerce in the bazaar. Moreover, it has rendered financially attractive the ownership of buildings in the town for rental to government offices, non-resident civil servants and shopkeepers. Secondly, it has enhanced employment prospects in the district administration, and, especially, allowed local people for the first time to pursue secure and lucrative careers as high-ranking civil servants.

These possibilities, coupled with a series of government land reforms setting limits on agricultural holdings, have led many affluent villagers to enter for the first time the traditional occupational preserves of townspeople. In increasing numbers they have sought posts at the higher levels of the administration, purchased property in the town, and become merchants, without, however, surrendering their village homes or lands. Townsmen have been no less quick to take advantage of these new opportunities, but partly in response to these peasant incursions, they have also begun to increase their holdings of land. To meet this growing commitment to agriculture, and at the same time exploit fully the expanded benefits available in commerce and government service, townsmen are having to make adjustments in their traditional household organization.

What is clear is that these macro-developments in the post-Rana period have resulted in less occupational differentiation between townsmen and at least some villagers. Of special importance, relations of interdependence have been transformed into those characterised by intense competition.

Townsmen and villagers now confront one another politically as well, primarily within contexts defined externally, first by political parties, and latterly by the structure of elected councils or 'panchayats'.

Without negating the dynamic of forces internal to the society, then, social change in and around this small township in the far western hills of the kingdom may be understood primarily as a response to exogenous factors.

In an important sense, this book is a companion piece to my previous analysis of Hindu-tribal relations in rural eastern Nepal (L. Caplan 1970). For that, too, was concerned to demonstrate the importance of considering how currents and events in the wider society impinge on the small-scale community. But while the kinds of post-Rana developments noted in these paragraphs have also contributed to shaping the relations between the tribal Limbu and their Hindu co-villagers, other catalysts such as government land policy and 'Gurkha' army service, which are irrelevant in the present context, were identified as of primary significance in the former study. This is not to say that conditions in eastern Nepal are fundamentally different from those west of Kathmandu, but that in examining change in a particular setting, we abstract from the complexity of social phenomena only the most important causal factors (Ginsberg 1958).

I have spoken of villagers as an undifferentiated category, but an important theme of this study concerns the highly selective manner in which the benefits of externally-induced changes already noted are distributed among the population. A concept utilized by urban geographers to identify the variety and intensity of links between town and countryside is relevant here. They plot the area an urban locale serves and is served by, and so delineate what has variously been called an 'urban field', 'catchment area', or 'umland' (see R. L. Singh 1955). It is asked, for example, how large a section of hinterland a town's educational or medical facilities serve, from how far away its peasant suppliers or customers originate, and so on.[3] Thus, Janaki and Sayed (1962) note how the primary zone of influence of a town in western India extends for a distance of some ten miles by road, beyond which another zone of diminishing influence can be delineated.

That portion of the wider hinterland with which Belaspur Bazaar interacts most intensively is, for reasons to do with the lack of motorized transport in the western mountains, confined to those villages within a two–three hour walk of the town—this is the maximum time villagers are able to spend journeying daily to and from the bazaar. Of special relevance for the present discussion, the principal challenge to the traditional occupational monopoly as well as the political ambitions of townsmen has come not only from the wealthier segment of the peasantry, but, in spatial terms, from the category of villagers resident in this 'umland'. It is townsmen and their immediate neighbours, therefore, who are the principal competitors for the new opportunities and benefits available locally.

Because of its proximity to the town and the educational facilities there, and a series of historical circumstances which conferred substantial wealth and prominence on a number of its inhabitants, one rural settlement, called Bhuka, has been in the forefront of village economic encroachment on the town and has provided its main political opposition. The consideration of town–village relations is essentially a discussion of the confrontation between members of these two communities.

The significance of an administrative presence in the town cannot be over-emphasized. I have already noted the bazaar's genesis as an administrative centre, and hinted at the manifold ways in which it affects directly the lives of those resident in and around the district capital. Insofar as this study attempts to assess the implications for local people of the administration in their midst, it can be set apart from others concerned with small towns whose principal function is trade or commerce. In view of the virtual absence of sociological studies of administrative centres,[4] this book, willy-nilly, breaks new ground. Further, in the light of the obvious importance of the public sector in general and the public service in particular as a 'source of status, wealth, prestige, and security' in so many of the new states of Asia and Africa (see Scott 1972:12–13), this discussion will, it is hoped, have relevance beyond a remote region in the Nepalese mountains.

Although social scientists have written extensively about the nature of public administration, its relation to political structures and to stages of development, its links with elites, and so forth, their approach has been holistic, and their conclusions of the macro-political and sociological kind (see, for example, Riggs 1964; Heady 1966; Tung Tsu Chu 1962). The anthropologist, working at the very base of an administrative organization in the midst of a small-scale society must ask a different set of questions: What is the extent and economic importance of government service for local people? How do they obtain and hold on to their jobs? What are the implications for prospective employees of greater bureaucratization of the civil service? What are the consequences for the household of a locally-resident civil servant of his transfer away from home?

Other questions might relate to the political concomitants of government service. Anthropologists concerned with bureaucracies in colonial Africa focussed on certain key structural positions—mainly those of chiefs or headmen—and stressed their dilemma in the face of conflicting demands and even ethical systems brought to bear by administrative superiors, on the one hand, and tribal followers on the other. This paradigm has been challenged by Kuper (1970) who calls for greater attention to be paid to the manoeuvrability of those occupying such 'inter-calary' roles. In this connection, the present analysis of political activities looks, for one

thing, at the ways in which a whole range of locally-resident government servants turn their official positions to personal and group
advantage, and alternatively, at how politicians outside the administration utilize ties to officials, both local and outsider, in seeking to
achieve their particular aims. Attention is therefore focussed not so
much on the administration as a structure, *per se*, but on its importance for local people as a fund of valuable resources to exploit in
furtherance of their politico-economic interests. We thus go some
way toward meeting the problem of how to take account, when
studying a small community, of the presence of an organization which,
metaphorically speaking, lies outside that community.

In the broadest sense, this book deals with the transformation of
small-scale into large-scale society. Most commonly, anthropological
studies of 'incorporation' processes have focussed on the integration
and absorption of diverse ethnic entities into colonial and post-
colonial states (see Cohen and Middleton 1970; Bailey 1957; 1960;
Kuper and Smith 1969). In Nepal, the unification of numerous
independent and semi-independent polities into a single nation
occurred almost two centuries ago. Yet despite adherence to a
common authority, the country, because of its politico-economic
structure, remained until 1951 an amalgam of relatively discrete
face-to-face communities. The post-Rana changes already alluded
to represent, from one standpoint, therefore, an expansion of the
scale of Nepalese society, and underlining this study is the question
of how people involved in and encompassed by such a transformation
cope with its local manifestations.

The book is divided into three parts. Part One provides relevant
background on the district capital. First, Chapter 2 considers the
physical and historical setting of the town. Chapter 3 then examines
the district administration in the Rana and post-Rana periods. The
second part deals with the occupations of townsmen. Chapter 4
looks at their involvement in government service and relates this to
the nature of household organization. The following chapter dis-
cusses the economic concerns of untouchables, and notes the effects
of post-Rana developments on their relations with other castes.
Chapter 6 then traces the growth of commerce in the bazaar and
analyses the nature of shopkeeping and its significance for townsmen.
The chapter concludes with a discussion of the growing investment

in land among bazaariyas and the implications of greater occupational diversity. The final, and longest part of the book considers the relations between townsmen and villagers, especially those resident in Bhuka. Chapter 7 examines the encroachments of rural dwellers into the traditional occupations of bazaariyas, and notes the growth of hostile feelings between them. The next chapter considers the nature of their political ties, first in the Rana period and then in the immediate aftermath of the revolution which saw the coming of political parties. This is followed by a discussion of political competition between townsmen and villagers within the context of a Village panchayat (Chapter 9) and then, in Chapter 10, at the district level.

Notes to Chapter 1

1 Although it was peripheral to his main research interests, Abrahams felt compelled to 'present some facts about a very small town . . . a subject upon which little if anything, seems to have been written' (1961:242). Since he wrote, although Africanists, like their Indianist counterparts, have concentrated much attention on large urban localities (see Epstein 1967), there has been very little research in small townships. Recently, Vincent (1971) and Parkin (1972) have worked in small trading centres in East Africa.

2 In West Africa, however, even the largest cities have traditionally included a large proportion of the population engaged in agriculture (see, for example, Little 1959).

3 Cohn and Marriott (1958) have attempted, in a not dissimilar way, to note how urban centres are linked to various hinterlands according to their different functions.

4 Uberoi has, as yet, published only a preliminary report of his research on district administration in Afghanistan (1968).

Part One
The District Capital

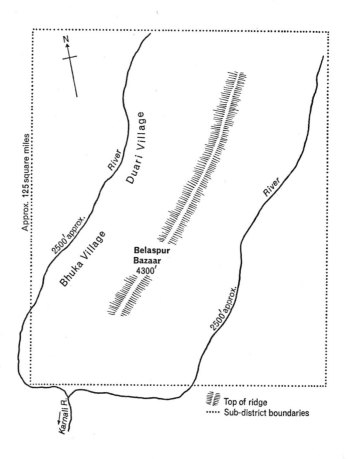

N

Approx. 125 square miles

River

Duari Village

2500' approx.

Bhuka Village

Top of ridge

Belaspur
Bazaar
4300'

River

2500' approx.

Karnali R.

░░░ Top of ridge
····· Sub-district boundaries

2

The Setting

The district

BELASPUR Bazaar is situated in the south-central part of Belaspur district, of which it is the administrative capital and market centre. The district is part of the far western hills, one of the most economically backward areas of the country. Although its population is largely reliant on agriculture, less than a quarter of the arable land in this region is irrigated, the forests below an altitude of 8000′ (where most of the population resides) have almost wholly disappeared, and poor soils combine with a low annual average rainfall (40–45″) to produce the highest per capita deficit of grain in the kingdom (Sample Census of Agriculture 1962). In the district, as throughout the far western hills, the main crops are paddy, maize, wheat and millet.

Belaspur district is not only economically handicapped, but physically isolated from the main centres of commerce and administration as well. There are no roads for motor vehicles nor any railways in the mountains of western Nepal. It is a week's journey on foot from Belaspur Bazaar to the nearest major town (which I call Balnagar) in the terai—as the low-lying plains in the south are referred to. This is the source of most manufactured goods found in the shops and homes of Belaspur district, and the immediate destination of most of its agricultural (mainly dairy) exports. Since 1967, there has been a twice-weekly plane service during the dry season (October–June) from Lakandra, a valley some 28 miles south of the bazaar, to Kathmandu via the terai (see Map 1). This has reduced considerably the hazards and difficulties of the trip to the plains for the small minority of travellers who can afford the fare. For the first time, it has brought the district, some 250 miles from Kathmandu, to within comparatively easy reach of the nation's capital. From 1950, Belaspur has also been linked by radio telegraph to the terai and Kathmandu and, from 1965, through an expanded system, to a dozen other stations. But these facilities, too, are available because of their high cost, only to the administration and the wealthiest members of the local community.

Prior to 1962, Belaspur was one of 35 districts into which the country had been partitioned in the early part of the nineteenth century. At the time of the 1961 Census it contained an area of approximately 1800 square miles, and a population of about 300,000. In 1962, a major administrative reorganization which divided the kingdom into 75 new districts reduced the area and population of what had been Belaspur by more than half; by 1969, at the time of my fieldwork, numbers in the newly bounded unit were an estimated 137,000.

The traditional division of districts into smaller units for revenue purposes was not abolished with the 1962 reorganization, although their importance has subsequently eroded as a result of alterations in the system of revenue collection (see Chapter 9). The new area of Belaspur contains six sub-districts (*dara*) and the bazaar is situated in the Simta sub-division which encompasses 125 square miles and contains approximately ten per cent of the district population. Simta comprises a ridge (running north to south) defined by rivers which surround it on three sides (south, east and west) and a section of the Mahabharat range which forms its northern boundary (see Map 2).

The district's population, like that in most parts of Nepal, may be divided into a number of caste (*jat*) groups, each of which is associated with one of three main, ranked ritual categories. At the top of the hierarchy are the 'twice-born' castes, usually referred to as *tagadhari* because they wear the 'sacred thread' of Hinduism. These are internally ranked, with the Brahmins accorded the highest status and, in western Nepal, the Joggis—mainly the offspring of ascetics who have given up their celibate lives and become 'householders'—granted the lowest.[1] The Jaisis, who are originally descended from the marriages of Brahmin men and Brahmin widows, and Thakuris, who claim Rajput ancestry and are associated with royalty (see below) both claim a place next to the Brahmins, as do certain kinds of Chetri who refuse commensal relations with all but members of this priestly caste.[2]

The groups collectively referred to as '*matwali*' or 'drinking' castes comprise the next category in the ritual hierarchy. This is the level at which Nepal's indigenous tribal groups have been absorbed into the caste system. The Newars who, in their native

Kathmandu Valley, have an elaborate system of stratified groups
(see Furer-Haimendorf 1956) are, with a single exception noted
below, classified in the Belaspur context, as a single 'drinking' caste,
although they are ranked above such tribal groups as the Magars and
Gurungs. None of these castes wears the sacred thread, but all are
regarded as ritually clean, which means that they can be served by
Brahmin priests, and that all other castes will accept water from their
hands. 'Twice-born' groups, however, will not take ritually relevant
foods (such as rice) cooked by members of 'drinking' castes.

The lowest place in the hierarchy is granted the untouchables,
who are regarded as ritually impure, so that those associated with

TABLE I

*Population of Belaspur district**

'Clean' Castes			
'Twice-born' Castes	*Approximate Nos.*	*Percentage*	
Chetri	44,900	32·8	
Thakuri	17,800	13·0	
Jaisi	14,400	10·5	
Joggi	2,600	1·9	
Brahmin	2,300	1·7	
		82,000	59·9
'Drinking' Castes			
Magar	16,200	11·8	
Gurung	1,100	·8	
Newar	500	·4	
Other	100	·1	
		17,900	13·1
'Untouchable' Castes			
Smith (Kami)	15,900	18·8	
Tailor (Damai)	6,900	5·0	
Cobbler (Sarki)	3,800	2·8	
Other†	500	·4	
		37,100	27·0
		137,000	100·0

* These figures are based on voting lists collected by the district authorities in 1969.
These provided the approximate percentages of adults in each caste and they were
then applied to the figure of total population estimated by the district authorities on
the basis of informal census data sent them by village councils. The population
figures, here taken to the nearest hundred, must therefore be regarded as extremely
tentative for a variety of reasons too obvious to mention.
† Includes Butchers (Kasai) and Muslims.

the two higher categories will accept no food or water from them nor allow them entry to their homes. Members of twice-born castes recall how, in the past, they would sprinkle water on their bodies after physical contact with an untouchable. Even now, in the bazaar, an untouchable must sit outside a tea shop and when finished with his drink, wash the glass, after which the tea shop owner drops a hot cinder into it to destroy the 'impurity'. In this area, the untouchable category includes, aside from Cobblers, Tailors and Smiths found throughout the Nepalese hills, Newar Butchers and Muslims, who are treated as a caste.[3]

Only the untouchables (excluding Muslims) and the Brahmins who serve the clean castes as family priests are associated with traditional occupations other than farming.

Table 1 gives the approximate numbers in each caste and ritual category and the percentages they represent of the total district population. Individual castes within each category are listed according to size and not rank.

Background

The area of what is now Belaspur district has been settled continuously for at least ten centuries. A plethora of extant stupas, monuments, inscribed stelae and other stone structures throughout the region attests to its inclusion in the powerful Malla empire. Built by emigrant Khas (or Khasiya) hill tribesmen from Garhwal and other Himalayan areas to the west, this empire, which emerged around the tenth century, came to rule over most of western Nepal and western Tibet until its collapse three centuries later (Tucci 1962). That part of the empire which extended over western Nepal was gradually replaced during the fourteenth century by a number of petty states established by Hindu immigrants fleeing the Muslim invasions of North India. These were divided into two main clusters: the Chaubise states (or 'group of twenty-six') to the east, and the Baise states (or 'group of twenty-two') on the west, between the Mahakali and Piuthan rivers. Much of the Belaspur region was a part of one Baise state until the mid-sixteenth century, when the latter was divided into several units, and the area in the immediate vicinity of what is now Belaspur Bazaar, became an independent state with its own ruler.

Little is known of the social organization of these principalities save that their royal families were members of Thakuri dynasties which claimed Rajput descent. However, because of the limited size of most of them, including the Belaspur polity, which extended over an area of perhaps 100 sq. miles, the status and power of the majority of such rulers, as one historian put it, 'could . . . not (have been) greater than that of a chief of a group of villages' (D. R. Regmi 1961:41). The ruler of Gorkha, however, a Chaubise state north-west of Kathmandu, was strong enough by the middle of the eighteenth century to conquer and unite into the Kingdom of Nepal all the independent and semi-independent principalities and tribal groups in the Himalayan regions between Sikkim and Kumaon, Tibet and India. This Shah dynasty still provides the monarchs of Nepal.

Belaspur, along with all the Chaubise and Baise states, fell to the Gorkha armies during the final two decades of the eighteenth century, and the rulers lost their sovereign rights in their former territories. Most, however, like the Belaspur king, were given small grants of land, called *manachamal* (literally, 'a measure of rice'), which stipulated either that they could enjoy the cultivation rights and a degree of tax relief on these lands, or that they would be assigned the taxes paid by the cultivators. Along with the latter kind of *manachamal* grant went the privilege to exact corvée, as many as 22 days a year, from each cultivator/household.[4]

These grants were designed to placate the defeated rulers and ensure their support for the new Nepalese state in its embryonic stages (M. C. Regmi 1964:21). But their descendants, called *chautariya*, were generally able to press, successfully, for the con-tinuation of these grants. The patrilineal successors of the Belaspur king, for example, retained their privileges through four generations. An excerpt from a document in the possession of the son of the last Belaspur *chautariya* sums up the succession process:

Some years ago my grandfather, D.N., was a ruler of Belaspur. When His Majesty (the Gorkha king) entered and conquered our state His Majesty made a royal proclamation granting (the right to revenues from certain) lands to D.N. After his death it was transferred to my grandmother (D.N.'s wife). After her (death) it was passed to my father, C.B. Now (because of C.B.'s death) it must be given to me, R.D.

The death of a title-holder did not automatically confer the title on his successor, but necessitated an elaborate and lengthy cor-respondence with Kathmandu before the supplicant was allowed to assume the prerogatives of *chautariya*. Almost invariably, however, before transferring a title the authorities took the opportunity to reduce somewhat the area of land within the grant, and so the amount of tax which would accrue to the grantee.

In the case of the Belaspur *chautariya*, the petitioner R.D. received the land grant, which was later given to his son, who held it until his death in 1927, at which time it was abolished. This was apparently in keeping with a policy instituted by the then Prime Minister to allow the retention of land grants only by those who were especially favoured by the Rana family which, in 1846, had succeeded in winning control of the instruments of government from the royal ruler, at the same time retaining the Monarch as a figurehead. (The Rana regime was finally ousted, and the power of the royal family restored, in 1951.) Descendants of the Belaspur *chautariya* argue that they lost their grant because they had refused to marry with the Ranas, who were Chetris and thus considered of inferior caste status.[5]

People still relate legends about the might of the former Belaspur rulers, their wars, their valour and their generosity (see P. Caplan 1972:13). But the patrilineal offspring of these men no longer enjoy any special status or position in contemporary Belaspur society, although on occasion, if the need arises, they do not hesitate to remind others of their 'aristocratic' ancestry. They are now well-to-do peasants living in a village (called Bhuka) near the bazaar, in the shadow of a hillock which is generally believed to have been the site on which the Belaspur king's palace stood. To-day there is a small temple on its otherwise desolate summit.

Growth of the town

All the evidence points to the establishment and growth of the bazaar following the incorporation of the Belaspur principality into the Nepalese state.[6] In the southern portion of the town, on a slight rise to the east of the main road, is the area's most prominent structure, a hexagonally-shaped stone fort, with a circumference of approximately 100 yards, which dominates the bazaar and surrounding region. Still used by the local garrison of the Nepalese army, it was built in the latter part of the eighteenth century by the conquering Gorkha forces as one of a series of military posts to protect the far western sector of the newly forged kingdom.

Belaspur Bazaar probably arose initially as an administrative station around the military fort, and then gradually became a small market centre as well. The development pattern of the town supports such a view for it has grown in a northerly direction from the area surrounding the fort. The earliest settlement took place in the area immediately south of the fort and along the main road as far as the town's oldest temple (to Bhairab—a 'terrible' manifestation of Shiva) which, according to documents and inscriptions, was built in the first decade of the nineteenth century. During the last quarter of the century settlement along the principal street began north of the temple, and continued as far as the public green (see Map 3). From the middle of the century the area east of the main road between the Bhairab temple and that dedicated to Narayan (Vishnu), which was built in 1878, was also opened up. The latest extension, called New Bazaar, along the main road beyond the green, was begun only in 1964, and now forms the northern end of the town.

From a distance, the dwellings of Belaspur Bazaar seem perched precariously along the top of a 4500′ ridge. They look out, on both sides, over spurs and slopes which drop steeply away from the crest of the ridge to valley floors 2000′ below, through which flow tributaries of the Karnali, one of the largest of Nepal's river systems, which eventually joins the Ganges in north India. Beyond, towards both east and west, the view is of other ranges, with their terraced slopes and scattered villages, as far as the eye can see.

In its compact settlement pattern the bazaar provides a striking contrast with the surrounding countryside of widely dispersed peasant houses and farms. Approximately 60 per cent of the 217 privately-owned dwellings in the town line both sides of the main street which averages about 25 feet in width.[7] The custom, especially in the oldest section of the bazaar, is for dwellings to be constructed against one another, with no gaps in between. A parade of houses may be broken occasionally by a small temple, a side street intersecting with the main road, or a path leading to a nearby village. Near the northern end of Old Bazaar, on the west side, the row of dwellings is interrupted by an elevated, flat, tree-lined platform of land some 75 yards in length by 25 yards in width. This serves as a parade ground and rallying point for the public on national holidays and other special communal occasions. Further north, on the east side of the main road, is the public green which, because it is partly in the shade of a magnificent pipal tree and adjacent to the district court, is a favourite point for informal meetings of bazaar residents and visitors to the town from surrounding villages, and a locus of endless discussion, argument and gossip. Other such loci are provided by a number of tea shops in the town.

The main street of the town, which stretches unbending for perhaps three-quarters of a mile, sits astride one of the principal routes from the high Himalayas to the western terai. In the autumn, with the onset of the cold season in the north, hundreds of sheep caravans pass through the bazaar on their way to warmer pastures in the valleys and plains to the south, later to be driven north again by the intense heat of spring and early summer in these regions.

Dwellings in the principal road are mostly two-storey structures of wood frame, stone and mud walls, and slate roofs, although frequently the top floor is only added some time after the bottom half has been completed. Those who erect these buildings design them, where finances allow, to contain a shop on the ground floor and residential quarters above. Of the 122 dwellings in the bazaar's principal road which are occupied (14 are empty) just under half (59) do contain shops. (Indeed, there are only four retail businesses which are not located in the main road, and these are in a street at a right angle to it.) A further nine dwellings are used for some other business purpose such as a tailor's workshop. Twelve dwellings in the principal street are wholly or partly rented as offices to the district administration, and 42 are utilized solely as residences. These latter are generally the homes of the poor, most of whom live at the southernmost tip of the bazaar.

In general, a somewhat more haphazard, less geometric pattern of house distribution is to be found at this end of the bazaar, where terrain has allowed the development of settlement areas behind the main street, on both its east and west sides. Here are also found the houses of untouchables which serve both as residences and workshops, but not retail outlets. They are similar in construction to the houses of poor villagers in that they are mainly single storey (although they may contain a loft) with a small open verandah in front. But, as opposed to village dwellings and like most houses in the bazaar's main street, they are not widely dispersed and do not have any land attached even for simple gardening purposes. The dwellings in these residential sections (*tol*) behind the main street are joined by narrow footpaths, and in the monsoon, which begins in earnest about the first of July and does not abate until mid-September, these become ribbons of mud. At such times only the main street in Old Bazaar, which is paved with a marble-like local stone, is easy to negotiate.

In addition to private dwellings, there are perhaps a dozen public buildings which house the social centre, schools and, in the main, branches of the administration (see Map 4). Most are in the northern section of the town, along the main street, and are in appearance no different from the largest privately-owned dwellings. Generally, the ground floor area is utilized as office space, while the upper storey constitutes the living quarters for the senior-most official. Aside from the stone fort the only structure which is conspicuous by its size and design is that containing the district headquarters (*gaunda*). This is a large, three-storey dwelling faced in concrete and containing other unusual features (for this area) such as glass windows—although most are now missing and have not been replaced—and a large open sun porch in the rear, where the district's chief official entertains his guests.

The building is set in ample grounds which include a flower garden behind and a large flat area (*tundikhel*) in front. This contains a badminton court and occasionally entertainments or public meetings are also held here since a small hillock rises sharply away from, and so overlooks, the level ground, creating a kind of natural amphitheatre.

Since there is no electricity in the district, nor in all the hills of western Nepal, houses rely on tiny windows to provide daytime light and on kerosene-lit wick lamps after dark. There is no piped water supply to the bazaar, so that people must fetch their requirements daily from the several springs and wells on the slopes below the town. The bazaar has no sewage system, and residents do not build latrines but prefer to make their way, in the very early morning, to a remote and private place. In spite of such obvious health hazards, local inhabitants explain their apparent freedom from the dangers which the neglect of such fundamental services could bring in terms of the favourable weather conditions obtaining in the area most of the year. Indeed, many outsiders, with few compliments to pay the district, invariably cite Belaspur's moderate climate as its chief asset.

Residents

The resident population of Belaspur Bazaar totals 941 persons, some 88 (9·0 per cent) of whom were, at the time of this study, working on a more than transitory basis outside the town (see

Chapter 4). In the majority of cases the reasons relate to government or other long-term employment away from home, although other factors such as ownership of land in another area (see pp. 114–15) or adolescent rebellion against parental control (by, in particular, young men) can lead to the lengthy separation of families. There is no way of measuring with any precision the extent of permanent emigration from the town, but it would be a rare person who could not name at least one close kinsman who had left for good, generally to settle somewhere outside the district. The desire to retain links in the bazaar is signalled by regular visiting and occasional letters, and, of course, continuing interest in family property. The numbers given for persons resident outside but still of the town, therefore, must be understood as a statement of the intentions of such people to remain 'bazaariyas'. Table 2 gives the total population of the town, by caste.

TABLE 2

Population of Belaspur Bazaar

'Clean' Castes 'Twice-born' Castes	Numbers		Percentages	
Chetri	143		15·2	
Thakuri	50		5·3	
Joggi	10		1·1	
Jaisi	4		·4	
		207		22·0
'Drinking' Castes				
Newar	267		28·4	
Magar	14		1·5	
Gurung	11		1·2	
Other	4		·4	
		296		31·5
Total of 'clean' castes		503		53·5
'Untouchable' Castes				
Cobbler	173		18·4	
Tailor	147		15·6	
Smith	66		7·0	
Butcher	51		5·4	
Other	1		·1	
Total of untouchables		438		46·5
Total population		941		100·0

The caste composition of the bazaar is clearly quite distinct from that in the district as a whole (see Table 1, p. 15). Whereas twice-born groups make up almost 60 per cent of the district's population, they constitute slightly more than one-fifth of the town's inhabitants. Drinking castes, by contrast, are only 13 per cent in the district, but 31·5 per cent in the town, and the overwhelming majority of the latter are Newars, who are virtually unrepresented outside the bazaar. Finally, against an untouchable population of 27 per cent in Belaspur district, almost half of all townspeople (46·5 per cent) are so ranked. Again, within this category, those groups with the smallest numbers in the district as a whole are best represented in the district capital. Thus, Tailors and Cobblers, who constitute 5·0 and 2·8 per cent respectively of all Belaspuris, are 18·4 and 15·6 per cent of the bazaar's population, while the largest untouchable group in the district, the Smiths (18·8 per cent) are only 7 per cent of all townsmen. Moreover, virtually all the district's Butchers reside in the bazaar.

Briefly then, in contradistinction to the demographic pattern in the district as a whole, the town is characterized by a predominance of castes at the lower end of the ritual hierarchy, which are, moreover, otherwise sparsely represented in the area at large. This configuration is to a significant degree understandable in terms of the bazaar's settlement history.

It is impossible to say with any certainty who the bazaar's first permanent residents were. Speculation about the migration histories of the various groups at present settled in the bazaar, however, is aided by local documents, individual biographies and oral traditions.

Untouchable castes

Four untouchable castes together make up just under half of the bazaar's population. With the exception of the small Smith group, which is dispersed throughout the town, they live in separate neighbourhoods in the southern-most section of the town: the Butchers along the main road; the Tailors and Cobblers off the road to the east and south of the fort (see Map 3).

Other than the Butchers, who migrated from the Kathmandu Valley (see below), most of the untouchables in the bazaar claim different parts of east Nepal as their places of origin. They claim, also, to have been among the first of the permanent settlers in the town. The senior males of the nineteen named patri-clan groups[8] among these castes are two or more generations removed from the first migrating ancestor. Eight clan groups identify someone related as a paternal grandfather to their seniormost member as their earliest representative in the bazaar, while eleven groups claim a more distant forefather as the first arrival.

The reasons for their migration are not hard to seek. A few Tailors (who are musicians as well) and Cobblers (who do various kinds of leather-work) might have come as part of the militia posted to the local garrison. But the principal motive for population movements in Nepal over the past century has been, not surprisingly, destitution arising from landlessness. The poorest sections of the peasantry have provided much of the personnel for the endless waves of migration which have swept from one end of the Himalayas to the other, despite seemingly insurmountable mountain barriers. And the untouchable castes have traditionally been the most poverty-stricken.

Those who found their way to and remained to settle in the bazaar saw here the opportunity to provide services to a growing town, and because it lay on an important north/south route, to exchange these services for the Tibetan salt and other goods brought by transhumant shepherds moving between the high mountains and the plains. Moreover, in the case of the Tailors and Cobblers especially, the services which they monopolized were and still are in relatively short supply in the district (see Table 1). Their settlement was also encouraged by a government commutation of taxes on houses in the town.

Clean castes: Newars

The Newars, who comprise the largest single caste group, were also among the earliest settlers in Belaspur Bazaar. Taking as reference point the senior male in each of seventeen extended patrilineal families[9] into which the local Newar community can be divided, two came to Belaspur in their own lifetimes, in five instances the migrating ancestor was the father, in another five it was the paternal grandfather, while five families claim that at least three generations separate their senior member from the immigrant forefather.

Seven out of ten migrating ancestors who are either one or two generations removed from their senior living descendants, had come from one of the towns in Kathmandu Valley; there was less certainty about those who had come earlier, although these were assumed also to have originated in 'Nepal' (as the Valley is known in these hills), because it was and is the centre of Newar civilization.

Most Newars from Kathmandu originally came to Belaspur as part of the personal entourage of a senior member of the district administration, usually the governor. Depending on personal abilities and the strength of ties to the patron, these men were, on arrival, assigned jobs in his living quarters, or posts in one of the offices of the administration, including the local militia.

Those who stayed on after completion of their tour of duty, or resigned the protection of a patron on the latter's return to the nation's capital, did so for several reasons. One relates to the poverty of their home environment, as most who left Kathmandu in the first place, as clients of officials, did so out of economic necessity.

Settlement in the bazaar was also stimulated, as already mentioned, by a commutation of taxes on house sites in the town, and by growing opportunities for petty commerce. Finally, in more recent times, a number of unattached men were encouraged to settle by the possibility of marrying local brides and benefiting from attractive dowries. The fathers of four Newar shopkeepers resigned their government service rather than accept re-posting out of the district in order to marry bazaar girls and start businesses in premises erected by their fathers-in-law and given their wives as dowries.

Early administration records support the statements of some informants that most who remained to settle were from a number of low and economically depressed Newar castes, such as Nau (potters), Kau (blacksmiths) and Bada (coppersmiths), who in Kathmandu Valley would normally not have married with one another nor enjoyed commensal relations.[10] But local demographic considerations resulted in a not too great concern for such rules among the immigrant settlers in Belaspur. This led to the obliteration of distinctions between these groups and their common self-identification as 'Shrestha'. Rosser (1966) shows how, in Kathmandu Valley, the Shrestha caste has traditionally been a 'catchment' group for upwardly mobile individuals and for this reason the status of anyone calling himself 'Shrestha' without some qualification is highly suspect. (' "If a man says he is a Shrestha we never ask any further questions. It might prove very embarrassing" say the Newars' (ibid: 103).) In a remote area like Belaspur, this very ambiguity allows for the forbearance of practices which might otherwise not be tolerated. In many respects, the Shresthas resemble the Patidars of Gujarat who, as Pocock notes, are subject to infiltration at the lower levels and can tolerate a considerable degree of 'graduality', inasmuch as 'there is no unambiguous body of rules, customs and beliefs which enable us to identify that caste descriptively' (1972:54).

But this relaxation of group boundaries did not extend to those ranked as untouchables in the Newar hierarchy. The Butchers (see above) were prevented from concluding marital alliances with the 'clean' castes; the line between the two is 'clear, precise, immutable' (Rosser 1966:88). Indeed, the Butchers are not even regarded by the Shresthas, nor do they regard themselves, as Newars, and when this term is used in the bazaar (and in this book) it refers only to the Shresthas. Other than the few who have immigrated to the bazaar in their own lifetimes, neither Shresthas nor Butchers any longer speak Newari, a Tibeto-Burman language still flourishing in the Valley of Kathmandu. They know only Nepali, the kingdom's *lingua franca*, and the first language of the vast majority of people in the far western hills. Newars have also adopted the marriage, funerary and other ritual practices of the hill people (*pahari*) of twice-born status. 'We have lost our traditions (*ran san*)', they say.

Other clean castes

The other castes (Chetri, Thakuri, Joggi, Jaisi, Magar and Gurung) are more recent settlers in the town. Since by the time they established residence most bazaar lands were in Newar hands (even if not built on) they were compelled to purchase vacant house sites or dwellings from the owners. As a result they do not live in exclusive neighbourhoods but are dispersed among the Newars in the main street.

Whereas the first immigrants of all the untouchable clan groups are at least two generations (and in over half the cases, three or more generations) removed from the oldest living member, and whereas ten of seventeen Newar first immigrants are two or more generations removed, in the case of the other resident caste groups, the first immigrant is nowhere more than one generation back (see Table 3).

The kinds of areas from which these recently arrived groups originate is also to be distinguished from both that of the untouchables and the Newars. As already pointed out the three largest untouchable groups trace their origins to rural areas some distance from the district, while the Butchers, along with the Newars,

TABLE 3

Migration of Castes to Belaspur Bazaar

	No. of clans or 'extended families'	Relation of first migrant to oldest living member			
		Self	F	FF	Prior to FF
Untouchables	19	–	–	8	11
Newars	17	2	5	5	5
Other clean castes	23	10	13	–	–

emigrated mainly from Kathmandu Valley (even the four groups uncertain about their precise areas of origin assume it was the Valley). By contrast, the majority of members of other clean caste groups have come to the bazaar from villages near the town. Table 4 summarizes the data.

TABLE 4

Areas of origin of immigrants to Belaspur Bazaar

	No. of clans or 'extended families'	Kathmandu Valley	Hill areas (outside district)	Villages in District	Unknown
Untouchables	19	3	12	—	4
Newars	17	9	4	—	4
Other clean castes	23	–	8	15	–

Members of clean castes other than Newars, who came from hill areas outside Belaspur district were all of 'twice-born' status and there are several reasons they did not, until quite recently, settle in the town. Unlike the Newars, most of whom originated in a traditionally 'urban' ambience and belonged, on the whole, to non-agricultural castes, they were, despite their links to the administration, rooted in the peasant environment of the Nepalese hills and, more likely, if they remained in Belaspur, to settle in its villages. A number of prominent village families trace their beginnings in the district more than two generations back to a former member of the Rana or even pre-Rana administration who settled on the holding which, during his government service had been assigned to him as *jagir*, i.e. lands whose income he was entitled to enjoy, since until the latter part of the nineteenth century Nepalese civil servants were not paid salaries (see Chapter 3). The prerogatives of *jagir* 'originally included rights in the soil and not merely the right to appropriate revenue' (M. C. Regmi 1965:9). Some men, therefore, acquired permanent proprietary rights over at least some of these lands and were able to settle on them after leaving government service.

However such prerogatives would only have accrued to high-ranking members of the administration. Less elevated employees, who were paid out of the incomes of senior officials, had to acquire agricultural holdings by purchase. But considering the availability of land in the district until perhaps seventy years ago and the special opportunities for accumulating some capital enjoyed by even the more menial government servants, it is probable that members of these twice-born groups who decided to remain in the district after leaving service also tended, like the more senior officials and unlike the town-focussed Newars, to settle in villages. There is, however, adequate evidence to suggest that in fact the numbers who actually settled in the district in these ways were very small and it would appear that this is because they already belonged, on the whole, to families with ample land and a reasonable level of income.

Since the turn of the century, however, the increasing pressure on land resources in most parts of the kingdom has led to the growing impoverishment of many belonging even to the traditionally land-owning twice-born castes. It is not surprising, then, that a handful of men with diminishing advantages at home, who sensed the possibilities for advancement in new, non-agricultural pursuits should have decided to settle in the town.

Insufficient land to meet a rising population can also explain the growing interest in the bazaar on the part of members of clean castes whose origins are in the villages of the district itself. (According to census figures the population of Belaspur district had approximately tripled in the forty year period up to 1961 when it was partitioned.) But the very opportunities they pursue can be and are being exploited by fellow villagers who do not settle in the town (see Chapter 7). The motives bringing these Belaspur peasants to reside permanently in the bazaar must therefore be sought in the circumstances of the migrants themselves. Personal biographies reveal a number of motives for the decision to move residence from the village to the town. One reason frequently cited is family quarrels over inheritance claims leading to bitter and irreconcilable divisions between brothers. Another relates to marriages, usually second or subsequent ones, which are not readily tolerated within village society. These not uncommonly take place between members of different castes and may lead to the establishment of a residence for the woman in the bazaar, to her children being born there and regarded, as well as regarding themselves, as bazaariyas.

This suggests that the bazaar is seen by some villagers as more tolerant of, and therefore a sanctuary for their occasional maverick unions, a reputation earned as a result of the relatively high proportion of inter-caste marriages among townspeople themselves (see Chapter 6).

Whereas the severance of links with ancestral lands and home is abrupt for those from distant parts of Nepal who decide to settle in the bazaar, migration from surrounding villages generally involves a more gradual process. The immigrant who seriously intends to settle in town brings his family here, and usually sells or abandons his village house if not his agricultural lands. Over time, his links to the village diminish, he returns to visit less frequently, and alternatively, he identifies increasingly with other bazaar residents as friends, neighbours, and, in time, kinsmen.

The rhythm of daily life in Belaspur Bazaar is to a very large degree determined by the district administration. Men employed in its offices must complete a whole round of activities—bathing, breakfasting, visiting, even cultivating—before leaving for work. Shopkeepers adjust their opening hours to those of the administration, for many of their regular customers are government servants who make their small but regular purchases of cigarettes, betel nut, etc. on the way to their offices. At the end of the working day, the main street of the town, quiet save for a handful of visitors or shoppers during office hours (10 am–4 or 5 pm, depending on the season), fills with civil servants. They mill about the shops, trade news and pleasantries, or, if they work in the older established administrative branches (see next chapter) stroll for a time, in formation according to rank, behind the office head (*hakim*) before accompanying him to his residential quarters, where they disperse. On Saturdays, when government offices are shut, most shops close down as well, and a stillness settles on the town; it appears deserted.

But setting a tempo is not the only way in which the district administration imposes itself upon the town. For one thing it is and has been for many years a major influence on the occupational patterns and general economic position of those who live in the bazaar. To begin this discussion Chapter 3 examines the structure of district administration in the Rana and contemporary (post-Rana) periods.

Notes to Chapter 2

1 I have included the Joggis with the twice-born castes, since in this part of Nepal they are effectively treated as such, even though they do not wear the sacred thread. In the old Nepalese law code (replaced in 1963) they were ranked as a separate category immediately below the *tagadhari* groups. I am grateful to Marc Gaborieau for bringing this to my attention. For a further note on ascetics in western Nepal see Patricia Caplan (1973).

2 See Furer-Haimendorf (1971) for a discussion of caste in western Nepal.

3 Gaborieau (1972) points out that in the old legal code of Nepal a distinction was made between those castes whose very touch was polluting and required a cleansing ritual, and those from whom water could not be accepted but with whom physical contact was possible. Muslims and Butchers were in the latter category.

4 A few rulers continued to exercise extensive fiscal and judicial privileges. These included the right to appoint tax-collectors and keep a large proportion of the taxes collected in their former territories, to enjoy the revenues from courts of first instance over which they were allowed to preside, and to exact free labour services from each dependent household. In some cases, moreover, these powers were handed on to patrilineal successors who continued to be referred to, even by the central authorities, as 'kings' (*raja*). These prerogatives were finally abolished only in 1960, to be replaced by an annual allowance from Kathmandu.

5 In an undated communication to the district administration from the Rana authorities the latter demanded that all *chautariya* request permission from the governor of the district before arranging marriages for their daughters, and instructed the governor to 'see their daughter and inform us if she is fit for us. If she is not fit for us, give them permission for her marriage.'

6 It is, of course, entirely possible that a small service-cum-administrative centre had grown up around the palace of the Belaspur kings before the Gorkha conquest, but we have no way of knowing who its inhabitants might have been. What is certain is that if it did exist, it was not on the same site as the present town.

7 Of these 217 dwellings, 53 are owned by persons not normally resident in the bazaar (see Chapter 7).

8 In the case of the Butchers, who do not have clan groups, I distinguish 'extended families'. See note 9 below.

9 Furer-Haimendorf points out how 'Newars in the diaspora tend to lose any consciousness . . . of the clan names their ancestors must have had' (1962:27). For the purpose of examining migration processes, it was necessary to distinguish these 'extended families' in an *ad hoc* fashion, on the basis of genealogies. Since they do not marry those to whom a patrilineal link can be traced the main criterion for distinguishing one from another is that no agnatic connection appears to be recognized between them. I am not suggesting, however, that the Newars themselves regard these units in an economic, ritual or any other sense as corporate groups.

10 See Rosser (1966:85–6) for a discussion of the Newar caste organization.

3

The District Administration

In much of South Asia, the formation and early development of urban or peri-urban communities can be attributed to local princes or zamindars (Fox 1969:70). In Nepal, however, it was the central government itself which, by establishing a number of administrative outposts throughout the kingdom, stimulated the growth of towns. Indeed, the history of such communities largely reflects that of the administration.

Very little is known of the administrative organization of the country during the 50 years following unification under the Shah dynasty of Gorkha, save that it was based on a number of military posts, such as the one in Belaspur. During this period, however, the kingdom was divided into a number of districts which, with a few subsequent adjustments, were to serve as the principal units of administration for the next century and a half (Kumar 1967: 93, 107).

Rana administration

The picture becomes clearer with the accession to power of the Ranas in 1846, and the gradual codification of governmental regulations. Administration in the 104 years during which they controlled the country had two main purposes: the maintenance of law and order, and the collection of land revenues. The revenues of the state during this time were apparently not distinguished from those of the Rana prime ministers, and treasury surpluses were regarded as their personal incomes (Goodall 1966: 609). In the light of such fiscal policies, it is understandable why, as one foreign observer remarked, 'the minute supervision' (exercised by the first Rana prime minister) 'over the management of all departments of the state is most extraordinary . . . not a rupee is expended from the public treasury . . . without his knowledge and sanction' (Cavenagh 1851: 74. See also Kumar 1967: 78).

In Belaspur, which was not untypical, the district headquarters, at the apex of which stood a governor (*bada-hakim*), was responsible for all administrative functions. The governor had direct jurisdiction over the military garrison which policed the district, and, in fact, was often a high-ranking army officer.

Revenue matters were also the responsibility of headquarters, which appointed a number of village and sub-district headmen to collect taxes on a commission basis. An administrative reorganization in Kathmandu led to the separation, in 1926, of tax-collection duties from headquarters and their assignment to a special revenue office in the district. This relieved the governor of the burden of organizing the collection of taxes, but not his final responsibility for land revenues.

For a time following the establishment of Rana rule, the governor was also the principal judicial figure in the district, hearing appeals from decisions made by a variety of mediators. Among these were senior government servants whose 'salaries' were still in the form of cash rents or taxes from lands (*jagir*) assigned to them, although in many parts of Nepal these were paid in grain. This system, which was undoubtedly based on Moghul practice in other parts of South Asia, was introduced by the Shah rulers and inherited by the Ranas, who gradually replaced it by cash salaries for government employees.[1] While it obtained, however, senior officials had the right to settle minor disputes among, and impose fines on, those who cultivated their land assignments (Cavenagh 1851, Malhotra 1958). Similarly, headmen enjoyed the same rights *vis à vis* the peasant cultivators from whom they collected taxes (see Chapter 8).

Criminal and other serious offences, such as those dealing with caste, were brought before a special arbitrator (called a *faujdar*) appointed by the governor. Such a person was not, strictly speaking, a member of the administration, but rather a kind of legal sub-contractor, who received a commission (six per cent is the most frequently quoted figure) on the fines he collected.[2]

In 1887, a judicial reorganization of the country saw the establishment of district courts, including one in Belaspur, whose decisions could be referred to an appeal court situated in Doti, a district farther to the west. This did not mean the complete severance of the district headquarters from the judiciary, however, for the governor not only retained within his office substantial judicial powers, but continued to exercise control over the operations of the court as well. Only in 1939 was the judiciary formally separated from the executive (Shrestha 1965: 44).

By the end of the Rana period (1950–1) the district administration consisted of a court (*adalat*), land revenue office (*mal*), branch of the national postal service (*hulak*), and headquarters (including the district's military garrison). Although virtually every decision and action taken by the administration had to be vetted by Kathmandu, the almost total isolation of the district from the capital rendered such control less than effective, and in a *de facto* sense, the Rana governor enjoyed a considerable measure of autonomy.

Appointments and tenure

Just as public revenues were treated as part of the Rana ruler's private purse, top appointments in the administration, including the post of district governor, were conferred personally by the prime minister. Districts were graded (A, B or C) according to their distance from the capital, population and revenue potential. The prime minister's closest kinsmen of 'pure' Rana status,[3] and his most loyal followers, were kept in Kathmandu or sent to govern the more important districts. Ranas of lesser, i.e., mixed, breed or those whose presence in the capital was not desired, were assigned the least sought-after governorships in places like Belaspur which, along with most districts in the far western hills, was in the lowest ('C') category. But few who were not members of this ruling family were ever entrusted with senior administrative posts. With only one exception, all the governors of Belaspur district during the Rana period were themselves Ranas.

Other senior officials in the district administration, such as those in charge of the court and the land revenue office (after their separation from headquarters) were appointed by their respective central departments in the capital or, more precisely, by the Ranas at the head of these departments. They also fixed the numbers of personnel in each district branch office and their salaries, but recruitment to menial and lower clerical ranks was entirely the prerogative of the governor himself.[4] And there were no rules regarding qualifications, nor any formal open competition for these posts. Before leaving Kathmandu (or a district where he had previously been posted) to take up his assignment, a governor-designate might recruit a number of followers with the promise of jobs in his new administration or personal household. The bulk of the personnel below senior rank, however, would only be chosen after arrival in the district from among the local inhabitants. The process of dismissing some incumbents to make room for his new appointees was provided for by the institution of *pajani*, whereby all appointments were regarded as being valid for only one year, and therefore could be renewed or terminated at such time.

This custom which, according to Kumar (1967: 82) probably had its origins in the principality of Gorkha, was practised throughout Nepal and resulted in the 'continuation or confirmation of . . . previous appointments, or modifications in the nature and tenure of existing appointments, or dismissals and new appointments' (ibid: 28).

In Belaspur, the *pajani* for the district headquarters was a formal and public occasion, held in the autumn, during the Hindu festival of Dasein. On the appointed day, all low-ranking office employees, including members of the militia, who turned out on parade, and a variety of hopeful candidates, appeared before the governor and heard the verdict concerning their immediate future. The tenure of employees in other branches of the administration was also subject to annual review, although there was no single such occasion on which decisions in regard to their positions were made known. The governor could not dismiss or in any way alter the status of senior officials who had been appointed from Kathmandu, although, of course, his reports could influence the head of department in the capital. Theirs was not the governor's *pajani* (as informants phrase it), but their own department heads'. The governor himself was in the hands of the prime minister.

The highest turnover of personnel would occur following the arrival of a new governor an event which took place every few years. Thus, during the final 46 years of Rana rule, about which I have information, governors spent an average of 2·7 years in the district. An abbreviated account given by one man of his career in the district administration illustrates the kind of insecurity experienced by most of its employees.

Governor G.P. gave me a job, but I was dismissed from service by R.L. (his successor). Later I got another job, but then B.B. came (as governor) and threw me out at *pajani* time. I hadn't done anything wrong. It was just that whenever a new governor came he dismissed old employees and hired new ones.

But even in a year when no change took place at the top of the district administration, as many as 10 per cent of government servants would be removed to make way for new appointees, who would, in turn, be subject to review the following year. A number of local inhabitants remember being given posts by a governor, only to be dismissed the following year by the same official.

A governor's apparently boundless power to remove incumbents and replace them with new personnel of his own choosing was constrained, in the final analysis, by Kathmandu's insistence, firstly, that peace be kept in the district, and secondly, that its revenue potential be fully realized. To achieve these goals, the governor needed a number of loyal and experienced employees to ensure a measure of continuity and efficiency in the district administration. He had, also, to rely on the co-operation of leading families in the district, and one way in which such co-operation could be assured was by placing at least some of their members in administrative posts, and granting them a modicum of security in these posts.

These constraints on the governor's freedom of action were minimal, however, and affected the tenure of only a handful of those employed in the administration, which, in any case, could not be guaranteed after his departure from the district.

The existence of *pajani* emphasizes, too, that winning the personal favour of a high official counted more in determining tenure than any demonstration of ability.

The same principles underlined the recruitment of local employees. Since there was no formal mechanism for evaluating persons seeking posts as government servants, selection was based on subjective factors. But senior officials were from outside the district and so had no personal acquaintance with members of the local public. What, then, were the bases on which candidates were chosen? Alternatively, how did Belaspuris go about obtaining jobs in the district administration?

Such employment may be regarded as part of an exchange of prestations between the governor (or an official able to influence him) and a member of the local population. In rare instances, as I have indicated, a post in the administration would be offered in return for the support and co-operation of a district notable. Similarly, local Brahmins who were required to provide priestly services, or other residents called on for special favours were in a position to urge reciprocity in the form of a job for themselves or others near them. Since senior officials from outside the district were compelled to rely on local sources for their food supplies this could have led to their dependence on a number of wealthy peasants in the district, with far-reaching consequences. This situation, however, did not arise for two main reasons: firstly, because (after the abolition of the *jagir* system) all branches of the district administration had some lands attached to them, and grain rents from the tenant cultivators were appropriated by senior government servants; secondly, officials had the right to requisition supplies from surrounding villages when necessary, for which payment was made (see Chapter 6). On the whole, then, there were few situations in which officials made demands on members of the public which would have allowed counter-demands for administrative employment.

The numbers of local inhabitants who obtained work in this way were therefore extremely limited. Once inside the administration, however, residents of the district were able, by means discussed later in this chapter, to intercede with senior colleagues on behalf of kinsmen or neighbours seeking employment. But the generally high turnover of senior staff and the institution of *pajani* restricted the extent to which such links could be utilized.

More commonly, when seeking a government post, members of the public sought to place the governor under an obligation through the process of *chakari*, which meant attending him regularly, presenting him with small gifts, or performing unsolicited services, over a period of time. Some report having followed the governor wherever he went for months on end (and portering his baggage when he toured the district), others remember bringing him fruit, vegetables, curds and other foods several times weekly, while a few recall attending his household chores. One successful applicant summed up the exchange thus:

I sat outside (governor) H.J.'s office for many weeks, and each time I went there I brought something, and greeted him whenever I saw him. At first he took no notice because there were others like me there, all doing the same. Then one day he asked my name and where my home was. After a few weeks had passed, he asked me why I attended him and I told him about my poverty and that I needed a job in the administration. He told me to show up at *pajani* time which was in a month. That is how I got my job.

A governor was not obligated at the outset to grant a supplicant his wish and could, without loss of esteem, signify a desire to see the offerings cease.[5] But as time went on and the weight of prestations grew, there came a point when to refuse the hoped-for counter-prestation would have compromised the official's reputation.

In theory, there was nothing to prevent a Belaspur man bypassing the district administration and making his way to Kathmandu, there to 'do *chakari*' to the prime minister himself in the hope of securing an appointment which would enable him to rise to a position which he could never achieve through recruitment by a governor in the district. Some informants state that during the latter years of Rana rule, public examinations—in such subjects as law, grammar, literature, geography, and accounts—were held annually in Kathmandu, and successful candidates would then have a good chance of being appointed to a clerical post by a Rana patron.

But even to sit such examinations required a degree of literacy and knowledge which no local resident had acquired prior to 1922, when the first of two 'religion and language' schools (*bhasa pathsala*) built in the district during the Rana regime was established in Belaspur Bazaar. By the end of the period only a tiny fraction of the district population had attended these schools and even fewer had completed the courses offered.[6]

Furthermore, to set out on such an expedition required consider-able wealth and stamina, for it could take as long as a month to reach Kathmandu on foot, and many more months in the highly competitive atmosphere of the capital attempting to forge, by *chakari*, the necessary links to the head of government. Very few people from a remote and backward area like Belaspur could expect to meet with any success in Kathmandu, and very few made the attempt.

The process whereby prospective employees ingratiated them-selves with senior officials did not cease after appointment, but continued for some time afterwards, both in the hope of avoiding or reducing the risk of dismissal at the time of *pajani*, and of gaining promotion. Prestations from inferior to superior, after appointment, however, took the form, not of gift-bearing, but of being in attend-ance on the senior official. According to one expert on Nepalese public administration: 'During the Rana regime government servants (in Kathmandu) gathered at the residence of their chief after a day's work to pay their respects and often waited hours for their senior to appear (Goodall 1966: 610 f.n.). The lowest ranking members of a department might also perform a variety of unofficial services for their superiors, a practice which still obtains (see p. 49).

For a member of the Belaspur public without personal links to someone already in the administration able to speak on his behalf, and who had neither the time nor inclination to engage in the lengthy and uncertain process of *chakari*, there remained one other avenue to a job in the administration: this was to offer the governor a cash payment (*ghus*).[7] Such an offer, if accepted (or, indeed, demanded by the official in the first place) brought immediate results in the form of a post.

The offer and acceptance of cash in exchange for a job, unlike other forms of prestation to achieve the same goal, was and is condemned as reprehensible behaviour. Therefore, quite apart from its importance in determining appointments to the administration, the issue of bribery is of interest sociologically in so far as it is cited to demonstrate the moral degradation of enemies in general and specific rivals in particular. I return to this point later in the book.

Post-Rana administration

Following the revolution of 1950–1 the administrative structure in Nepal underwent considerable expansion and reorganization.

In Belaspur, the first post-Rana decade saw the establishment of an education office to oversee the growth of primary schools, a high school, health centre and radio telegraph station. In addition, a new police force relieved the army of responsibility for the maintenance of law and order. With the founding of a national system of elected councils (panchayats) in 1961, the administration went through a further phase of expansion. A secretariat for the district council was created, and its head, the chief district officer (CDO) given responsibility for co-ordinating the various development programmes in the district. The new panchayat system also called for the establishment of seven 'class' organizations, to represent the interests of labourers, children, students, ex-servicemen, women, farmers, and youth; this required the opening of yet another administrative office. Other governmental programmes leading to the establishment of departments in Belaspur in the mid-1960s were a land reform scheme and another to eradicate malaria (see Appendix A).

There are to-day sixteen government or quasi-government offices and agencies represented in Belaspur district, employing a total of 334 persons.[8] If account is taken of the transfer of military headquarters for the region out of Belaspur in 1968, which reduced the numbers in the local garrison by over 100 men to only a token guard, the present figure represents roughly a trebling of the number of government servants in the district administration at the end of the Rana period—notwithstanding a decrease in the size and population of the district unit since that time. The numbers employed full-time in each administrative branch are given in Table 5.

TABLE 5

*Employees of the district administration**

Branches established before *1951*	Numbers†
Post Office	42 (25)
District Headquarters	23
Court	23
Land Revenue	15
Army	9
Jail	7
	119 (25)
Branches established after 1951	
Malaria eradication	63 (30)
Police	61 (15)
District Council Secretariat	26
Land Reform	26
Health Centre‡	12
High School	8
Education	7
Bank	7
Telegraph	3
Class Organizations	2
	215 (45)
TOTAL	334 (70)

* Figures in brackets represent the numbers employed outside Belaspur Bazaar. Thus, 25 of the 42 postal workers are attached to sub-post offices in various parts of the district; 30 of the 63 employees of the Malaria eradication office are in branches outside the district capital, as are 15 of 61 policemen.

† Persons employed on a seasonal or occasional basis are not included in these figures.

‡ The majority are employed as vaccinators, under a recently inaugurated programme of immunization against smallpox.

Leaving aside the army figures, both past and present, the total numbers now employed in administrative branches established prior to 1951, have remained the same (although a few offices have expanded, and others reduced their personnel). Expansion, in other words, has been in the form of new offices and the jobs they have created, rather than in the growth of established administrative branches (see Map 4 for the distribution of these branches in the town).

The introduction of a panchayat system was accompanied by a reorganization of the kingdom into 75 'development districts' (*jilla*) grouped into 14 'development zones' (*anchal*). Belaspur, along with two adjacent districts to the east and south, and two others in the terai, became part of a single zone, whose capital is at Balnagar in the terai. The district governor was replaced by an assistant zonal commissioner (*saik-anchaladhis*), based in Belaspur but with jurisdiction over the two other adjacent mountain districts, and responsible to the zonal commissioner (*anchaladhis*).[9]

Within the district the assistant commissioner retains responsibility for law and order through control of the police, but the local army garrison has been placed under the direct jurisdiction of the defence ministry in Kathmandu. Moreover, apart from internal security, and the land reform programme, whose implementation is also entrusted to him, all other aspects of district administration have been placed in the hands of the chief district officer. Although the boundaries of jurisdiction between the two sectors of the administration are by no means clear,[10] and for members of the public, non-existent, the effect of this division of responsibility has been to limit the powers vested in any single district official. In addition, recent improvements in communication between Kathmandu and the outlying areas has made it possible for central (and zonal) departments to exercise greater control than ever before over the activities of district offices and has consequently eroded the authority of senior district officials. Compared to the autocratic governors of the Rana period, the heads of branches in the district to-day are much more constrained by an encompassing national administration.

The growth of bureaucracy

Further constraints are imposed by the growing formalization of rules and practices affecting the treatment of government employees. The Civil Service Act of 1956, which created a Public Service Commission (PSC), signalled the government's intention to replace the personalistic administration of the Rana period with an impersonal bureaucracy. Government employees were guaranteed security against arbitrary dismissal; promotion committees were provided for, and their procedures spelled out in great detail; leave entitlements were determined;[11] and a pension scheme and a contributory health fund were established.[12] Finally, administrative posts were classified as gazetted or non-gazetted, each category internally graded, and a uniform salary structure, including a system of annual increments, introduced.[13]

Table 6 gives the distribution of government employees in the Belaspur administration according to three main categories of rank: 'senior' (including administrative and technical divisions), 'junior' (mainly clerical), and menial. The basic salary range is also given, along with the average income of employees in each category. The latter figure includes, as well as basic salary, increments and special allowances. Those posted to Belaspur from outside the district, for example, receive an additional 35 per cent of their basic salary as a cost-of-living allowance.

TABLE 6

*Employees in the district administration according to rank**

Rank	Numbers	Basic Monthly salary range† rupees	Average Monthly income (to nearest 5 rupees)
Senior—administrative	48	150–600	300
Senior—technical	19	150–500	300
Junior—clerical	73	85–100	110
Menial	124	70–75	85
All ranks	264		150

* This table (like subsequent ones) does not include the 70 employees posted outside the bazaar in other parts of the district (see Table 5) who I was unable to interview.
† In 1969, one pound sterling was equal to rs 24.20.

Senior (administrative)

What I have designated 'senior' (administrative) includes grades ranging from the highest in the district, that of assistant commissioner (later 'special officer') and chief district officer (CDO) which are gazetted, second class posts to *kharidar*, a non-gazetted second class post.

Senior (technical)

'Technical' grades comprise a variety of posts which carry minimal administrative responsibilities, but require special training or qualifications and so offer good salaries: high school teacher, medical officer, telegraph operator, agricultural advisor, bank accountant, etc.

Junior

'Junior' grades include the clerical ranks of *mukhiya* and *bahidar*, which are non-gazetted, third and fourth class, respectively.

Menial

'Menial' posts are those which require minimal skills; they include messengers, peons, stable boys, police constables, army privates (*sipoy*), and postmen.[14]

Educational requirements New appointees to the district administration must meet certain minimal standards expected of all government employees above menial rank to-day. The most important are those relating to education.

For some years now the PSC has demanded of those seeking what have been termed senior posts in the administration at least a School Leaving Certificate (i.e. tenth grade or high school graduation). Those applying for gazetted posts must have a university degree or, as in the case of non-gazetted 1st and 2nd class posts requiring SLC, their equivalent from a religious institution. These standards apply only to new recruits and not to those who have risen to these posts over the years. Appointments to equivalent non-PSC jobs (see below) tend also to be awarded to those with similar qualifications. No specific schooling requirements are set out for junior posts, but the PSC exams (which are also given, usually as abridged oral tests, to candidates for corresponding non-PSC jobs) assume at least a primary school education (five years) and perhaps a year or two of middle school (up to eighth grade). Although a certain flexibility is called for in the application of these regulations to candidates from a remote and backward area like Belaspur, the government has undoubtedly succeeded in its goal of raising the educational level among employees of the administration. Senior government servants in the district administration who were recruited into the civil service after the introduction of the PSC have an average of 10·2 years of schooling, while those in junior posts average 7·5 years, as compared with the average of 6·9 years for senior and 5·4 years for junior employees recruited before 1956.[15] Table 7 indicates the extent of literacy and the level of education among members of the district administration in Belaspur.

The rise in the educational level of government servants has, of

TABLE 7

Education of district administration employees

Ranks	Illiterate %	Literacy acquired at home %	in school %	Average no. of years in school*
Senior	—	1·5	98·5	9·8
Junior	1·6	8·1	90·3	6·3
Menial	24·3	11·2	64·5	3·7
All ranks	11·5	7·7	80·8	6·1

* The average is for those who attended school.

course, been made possible by a dramatic increase in schooling facilities since the otherthrow of the Ranas. Prior to 1951, fewer than fifty primary schools, mainly of the *bhasa* type (see page 37) and only a score of secondary schools had been built in the kingdom. A large proportion were in the Kathmandu area, so as to benefit the Ranas and their favourites. The census of 1952–4 revealed that in a population of approximately 7 millions above four years of age, only four per cent could read and write, while 1·7 per cent had completed primary school. By 1968, there were thousands of primary schools in the country, and the government claimed (perhaps over-optimistically) that a third of primary school age children were attending such institutions. In addition, there were 475 middle schools and 380 high schools by this time, and the numbers of high school students alone had increased by an annual average of 7,700 to some 94,000. Tribhuvan University, also a post-Rana creation, to-day has a number of affiliated colleges in various parts of the country teaching to intermediate level (two year) and bachelor level (four year) degrees.

Although by comparison with most other areas of the kingdom educational progress in Belaspur has been modest, the district's record is nevertheless impressive. Whereas there were only two *bhasa* schools prior to 1951, with places for approximately 160 students, there are to-day 75 primary schools with about 4000 places. In addition, two middle schools and a high school have been built; the latter, with places for 150 students, was established in the bazaar in 1961.[16]

The benefits of this growth have not been distributed equally among all sectors of the district population. Profiting most have been members of the highest castes, more of whom can now send their (mainly male) children to school. Those at the lower end of the caste hierarchy, particularly the untouchables, have benefited least from these new opportunities. In a total register of some 200 children in the two primary schools situated in Belaspur Bazaar, fewer than 10 per cent are untouchables, although these castes constitute almost half of the resident population in the bazaar. A similar situation appears to exist in primary schools in the villages (see P. Caplan 1972). Only four of the 153 high school students belong to untouchable groups.[17]

In Rana times untouchables in Belaspur were actively discouraged from aspiring to literacy by the Brahmin teachers in the *bhasa* schools who were loth to accept them as pupils on grounds of caste. Nowadays, other factors prevent them from competing for school places. Some are financial: the fees which have to be paid, the school uniforms which have to be bought, and the loss of valuable agricultural or craft labour which school children represent to their families keep most untouchable youngsters out of school.

But even those untouchable families who are sound financially (see Chapter 5) are reluctant to send their children to school. Firstly, it is feared that they will not be made welcome and may even be discriminated against by the teachers who are all of high caste. Secondly, and of greater importance, they argue that education will not result in increased opportunities to enter government service above the rank of menial, which in any case requires no educational qualification. They see an almost total absence of untouchables in junior and senior administrative posts in the district, and conclude that such posts are closed to them (see Table 8). Members of other castes, anxious to exploit these scarce benefits themselves, do nothing to discourage such a view. Moreover, the Nepalese government, unlike the Indian, has no legislation discriminating in favour of these underprivileged sections of the society. The untouchables of Nepal, to their detriment, have to compete for government jobs on an equal footing with members of higher caste groups. The result is a reluctance to send children to school, which in turn effectively prevents them even from applying for non-menial jobs in the administration. Although they constitute 27 per cent of the district population, fewer than 4 per cent of local administrative employees are untouchables, the vast majority of these in menial jobs. Of 140 posts above menial rank, only one, a technical post, is filled by an untouchable (from outside the district).

TABLE 8

Employees of the district administration by caste category

Rank	Numbers	High castes* %	Other clean castes %	Untouchables %
Senior†	67	82·0	16·4	1·6
Junior	73	83·6	16·3	—
Menial	124	78·2	14·4	7·3
All ranks	264	81·1	15·1	3·8

* Twice-born castes.
† Includes technical staff.

Recruitment A number of changes in recruitment procedures were also suggested by the Civil Service Act. All permanent employees of the administration above menial rank were to be appointed by the relevant department in Kathmandu only after approval by the PSC, which would require candidates to pass entry examinations and undergo special interviews.

The aim of the government to recruit into the civil service, by objective assessment, the best qualified candidates has by no means yet been fully realized in the district. One reason is that the new regulations regarding appointments were, at least for a time after their introduction, largely ignored by administrative departments in Kathmandu (Shrestha 1965). Second, until 1963, when a branch of the PSC was established in the zonal capital, entry examinations could be taken only in Kathmandu, which made the implementation of these rules virtually impossible in the district. A third reason delaying the realization of these goals relates to the acquisition of tenure by government servants recruited before the introduction of the PSC. Men who had gained entry into the administration before 1956 were not summarily dismissed when the Civil Service Act was introduced. Therefore a number of officials in the district administration today were appointed and/or promoted personally by a governor prior to 1956 and, where necessary, were given repeated chances to pass the PSC exams enabling them to acquire tenure, thereby reducing the amount of recruitment under the new regulations. This applies mainly to posts in the older established district offices.

Fourthly, there are a number of posts in the district administration not under PSC jurisdiction. Recently introduced government programmes such as malaria eradication, land reform and innoculation against smallpox are not regarded as permanent, are financed by the development budget (composed largely of foreign aid funds) and not regulated by the PSC (see Appendix A). Even the district panchayat secretariat and class organizations—established in connection with the panchayat system—have not yet been fully incorporated into the regular administration, and consequently, many of their employees, save the most senior, are regarded as 'temporary', or under special contract. Indeed, because of the occasional movement of personnel between administrative branches in the district, it is possible to find PSC and non-PSC regulated employees in the same office.[18]

A few other offices and agencies in the district are only indirectly linked to the regular administration, and their employees, too, are recruited without reference to the PSC. Thus, although the high school in Belaspur is government-aided, it is not supervised directly by the Ministry of Education; its teachers are recruited by a locally-appointed management committee. The bank also employs and trains its own personnel.

Apart from those in menial jobs, as many as half the employees in offices established since 1951, therefore, are not subject to PSC rules, even if they enjoy many of the benefits of those who are.

Finally, and perhaps of greatest significance, the PSC, even where it has jurisdiction, does not itself originate most appointments to the district administration, but only vets them. Local applicants for vacancies to such posts are interviewed by a panel composed of senior officials from both the office in which the vacancy exists, and other branches of the district administration. The panel appoints someone for a temporary period (usually six months, although this may sometimes be extended) and requests the department in Kathmandu, with the approval of the PSC, to make the appointment permanent.[19]

When filling vacancies which do not involve the PSC, a similarly constituted interview board makes a temporary appointment, after which the relevant department in Kathmandu considers an indefinite (but not permanent) extension of employment based on recommendations received from the office head in the district.

The fact that initial appointments to both PSC and non-PSC posts are made on the basis of interviews gives local candidates the opportunity to establish links to one or more members of the panel, generally through intermediaries. These brokers (Mayer 1963) are kinsmen, neighbours, or, increasingly, friends already in administrative posts who 'speak for' the candidate. In addition, since Belaspur residents now can and do attain high office in the district administration,[20] they are in positions to influence members of interview panels and, not infrequently, sit on such panels themselves.

Local dignitaries who are not administrators are occasionally invited to sit on interview panels, as well, thereby giving certain candidates potential advantages over others. In 1967, when the land reform office opened in Belaspur, the president of the district council was one of four members on the board set up to interview local candidates for jobs. Of the 14 senior officials who were recruited by the panel, three were his close relatives and two more his neighbours.

Whereas perhaps half of all government employees who obtained posts on the basis of such interviews admit to having counted on someone's personal intervention, none indicated that *chakari* had anything to do with his success. *Chakari*, which far outweighed in importance the use of personal ties and influence during Rana times, has all but been eclipsed as a means of gaining entry to the present-day district administration. This is due, paradoxically, to the growing bureaucratization of the administration, which has, first of all, made it possible for people in outlying areas like Belaspur to pursue a career in the civil service, and secondly, created the conditions of security and permanency necessary to enable relationships and attendant patterns of obligation to develop both among administrators and between them and members of the public.[21]

The trend away from *chakari* and toward the utilization of various personal links as the means to obtain government service is especially evident when we examine the manner in which menial posts, i.e. almost half of all administrative jobs in the district, are filled. Appointment in such cases is entirely the prerogative of the head of the district office concerned, although police and army recruits are vetted by zonal officials. The office head, however, does not enjoy the right of arbitrary dismissal; after a six month trial period, the incumbent acquires tenure.

Those who have been in their jobs since before or just after the end of the Rana period mainly cite *chakari* as the reason for their appointment. Those hired during the last dozen or so years, however, came by their jobs differently. Approximately four in five attribute their success to a personal link, direct or indirect, to the source of the appointment.

Where administrative branches are headed by permanent residents of the district, intermediaries are not necessary and favours go directly to those linked personally to the grantor. The two messengers working in the radio telegraph office are close relatives of the operator and office head; four of the five menials on the jail staff are neighbours of the keeper who hired them; the three latest recruits to the post office are the postmaster's (real) sister's husband, his (real) mother's brother's son, and his (real) younger brother; while the first peon post to fall vacant since the arrival of the new head of the land revenue office—like the others mentioned above, a resident of the district—went to his (real) sister's son.

If office heads are not personally known in these ways to prospective employees, intermediary links must be activated. On occasion, prominent members of the local community outside the administration act as brokers. Several employees of menial rank attribute their appointments to the influence of a sub-district headman, district panchayat executive, or even the Brahman priest of a senior government official (see P. Caplan 1972: 67). Links most frequently activated, however, are to officials in the office concerned, related in some manner to the applicant, who intercedes, on the latter's behalf, with the office head. Thus, of the men now occupying menial posts in the district headquarters, all but one are residents of a single settlement, and were recommended by two clerks in the office who live in the same locality. One third of the menial jobs in the district council secretariat and the court were also obtained in this way, as were half of those in the land reform office.

Another method is for someone who obtains a menial job to recommend others when further vacancies arise. Three members of an extended family from the same settlement came to be peons in the education office by this process, and one postman is responsible for getting at least three neighbours similar jobs.[22] Even where such opportunities do not arise, a man leaving a menial job will generally recommend a relative, neighbour or friend to succeed him.

The ability of the lowest-ranking members of the administration to influence their senior colleagues in this way is explicable to some extent in terms of a variety of petty out-of-office tasks and favours which the former perform for the latter.

Top officials from outside the district no longer have the right, as in Rana times, to requisition food from the surrounding countryside (see p. 36), so that arrangements must be made with local peasants to provide them regularly with dairy products, vegetables, fruit, meat and grain. But there is no regular market in Belaspur Bazaar, and moreover, local supplies of most foods are sporadic and unreliable. To ensure a steady flow of provisions, therefore, requires a fair amount of foraging in the villages. This is a task which usually falls to lower ranks in the administrative offices.

The latter also serve as cooks, water carriers, cleaners, dish washers, etc. for their superiors in the latters' residential quarters. Virtually every senior official from outside the district and a few locally-resident administrators as well, use subordinate office staff of menial rank as domestic help.[23] Some do so only before and after office hours, others on a full-time basis. Those who do such work receive only their government salaries, and the officials for whom they work generally provide them with a new set of clothing annually.

By these and similar means, low-ranking members of the district administration offer prestations to their superiors which not only increase their security and enhance their promotion prospects by ensuring good reports to head office, but which are also countered by occasional favours such as the conferment of a menial post on a recommended friend, kinsman or neighbour.

Administration finances

To complete the chapter I will say a word about the financial implications of the growth of Belaspur's district administration. The scope of administrative concerns during Rana times required a minimal budget, mainly to meet the costs of the militia and the small civil staff. In 1934, for example, a year for which fairly comprehensive figures were available in the district records, salaries and allowances of the 207 government employees totalled approximately rs 18,000, and this figure accounted for some 90 per cent of the entire expenditure of district offices that year (rs 20,000). These costs were met out of locally derived income which amounted to approximately rs 51,000—made up of land revenues (rs 35,000) and an additional rs 16,000 from judicial, postal and other revenues. Income, in other words, exceeded expenditure by more than two-and-a-half times. By 1950, the last year of Rana rule, the proportions of income and expenditure, which had both risen only slightly since 1934, were roughly the same.

By the time of this study the balance of income and expenditure had changed dramatically. Over a period of 35 years the expansion of administrative personnel and services, coupled with general inflation[24] has led to a 32-fold increase in the total annual expenditure of the administration (to rs 645,000) notwithstanding, it will be recalled, a considerable retraction in the size of the district unit. Most of this money (84 per cent) is spent, as in the past, on salaries, although significant amounts are now used for office equipment and stationery, to pay rents, and make emergency welfare grants. But during the same span of time administrative income has risen barely three-fold to rs 144,000: land revenues have only doubled because, in the interim, there has been neither a tax settlement (*jac*) nor any rise in the basic rates on cultivated land.[25] As a result, income now covers only 22·3 per cent of the administration's outgoings. The deficit is met out of national revenues and externally-aided budgets earmarked to meet the costs of special projects such as malaria eradication.

Table 9 summarizes the figures. Because of the re-drawing of district units in 1962, the entities being compared are not strictly comparable. Were the same boundaries to obtain today (1969) as in

TABLE 9

Income and expenditure of the district administration
1934 and 1969
(to the nearest 1,000 rupees)

		1934 (rupees)	1969 (rupees)	
Expenditure	Salaries	18,000	543,000	
	Other	2,000	102,000*	
		20,000		645,000†
Income	Land revenues	35,000	72,000	
	Other	16,000	72,000	
TOTAL		51,000	144,000	
Income as a percentage of expenditure		255·0	22·3	

* These figures do not include a special grant to the district for development projects which in 1969 totalled rs 69,000 (see Chapter 9).

† See Appendix A for a breakdown of this figure by administrative branch.

the past, the difference here noted would be even greater. These figures, then, must be understood mainly as indicative of trends in the financing of district administration.

From the point of view of Belaspur residents the dramatic increase in administrative finances since Rana times has meant that government is today a cash source of crucial importance. Other ways in which cash traditionally entered, and still enters, the area was through military service, seasonal labour in the terai or India, and the export of clarified butter. Belaspur has not sent large numbers to serve in the 'Gurkha' regiments of the British and Indian armies, and this is probably because of the relatively small 'tribal' population it contains. Records of the ex-Servicemen's Association, while probably underestimating the numbers, suggest that only about 700 men resident in the district (400 of them Magars and Gurungs) have a history of Gurkha service, and those among them eligible for pensions receive just under rs 160,000 annually. It is impossible to estimate the amount of earnings from other kinds of migratory labour outside the district, or sales of dairy produce. But it should be noted that the latter are gradually diminishing as a result of over-grazing and the destruction of vast areas of what was previously forest, while the former, though probably on the increase, involves inhabitants of the district in long absences away from home without any guarantee that their rewards will compensate for the hardships they face in a strange and hostile environment (see P. Caplan 1972).

The importance of substantial administrative injections of cash directly into the district in the form of salaries, aid for development programmes, the purchase of supplies, etc. cannot be over-emphasized. Indeed, they may be seen as the most significant new source of wealth in the district, and the struggle to exploit and benefit from them has been a critical ingredient in the pattern of political events focussed on the district capital during the 20 years since the end of Rana rule.

Conclusion

This chapter has traced the growth in the scope and functions of district administration in Nepal and especially in Belaspur over the past century or so. Attention was drawn, in particular, to an important distinction between Rana and post-Rana procedures surrounding recruitment and tenure. From the viewpoint of the local populace, the previous system was based on the establishment of direct, personal links to a handful of outsider officials (usually the governor himself) primarily through a prescribed series of prestations known as *chakari*. Indeed, this institution was recognized throughout the country as a means whereby subordinates created relationships with persons of super-ordinate status when their personal spheres or networks of social ties did not normally intersect.

By contrast, the present system relies, in the preliminary stages at least, on the utilization of existing personalized links to the sources of appointment, created not *de novo*, as it were, but in the context of existing 'multiplex' relationships. Thus, the initial conferment of administrative posts is incorporated into traditional patterns of exchange and becomes part of an ongoing system of obligations.

Paradoxically, it is the growing bureaucratization of the administration which has enabled these 'nepotistic' practices to expand. Local residents, who in the past could not rise above modest clerical jobs can now aspire to the highest ranks in the district administration, provided, of course, they possess the necessary qualifications. Moreover, with new rules guaranteeing security of tenure, government servants are no longer subject to arbitrary dismissal which obtained under the Ranas. Thus, not only can already existing multiplex links between locally-resident administrators and members of the public be more fully exploited, but the former have more time and opportunity to create 'informal' ties of friendship or clientship with non-local officials within the administration itself, which redound ultimately to the benefit of local people seeking employment in the district administration.

Alongside an increasing emphasis on formal, mainly educational qualifications, bonds of kinship and neighbourhood have replaced those forged (more impartially, perhaps) by *chakari* as of crucial significance in determining how administrative office is awarded. As Stirling observes in connection with southern Italian administrators, '(they) belong to the local network and share the local morality. Thus notions of impartiality . . . simply do not form a part either of the public's or of the officials' expectations of bureaucratic conduct' (1968:63). Making a more general observation, La Palombara points out how 'particularism' is one of the 'integral characteristics of all systems or organizations, primitive or modern' (1963:50).

Finally, a word might be said about the use of the term 'bureaucracy'. Although it represents not one but many concepts (Albrow

1970) the word is most commonly associated with Weber, who identified it, in its most rational form, with a number of specific characteristics such as hierarchy of offices, selection of personnel on the basis of technical qualifications, security from arbitrary dismissal, promotion by merit, etc. In the remainder of this book, the terms 'bureaucrat' and 'bureaucracy' will be employed simply as descriptive synonyms for 'government servant' and 'administration', without intending to imply that the present Nepalese system fulfils Weber's criteria. Indeed, from the foregoing discussion it is clear that it more closely approximates the Weberian ideal in its principles than in its practices; but the same could probably be said of most administrative organizations.

To begin Part Two—which is concerned with the economic activities of townsmen—I consider the extent of government service by and its significance for residents of the district capital.

Notes to Chapter 3

1 In the land revenue records of Belaspur district taxes on certain lands continued to be listed as designated for the upkeep of the troops, or the post office, etc.—but not assigned to particular individuals.

2 Hodgson reports the existence of *faujdar* throughout Nepal (see Kumar 1967:128–9). To this day, court cases are classified as *dewani*—having to do with disputes over land and financial matters—and *faujdari*—those dealing with all other matters (assault, theft, defamation, etc.)

3 Many Rana men (Ranas were a part of the Chetri caste) married women of lower 'drinking' castes. The offspring of such women could not succeed to the highest posts in the land, which were reserved for the children of Chetri women only.

4 Governors could make appointments (and promotions) up to and including the rank of *bahidar*, the lowest clerical grade, and the first above a menial.

5 Firth has rightly questioned the Maussian view of obligations to give, receive and reciprocate as implying 'almost automatic, behaviour and response' (1967:17). He also suggests that Mauss's discussion deals essentially with exchanges between persons of 'broadly equivalent' social status (ibid: 12).

6 This school prepared students for the certificate of *Pratemik Paritcha*, to which the civil service nowadays assigns the same status as a 'middle school', i.e., eighth grade education. The second *bhasa pathsala*, established in 1939 in the western part of the district, was roughly the equivalent of a modern primary school, i.e. five grades.

7 This should be distinguished from payments which government servants were obliged to make to the governor after appointment. The lowest ranks in the militia, for example, were required to pay to the head of the district (who was also the militia commander) a special fee called *'salami'*.

8 I include in this figure institutions such as the high school and bank, because

they are partly or wholly financed and controlled by the government and because their employees are also regarded as government servants by members of the public.

9 Towards the end of 1969, assistant zonal commissioners were in turn replaced by special officers (*bises adhikirt*) but these retained the same functions as the previous officials. Shortly after I left the field, this office, too, was abolished and the C.D.O. became the most senior administrator in the district.

10 This system, which at the time of this study had only been in operation for about three years, had led, in many districts, to administrative stalemate and to serious tensions between the assistant commissioner and the C.D.O. Nothing of the kind, however, had happened in Belaspur.

11 In addition to public holidays, government servants are entitled to 15 days casual leave, 26 days sick leave, 26 days home leave, and 15 days mourning leave, all on full salary in any one year. In addition, they can request special leave of up to one year on half pay after two years' service (but only once in their service career), extraordinary leave without pay, and study leave as agreed with the department (Civil Service Act 1956).

12 Government servants are compelled to retire at 63, and entitled to a pension after 20 years' service. In 1945 the Ranas had introduced a pension scheme for those having served the administration for 25 consecutive years. But given the insecurity of government employment at that time few people benefited from the scheme.

13 A conference of district governors meeting shortly after the creation of the Public Service Commission, complained bitterly to the Home Ministry about the diminution of their rights to appoint, promote and dismiss government servants in their areas.

14 The administrative structure in Nepal is apparently unique in having such a large proportion of its personnel (51 per cent of the total in the country as a whole) in the menial grades (see Shrestha 1969:74).

15 On the whole, senior administrative (i.e. non-technical) officials in offices established before 1951 are older (over 40 years) and less well-educated (average 6·9 years of schooling) than those in post-1951 offices (30·8 years of age and 9·6 years of school). Men in technical posts are youngest of all (average 24·8 years) and, as might be expected, best educated (average 10·9 years of schooling).

16 The average number of high schools per district in the country is five; seven districts out of 75 have none at all, while nine, including Belaspur, have only one.

17 The caste affiliation of students in middle schools was not possible to obtain, as these are situated outside of Belaspur Bazaar.

18 'Greater prestige attaches, for a variety of reasons, to a "status" job in the Regular Service than to even the more responsible jobs in the temporary or development service' (Shrestha 1969:70). It is doubtful if these distinctions are fully appreciated by local people or that they seriously influence choices about which branch to choose when applying for government employment.

19 Non-gazetted posts must be approved by the central department concerned, subject to PSC agreement, which is given after suitable results in the examinations and interviews. Appointments to gazetted posts are made by a special

committee of the government, subject (but perhaps less so) to PSC acquiescence.

20 In 1969, several senior court officials (but not the judge), the heads of the land revenue, postal, jail, telecommunications and class organizations branches, and (for several months) the acting heads of the police and education office were residents of Belaspur district.

21 In small-scale societies of the kind found in western Nepal 'positions of bureaucratic standing are seen as positions of power, for dispensing privileges and favours, or protection' (Stirling 1968:63).

22 Some links are created quite fortuitously. A peon in the bank got his job through the recommendation of the manager's mother who, while on her way to Belaspur to visit her son, had met the young man by chance on the trail, and the latter had fallen in with her party.

23 According to Taub (1969:147) Indian officials in the Orissan capital of Bhubaneshwar use office staff as servants in their dwelling quarters. The situation among civil servants in Kathmandu is apparently different in detail if not in intent. Goodall (1966:610) writes: 'To-day, loyalty to one's superiors is expressed through unassigned personal services only nominally voluntary, and include such errands and domestic service as runs for kerosene permits and the guidance of shipments through customs'.

24 For example, the annual salary of a private in the militia rose 15 times from rs 60 to rs 900 over the 35 year period.

25 Houses were registered, lands measured and taxes assessed during periodic revenue settlements (*jac*). In Belaspur district these were held in 1852, 1868 and 1889. Thus, paddy fields (*khet*) are still taxed at the same rates as when they were last registered in 1889. The increase in income has accrued from a rise in the number of households and new lands brought under cultivation.

Part Two
Townsmen

4

Administrative service

THE administration played a prominent part not only in the establishment of Belaspur Bazaar, but as the source of many of the town's earliest settlers. They came as government employees or as members of the entourages of those who were, and for a variety of reasons, stayed on to begin new lives in the district capital. The relinquishing of particular jobs or sponsors—the immediate consequence of settling locally—did not, however, mean abandoning government service as an occupation. They and their descendants in the town, especially members of clean castes, continued to regard the administration as a major if not their sole means of livelihood. The extent of this continuity is partly reflected in the fact that the fathers of 65 per cent of bazaar residents now in an administrative post had been similarly employed. By contrast, the fathers of only 38 per cent of Belaspur villagers currently in the district administration had been government servants before them.

The extent of service

In the district capital today, three out of every four males of clean caste, eighteen years of age and over, have served or are at present serving in some branch of the Nepalese administration, while a fifth of untouchable male adults have been or are so employed. Table 10 gives the relevant figures.

TABLE 10

Male adult townsmen in government service

	Total no. in bazaar	Former employees*	Present employees†	All employees
Clean castes	118	30	58	88 (74·5%)
Untouchables	102	16	6	22 (21·5%)
	220	46	64	110 (50·0%)

* In addition, two women of clean caste were employed for a time.
† In addition, three clean caste women are currently in government service, while five men belonging to such groups teach in primary schools in the district.

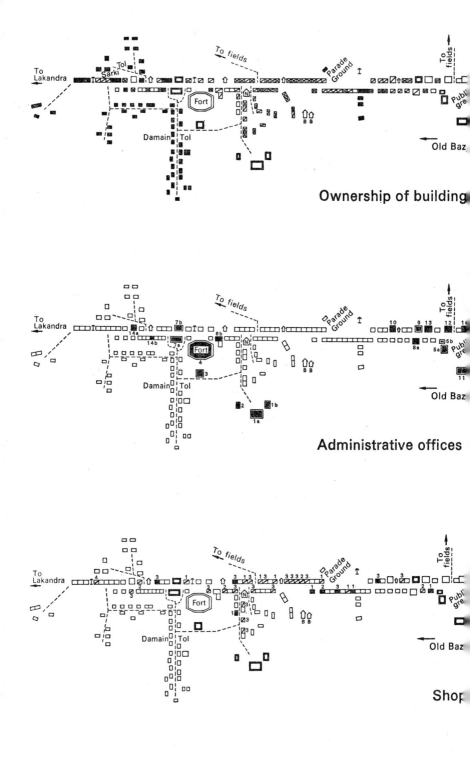

To Lakandra

Sarki Tol

To fields

Parade Ground

To fields

Publi gre

Fort

Damain Tol

B B

Old Baz

Ownership of building

To Lakandra

To fields

Parade Ground

To fields

Publi gre

7b

14a

14b

8a

8b

Fort

4

3

2

1b

1a

Damain Tol

10

9 13

12

8a

5a 5b

11

B B

Old Baz

Administrative offices

To Lakandra

To fields

Parade Ground

To fields

Publi gre

Fort

Damain Tol

B B

Old Baz

Shop

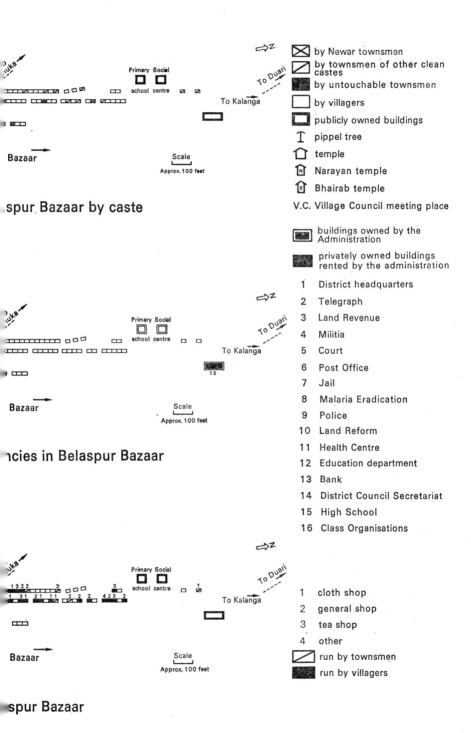

Primary Social
☐ ☐
school centre

To Duari

To Kalanga

⇨z

Bazaar

Scale
Approx. 100 feet

spur Bazaar by caste

⊠ by Newar townsmen
◪ by townsmen of other clean castes
▨ by untouchable townsmen
☐ by villagers
▭ publicly owned buildings
T pippel tree
⌂ temple
Ⓝ Narayan temple
Ⓑ Bhairab temple

V.C. Village Council meeting place

▦ buildings owned by the Administration
▨ privately owned buildings rented by the administration

1   District headquarters
2   Telegraph
3   Land Revenue
4   Militia
5   Court
6   Post Office
7   Jail
8   Malaria Eradication
9   Police
10 Land Reform
11 Health Centre
12 Education department
13 Bank
14 District Council Secretariat
15 High School
16 Class Organisations

Primary Social
☐ ☐
school centre

To Duari

To Kalanga

⇨z

Bazaar

Scale
Approx. 100 feet

ıcies in Belaspur Bazaar

15

Primary Social
☐ ☐
school centre

To Duari

To Kalanga

⇨z

1   cloth shop
2   general shop
3   tea shop
4   other
◪ run by townsmen
▨ run by villagers

Bazaar

Scale
Approx. 100 feet

spur Bazaar

In the past, untouchables were employed almost exclusively in caste-linked jobs: Tailors comprised the military band (since they are also musicians), Smiths were used as armourers, while Cobblers made ammunition belts and boots for the military garrison. With rare exceptions, untouchables were not hired—in Belaspur, at any rate—even for posts which required no qualifications of any sort. Only two untouchables resident in the town out of 29 now forty years of age or over were employed during Rana times in menial jobs not connected with any traditional occupation. Both are Butchers. The recent transfer of the main military garrison out of the district removed even these job opportunities from the occupational groups. Nowadays, although there is no official opposition to their employment in other areas of the administration, very few are in fact hired.[1]

Table 11 gives the castes of townspeople currently employed in administrative jobs (including three women).

TABLE II

Castes of government servants resident in town

Caste	Numbers	
Clean castes		
Newar	27	
Chetri	24	
Thakuri	6	
Magar	3	
Gurung	1	61
Untouchable castes		
Butcher	4	
Smith	1	
Tailor	1	6
		—
		67

The 67 bazaariyas at present in government service are almost equally divided between those working in and those working away from the district. Thirty-three, originally recruited mainly in Belaspur, have since been transferred to other areas. Over half of these are posted to neighbouring districts within the zone, including eight men in the army garrison who were moved south to Lakandra district in 1968. Fifteen civil servants whose homes are in Belaspur Bazaar are working outside the zone.

The remainder, thirty-four, are members of the district adminis-

tration in Belaspur. Although bazaar inhabitants constitute less than
one per cent of the district population, over 15 per cent of local
administration employees resident in the district are townspeople.
They form the largest contingent from any single settlement.

Clearly, townspeople have, over a long period, looked to the
district administration to provide employment. It is also evident that
they have been especially favoured, no doubt due to their close
association with the administration. As settlers and children of
settlers who came to the area as government servants, they have, by
following strategies outlined in the previous chapter, maintained a
disproportionately high representation among the personnel recruited
locally. Even in Rana times, when employment was fraught with
insecurity, a handful of townsmen served in the administration for
long periods at a stretch (see below) and undoubtedly exerted some
influence on senior officials. Then, the cumulative experience of
townsmen in administration, their control of shopkeeping and credit
and the simple expedient of constantly being 'on the spot' i.e.,
resident in the district capital, rendered their attempts to find and
retain employment more likely to succeed than members of the
district population without such advantages.

Moreover, because key schooling facilities were sited so close at
hand, townspeople were able to acquire a comparatively high level
of education, a factor redounding to their favour in the past, since
literacy was essential for a clerical post, and even more so in recent
years with the greater emphasis being put on educational standards
in the civil service. Table 12 gives the percentage figures for literacy
of adult males permanently resident in the district capital, and the
means by which literacy was acquired.

TABLE 12

Literacy of adult male townsmen

	Total no.	Illiterate %	Literate %	Literacy acquired in bhasa* %	in school %	at home %	by other means† %
Clean castes	118	6·5	93·5	44·8	43·9	2·8	2·0
Untouchables	102	76·2	23·8	7·1	7·1	4·7	4·9

* The *bhasa*, established in 1922, continued to operate until 1958, for a time alongside
the 'modern' schools, established after the revolution.

† The last category refers mainly to those who learned to read and write while working
in India, or serving in the Gurkhas.

The high proportion of male adults belonging to clean castes in the bazaar who are literate contrasts with figures for residents of Duari (P. Caplan 1972). There, just under half of male adult members of clean castes are literate; those resident in parts of the village nearest the town and so within easy reach of the *bhasa* school, have a higher rate than inhabitants of more distant areas. The literacy rate for adult male untouchables is under eight per cent.[2]

Apart from those now attending school, a total of 36 bazaariyas (35 of them members of clean castes) have achieved a middle school standard or better. Eleven have gone as far as eighth grade; nine have reached ninth grade; 14 others have reached tenth grade—four among them having received their School Leaving Certificate—and two more are at present in university. Not counting the latter two, who are still studying, and another who has joined the Indian army, all but five, i.e., 28 are presently in government service, and most (20) hold senior posts.

Indeed, a strong emphasis on schooling beyond primary and even middle grades helps to explain why such a high proportion of bazaar-resident government servants are above menial rank. As regards the personnel in the Belaspur administration, we note that 11 of the 38 senior officials (29 per cent) and 12 of the 70 junior officials (17 per cent) who live in the district are townsmen. Remembering the ratio of bazaariyas in the district population as a whole, it is clear that they provide a disproportionate number of the higher ranks in the district administration, a fact of some political significance (see especially Chapters 8 and 10).

Turning to the wider category of townsmen holding senior bureaucratic rank, both inside and outside the district, we note that of the 25 men and one woman, 21—most of whom are under 25 years old—have completed either middle school (three) or high school (18). The minority of five are all over 35 years of age and attended the *bhasa* school.

Bazaariyas are somewhat atypical in that education to post-primary levels cannot easily be correlated with great wealth. Certainly, the very poorest persons are virtually excluded from exploiting these opportunities, but otherwise the range of financial circumstances is fairly broad among the best educated townspeople. This is clearly related to the comparative ease and economy with which they can utilize school facilities. Thus, a family in town does not have to lose the labour of an adolescent member attending school located a few yards away, and need find only the fees, but no other boarding expenses which it would have to do were the school some distance away. But perhaps of even greater significance is the realization among most townspeople that without a stress on acquiring educational qualifications, whether through the *bhasa* in the past or the new secular system nowadays, no hopes for any but the most menial government service could be entertained.

Earnings in government service

Bazaar residents currently earn a total of just over rs 122,000 annually in government service. Those employed in the Belaspur administration receive approximately rs 46,700 which represents 10·5 per cent of the total amount spent on salaries (excluding allowances) by the district bureaucracy and approximately 22 per cent of all salaries it pays to residents of the district. The 33 bureaucrats posted away from Belaspur earn considerably more (rs 75,500), mainly because, with the exception of those in the terai, they receive special allowances for working and living away from home, in some cases as much as 100 per cent of their basic salary. The amount which actually finds its way back to their homes in the bazaar, however, is much less than the total earnings. The percentage of this figure which any particular individual remits is contingent on a number of considerations. First, it depends on his branch of service, for those in the militia and in certain sections of the police (mainly those performing guard duties) are housed, fed and clothed, and so need not incur any expenses on basic maintenance. (Fourteen of the 33 bureaucrats serving out of the district are in this category.) Second, it depends on the individual's rank; those holding top administrative posts are accommodated in government quarters; there are three such men serving outside the district. Most other bureaucrats away from their home area have to make their own arrangements for living, and at their own expense.

Another important consideration is the location of the posting, for the cost of living rises sharply as the distance from the terai increases. To give an example, a tin of kerosene selling for rs 15 in the terai will fetch a price of rs 40 in Belaspur Bazaar, and as much as rs 80 in Kalanga, an administrative centre some six days' walk to the north.[3] Food grains, especially rice, are also in scarce supply in such distant regions, and must be imported from the south, so that the prices of virtually all commodities are extremely high. Belaspur residents posted to one of these northerly districts (nine men have such postings at present) often complain of the inadequacy of their apparently generous cost of living allowances, and find themselves forced to use much of their salary just to meet daily expenses.[4]

A distant posting also reduces the chances of finding any close relatives on whom a bureaucrat can rely for assistance. Bazaar residents tend to marry near at hand (see Chapter 7) and so have few kinsmen or affines outside the district. On those rare occasions when such a relative does in fact live within commuting distance of the administrative office in which a Belaspuri works, the savings he makes can be substantial. One bazaar inhabitant, assigned to a northern district capital where his mother's brother happens to reside, lives in the latter's household at no cost. Even a less intimate relative would offer comparable accommodation and hospitality, although the bureaucrat guest might be expected to provide his own grain, which (if it were economic to do so) he would probably have sent to him from home.

The amount a government servant working away from home can save out of his salary will also depend on whether or not he brings some members of his family with him. In the early years of their marriage, a bureaucrat's wife is likely to accompany him to his post. Following the birth of their children (for which events she will probably return either to her home, or to that of her natal family), she is expected to assume a greater share of responsibilities within the household.[5] Thereafter she will probably only occasionally reside with her husband while he is away, although civil servants have generous amounts of leave (see Chapter 3, note 11), and so adequate opportunities to visit their homes. The frequency and duration of her stays with her husband will depend on such factors as the size of the household and the extent of its wealth (and so its ability to spare her labour). But her 'usefulness' to him in his professional capacity is not likely to be a consideration, especially outside Kathmandu. On the whole, wives of civil servants in district administration are not expected to (although they may) participate in their husbands' formal and informal functions and activities.[6]

A government servant's wish to have his wife and children with him in a particular posting will also be influenced by the attractions of the area itself. They are less likely to be invited to join him in remote regions where communications are difficult, school and health facilities poor, and as noted, the cost-of-living high by comparison with the home area. Thus, bureaucrats resident in the bazaar are more apt to have their families with them when they work in the terai than in the northernmost regions of the country. A third of the 21 married men serving outside the district have their wives and children with them at present, and only one is in an area north of Belaspur district. Bureaucrats accompanied by their families will of course not be in a position to contribute substantially to their domestic groups in the town.

The overall reluctance to bring families on assignments outside the district is demonstrated by the example of one townsman who has spent 23 years in the civil service, in six distant postings, in addition to two brief assignments in Belaspur itself. Although first transferred out of the district in 1952, it was only in 1959, while in an administrative centre in the mountains to the west of Belaspur, that he was accompanied for the first time by a member of his family. His second wife, whom he had just married, joined him for about a year. In 1964, she joined him again (with two of their young children) for a similar period in a terai district, because at that time his parents were still alive and moreover, his wife's natal home was not too far away, and she was able to spend part of this time with her parents. Since 1967, his eldest son has been with him in another terai town so that the boy, now nine years old, can attend a better school than is available in Belaspur Bazaar. When I asked him why he had not kept his family with him more often he replied 'In the end, we have only our homes and property to return to, and if we don't leave our families behind to care for them, who will do it?'.

Finally, the amount a bureaucrat posted out of his district (or indeed, one remaining within his home district) saves, depends in some measure, on his position in the household. At one extreme is the young man, unmarried and without major responsibilities at home, who is not heavily pressurized to remit his savings, especially if the household is reasonably well-off. At the other extreme is the married bureaucrat who is the economic mainstay of a poor household, and therefore whose principal concern is to save as large a proportion of his earnings as possible.

It may be estimated that between one-third and one-half of the total earnings of bureaucrats posted out of the district reaches their bazaar homes, i.e. perhaps rs 30,000.

To this point, I have noted the strong attachment of bazaar residents to administrative employment as well as the factors which have contributed to make such a commitment both necessary and possible. But a variety of circumstances arise in the course of an official's career which test his ability and determination to remain in government service.

The cycle of bureaucratic service

A man usually attempts to enter the administration immediately he meets minimum age qualifications, which is sixteen for most menial posts and eighteen for other categories. An examination of the histories of former officials resident in the bazaar reveals that 48 per cent had enlisted by the time they were twenty, 37·5 per cent between 21 and 25 years, and 14·6 per cent when they were over 25 years. A comparison of ages of first entry into the administration by townsmen currently in government service suggests a trend in recent years towards even earlier enlistment, encouraged, no doubt, by the high qualifications obtainable nowadays at an early age through schooling. Of the 67 persons now in bureaucratic posts, 46 (68·6 per cent) had entered the administration by the age of twenty, 18 (26·8 per cent) between 21 and 25, and only three (4·4 per cent) when they were over 25 years of age.

The period of young manhood is regarded as an appropriate one for 'service'. This becomes evident when the age structure of bureaucrats is compared with that for all adult males in Belaspur Bazaar. Table 13 gives the figures.

TABLE 13

Comparative age structures of bureaucrats and all adult male townsmen

	18–29 %	*30–39* %	*40–49* %	*50 and over* %
Government servants	70·4	15·6	7·8	6·2
All adult males	45·3	26·4	14·6	13·7

The age structure of government employees suggests that bureaucratic posts are surrendered as men enter their more mature years. This, of course, still does not preclude them from spending substantial periods in administrative service. The 33 former officials who are now 35 years of age or over, and therefore unable to rejoin the administration[7] spent an average of 12·2 years in government service. Over three-quarters had left government service for good by the time they had reached forty years of age, the average on 'retirement' being 36 years. Twelve men were employed from six months to five years, four between six and ten years, seven between 11 and 15 years, four men between 16 and 20 years, and six men over twenty years. Three in the latter category managed to remain in continuous employment for 25 years, spanning both the Rana and post-Rana regimes, and earned a pension from the Nepalese government. In one case, a Magar joined the court in 1934, when he was 19 years of age, and remained in the same clerical post until after the Ranas were overthrown when, under the new regime, he received regular promotions until his retirement in 1967 with 33 years of service, much of it spent, after 1952, out of the district. In another instance, a Newar's career which began in the Belaspur district headquarters, followed a similar pattern and he retired in 1962, at the age of 57, after 39 years of government service. However, the majority of those who served in former times and especially during the Rana era had occasional breaks between spells in employment (see Chapter 3). Several examples will illustrate the pattern:

T.B. a Chetri, joined the land revenue office in 1935, at the age of 22. Four years later he was dismissed but rejoined the same office in 1940 and worked there until 1950 (the time of the revolution), when, along with most employees, he left in anticipation of dismissal. He was again employed in the land revenue office for a year during 1951–2, at which time he left the service for good. He was then 39.

K.B. a Newar, worked in the land revenue office for three years from 1945–8, at which time he was dismissed. He returned, this time to the court, a year later and worked there for almost two years before being dismissed. A short time later, he rejoined the land revenue office where he remained for nine months. He left government service of his own accord during the troubles of 1950–1, but returned to work in the jail from 1953–4. He left government service for the last time at the age of 32.

J.L. a Newar, became a clerk in the telegraph office in 1954, but left in 1956 and six months later got a postman's job. He left this a year later. He was out of the administration for about a year, and then joined the police. He left this after five years and some months later got a clerical job in the district headquarters. He was dismissed (for misbehaviour) three years later at the age of 37.

The high concentration of bureaucrats in the 'under 30' age bracket, and the formidable drop in numbers over this age can be at least partly understood by examining the normal processes of household growth and development in the district capital.

Household

The definition of a household frequently presents difficulties for the anthropologist (Kolenda 1968). This is especially true when we attempt to identify such units in a setting like the bazaar, where out of a population of 941 persons, just under 10 per cent are absent on a more than temporary or seasonal basis. Some, as we have seen, are government servants posted away from Belaspur, others their wives and children who have gone to live with them, while several are brothers or sons of household heads who are in India, and with whom some minimal contact is maintained. In such circumstances the definition of a household in terms of a unit sharing a common budget (see Lynch 1969) can be useful only if it is not given a too rigid interpretation. Perhaps an additional criterion in this context is a common patrimony. For fathers and sons or brothers recognize their identification within a single household (*ghar*) until such time as steps are taken to effect a division of property. This is not to say, however, that the establishment or recognition of a separate unit is invariably accompanied by a *full* property settlement; on the contrary, it generally takes years before its finalization. But certain assets, at least, are shared out among those involved in the creation of a new household, and members of the latter thereafter assume responsibility for their own budgetary affairs.

Using these dual criteria (budget and property division), we can identify 152 households in Belaspur Bazaar. The 75 clean caste households contain an average of 6·7 persons, including those away, or 5·7 actually in residence at the time my census was conducted; the 77 untouchable units average 5·6 and 5·4 members respectively. The relatively small difference between the total numbers and those actually resident in untouchable households can be explained by (a) their virtual absence from higher ranked (and so transferable) administrative posts, (b) the fact that those working in India (16·5 per cent of untouchable adult males) seldom bring their wives and families with them, and (c) the higher rate of permanent emigration among members of these castes.[8]

Table 14 summarizes the composition of bazaar households (which are normally virilocal).

The developmental cycle of household groups among clean castes is clearly distinct from that of untouchables. Households of the latter tend to break up much earlier than those of the former. Each son separates soon after his wife has given birth to their first or

TABLE 14

*Household composition in Belaspur Bazaar**

	Clean castes	Untouchables
(a) *Simple nuclear*: husband and wife and their unmarried children	29	46
(b) *Supplemented nuclear*:		
1. Husband and wife and their unmarried children, and husband's unmarried or divorced siblings	5	3
2. Husband and wife and their unmarried children, and husband's mother	6	7†
3. Husband and wife and their unmarried children, and husband's mother and unmarried or divorced siblings	8	2
(c) *Sub-nuclear*: Widow(er) and unmarried children	6	7
(d) *Single person*: Widow(er) alone	2	1
(e) *Other*	2‡	1§
(f) *Lineal joint*: Husband and wife and married son and wife and children	9	7
(g) *Lineal-collateral joint*: Husband and wife and two or more married sons and their children	4	2
(h) *Supplemented collateral-joint*: two or more married brothers, their wives and children, and their mother	4	1
	75	77

* The various 'types' here identified are based on Kolenda (1968).
† In two cases, a man lives uxorilocally in a household containing his wife's mother.
‡ One household consists of orphaned siblings (all unmarried); the other of a woman, her married (and separated) daughter, and another (dead) daughter's son and his wife.
§ A widow in her natal home, and her sister's child.

perhaps their second child. The youngest son may remain with his parents if they are too old to care for themselves, or, as is more likely to happen, he has a widowed mother to look after by the time he comes to marry. A group of brothers will generally arrange a final property settlement, however, only after both parents have died.

The readiness to foreshorten the period of joint living and establish nuclear households relatively early is not due to any temperamental failings on the part of these low caste families. The reasons are economic 'in the sense that (with the exception of the Butchers) their resources consist essentially of occupational skills which can be practised to satisfactory advantage in small nuclear household groups. This will be discussed in greater detail in the next chapter.

Clean caste households, by contrast, tend to remain joint for longer periods of time. Married sons seldom split up before the death of their father and many continue to live in one household during the lifetime of their widowed mother; although they hardly ever remain together in a collateral or fraternal joint unit after both parents have died: there are no such households in the bazaar at present. But, as has often been pointed out, a too simple dichotomy between 'joint' and 'nuclear' reveals little of the developmental process of households. For many domestic groups characterized in the above table as of 'supplemented nuclear' types (2 and 3) were until recently joint groups which, on losing their eldest male, remained together. And it is the prolongation, first of the period of jointness, and then of co-residence of a widowed parent and his/her married son(s), which enables the clean caste household to deploy its personnel on several occupational fronts (see Chapter 6). For the moment we are concerned with its members who work in the administration. Forty-four clean caste households (58·6 per cent) and another five untouchable groups (6·5 per cent) have members serving in the bureaucracy; fourteen of these units (13 clean caste and one untouchable) have two or three persons so employed.

As might be expected, a large proportion (53·7 per cent) of the 67 bazaariyas in bureaucratic jobs are either single (including the three women) or only recently married and still without children. They belong to a variety of household types, but with only two exceptions,[9] all have in common a position of subordination within the domestic group. From the point of view of the young bureaucrat, he belongs to a household of orientation.[10] At this stage in his life he has few responsibilities at home and can easily be spared to pursue a career in government service. The young man himself is eager to do so: he regards this period as an opportunity to acquire knowledge of and develop contacts in the administration; travel to and perhaps work in other parts of the country; and bask in the prestige (and perhaps, power) of a job in the bureaucracy. Then, too, the higher his educational qualifications, the greater the expectation that school will be followed by at least a spell in service. Finally, if the family is less than prosperous, all members welcome the addition of a reasonable and steady cash income.

The birth of children, the death of parents, or indeed any developments which increase his responsibility within the household,[11] or, especially, place him in a dominant position within it, present obstacles to the continuity of a career in administrative service. The manner in which they are dealt with depends on the interaction of factors both within and outside the household.

An extremely important consideration for anyone attempting to combine government service with some measure of responsibility for household affairs is the location of a bureaucratic posting. Men who live within easy reach of their offices—and this obviously includes those both resident and working in the bazaar—can handle their administrative and household tasks with relative ease. These men have ample time during their days off, as well as before and after office hours, to deal with domestic affairs, and are always able to leave their offices for an hour or two to settle a crisis at home. Thus, the movement from a subordinate to a dominant position in the domestic group would not necessarily affect a bureaucrat working near his home. Of the 34 townsmen holding jobs in the Belaspur district administration, 17 are the eldest males in their domestic group, and 13 of them are the heads of simple nuclear households. Such men are, clearly, able to combine regular government employment with responsibility for household affairs.

But the transfer out of his home area of an official who is a household head, or, alternatively, the occurrence of some event which catapults a bureaucrat already serving outside his own district from a subordinate into a dominant position in the domestic group, may very well result in his resignation from the administration. Certainly the most frequently cited reasons for leaving government service relate to such events.

For example, the death of his father in 1962 led to the resignation of R.P., a Newar, from his clerical post in another district and his return to the bazaar. Two years later, his older brother decided to sell some land he had purchased and farmed in a village some days' walk from town and assume responsibility for the bazaar household. Soon after, R.P. re-entered the administration and was again sent to another district, a transfer he willingly accepted.

Another Newar, S.B., in 1960 the head of a household with six young children, left his job on being notified of his transfer to another district, since, as he explained, there was no one to care for his family. Several years later he obtained another post in the administration in Belaspur, which he still holds, but would probably leave again if he were to be transferred out of the district.

The composition of households to which those serving outside the district belong, reveal a significantly different pattern from the domestic units of those working in Belaspur itself. Table 15 gives the comparative figures.

TABLE 15

Households of bureaucrats serving in and outside district

Households types to which bureaucrats belong *	*Bureaucrats serving inside district*	*outside district*
(a) Simple nuclear	15	3
(b) Supplemented nuclear (1)	–	3
(2)	1	1
(3)	2	5
(c) Sub-nuclear	–	–
(d) Single person	1†	–
(e) Other	1	2
(f) Lineal joint	8	3
(g) Lineal-collateral joint	3	9
(h) Supplemented collateral-joint	3	7
	34	33

* See Table 14 for a description of these types.
† A divorced man.

The first thing to note is the considerable discrepancy in the numbers belonging to simple nuclear households (type (a)). The three men posted outside the district who are members of this kind of household are unmarried and so (from their point of view) members of units of orientation. None is a household head, whereas as I have indicated, 13 of the 15 men working in the district capital who belong to such groups are heads of what are for them households of procreation. In fact, although nine of the 33 men outside the district are the eldest males in their domestic groups, as compared with 17 of the 34 bureaucrats within the district, only three can be unequivocally identified as household heads. The remainder belong to domestic units in which their mothers play a key role; hence the relative importance of supplemented nuclear and supplemented collateral-joint households, i.e., types b (3) and (h) for those posted away from Belaspur.

Women as household heads

I have already alluded to the large numbers of bazaar inhabitants living away from home. If gross figures are broken down we note that 41 of the 119 adult men belonging to clean castes, or approximately 35 per cent, are away while only 8·4 per cent of their women are absent. This leaves a ratio of 142 women to 78 men actually resident regularly in the town among the clean castes from which, as we have seen, the great majority of bureaucrats are drawn. Such an imbalance is, of course, created by the involvement of townsmen in government service, but alternatively, it is only possible because of the critical part played by women in household affairs.

Studies of labour migration in peasant societies have noted the crucial role performed by women in the agricultural sector, thereby enabling men to spend lengthy periods away from home earning cash (Watson 1958). Women in Nepal, in addition to participating in all aspects of cultivation, save ploughing, also tend animals, are responsible for 'normal' domestic chores (cooking, cleaning, washing-up, etc.) and engage daily in the arduous and time-consuming tasks of foraging for cattle feed and firewood in the distant and increasingly sparse forests (see Macfarlane 1972). Of special significance for this discussion is the fact that when they reach their mature years, women are not infrequently called upon to organize the activities of a household, supervise its resident personnel, take whatever decisions are required and in general manage its day-to-day affairs, i.e., assume the role of household head.

There are a number of domestic groups in the town whose adult males are all away in government service. In one, a widow, with two unmarried sons in bureaucratic jobs, is alone; in another a widow, one of her daughters-in-law, and the latter's two children, are the only residents in a household which formally contains three sons, their wives, and eight children; in a third, a woman runs a household with the help of her daughter-in-law while her husband and son are away in government service. It is only because these women are fully capable of assuming the tasks of management that their households can spare its adult men to the bureaucracy.

Table 16 indicates where responsibility lies for the supervision of households to which bureaucrats working away from home belong.

To demonstrate that the significance of women in the management of domestic groups is not unique to this part of Nepal, I have provided comparative data for members of the Belaspur administration whose homes are outside the district. As the table shows, the households of eight locally-resident government servants working outside Belaspur are in the charge of their mothers (the majority of them widows), while the households of another three are supervised by some other mature woman (wife, grandmother, elder married sister). In other words, one-third of these households are run by women during their husbands' or sons' absences, and a not dissimilar proportion obtains in the case of outsiders working in the Belaspur district administration.

TABLE 16

Supervision of households of bureaucrats outside the district

Household supervised by	Bazaariyas outside Belaspur district	Outsiders in Belaspur district
Father	18	22
Elder brother	3*	3
Mother	8	6
Other mature woman	3	3
Other	1	2
	33	36

* In one case the elder brother shares supervision with their mother; in another, their mother is alive, but too old and frail to take part in active management.

Careers in government service

If we stress the importance of women for the successful pursuit of a career in government service, we do not thereby underestimate the role of senior male kinsmen in these matters. In approximately two-thirds of all cases, as the table above shows, bureaucrats rely on fathers and elder brothers to protect their interests at home. It is interesting, and a little puzzling, to note, however, that there are no domestic groups in which a married son or younger brother runs the household, leaving his father or elder brother free to pursue a career in the administration. This may have to do with the notion that government service is a young man's occupation and that if a household can only 'afford' one bureaucrat, all must defer to the youngest. But it is more likely related to the fact that the normal stresses leading to the break-up of a household cannot be held in check by a father or elder brother if he is in government service while his son or younger brother is at home.

A young man with a wife and children who would, in the normal course of events, establish a separate nuclear household must, if he is to pursue his career in the civil service, submit to a different household organization. For the precipitate creation of a simple domestic unit in which he is the dominant figure places the bureaucrat in an invidious position, where his responsibilities both to the job and the domestic group become difficult if not impossible to discharge, unless, of course, he is fortunate enough to be posted in his home area.

Bureaucratic rank is here an important factor, since there is less likelihood that men in lower posts will receive assignments away from their home district than those in senior ones. Nine of the 13 bureaucrats serving in the district who are the heads of nuclear households are of menial or junior rank. Since senior officials are transferred frequently,[12] domestic arrangements are required which allow for the continued management of their estates during their prolonged absences. Such bureaucrats must, therefore, delay partition and remain for as long a period as possible either in joint households or, after the death of one parent, in domestic groups which include the other. Clearly, the fact that they are attached to households supervised by their fathers, mothers or other persons with greater seniority than themselves enables the majority of bureaucrats posted away from home to continue their careers in the civil service. But the figures given earlier for average length of service and age structure of government employees suggest that many men are, in fact, still deflected from pursuing their careers by events which transform the composition of and their positions in the households to which they belong.

However, plans for a career in bureaucratic service do not depend wholly on finding solutions to problems of domestic organization. Indeed, decisions regarding such organization are likely themselves to be influenced by expectations about future prospects in the bureaucracy. It has been noted that government service has traditionally been plagued by insecurity and that even today many kinds of administrative employment are only of limited duration. As a result, most young men do not regard public service as a life-long career toward which they study and prepare. They expect that after a spell in an administrative job they will devote the rest of their lives entirely to their household affairs.

Until the end of the Rana period the likelihood of Belaspuris rising to senior administrative positions was extremely remote. As a result, only a small minority thought it worthwhile taking a post outside the district (which usually meant accompanying the district governor to his new assignment). Even nowadays, those in menial or junior ranks, while only infrequently transferred out of their home district, are most reluctant to accept such transfer when it comes, especially if they entertain no hopes for promotion. Unless they are still very young and in the early stages of both their domestic and administrative careers, they usually prefer to resign. In response to queries about their reasons for leaving, ex-officials often reply: 'Why go out of the district for a low post?'

This attitude is conditioned somewhat by the knowledge that little saving is possible from the salaries paid low-ranking officials outside their home district (see above), and that isolation and loneliness are usually the lot of men living and working far from their homes. But it also acknowledges the risks to the viability and good management of their households occasioned by their absences. Such risks are not felt worth taking if the prospects for advancement and success are not seen to be bright.

The tenacity with which a career in the civil service is pursued beyond the stage of young manhood depends also on the strength of the competition from alternative means of livelihood. As I indicate in Chapter 6, the growth of land ownership among bazaariyas, attributable in large measure to money earned in government service, has not only rendered them less dependent financially on employment in the bureaucracy, but has compelled them to devote more time and care to the management of these estates. Similarly, the past few decades have seen a substantial expansion of commerce in the town, also attributable in large part to the growth of administration, and to the extent that townspeople have become increasingly dependent on this means of livelihood, their stake in administrative service must be constantly weighed and re-assessed.

Conclusion

This chapter has attempted to convey the scale of townsmen's involvement in government service over a long period of time, explicable largely in terms of their 'strategic' position on the very doorstep of the administration. Because, increasingly, local bureaucrats are being promoted and transferred, it was necessary to stress the importance of relating the growth of an individual career in the civil service to the normal processes of household development. It was noted that a critical variable in the situation is the nature of the domestic group: career bureaucrats tend to be associated with households in which a genealogically senior kinsman continues to assume responsibility for their management. In this regard, special note was taken of the position of mature women, especially widows, in bazaar domestic groups. There has been very little written on the significance of this category of women in South Asian economies, although many of these economies are, in fact, heavily dependent on some form of migrant labour. In the literature on the joint household, for example, widows are generally regarded as 'supplements' or 'accretions' to the basic nuclear or joint unit, which terms tend to convey the impression, perhaps unintended, that these women are, in fact, peripheral. Thus, from a position of subordination to her husband in a joint unit, she is transferred, after his death (by the anthropologist), to a similar position in a nuclear group in which the focus is her son; her true role, indeed, the very nature of the resulting domestic group, may be completely overlooked.

Finally, it should be noted that some of the developments in household organization described in these paragraphs may very well presage a departure from practices in Rana times. Townspeople who benefited considerably from the first *bhasa* school, have been no less quick to take advantage of new educational facilities in the district capital, and so have been able to exploit the opportunities now available for advancement to higher and more lucrative levels in the civil service. As competition increases for these scarce and attractive posts, and as the prospects for promotion, greater security and eventual pension rights improve, bazaar incumbents may become more reluctant to surrender their jobs—even if these involve frequent transfers out of the district—than were their predecessors to leave their lower-ranking, less secure and less lucrative employment. Household arrangements will then increasingly have to be made to enable them to do so.

Indeed, I have the impression, gained from the biographies of former government servants, that because of the limited opportunities during Rana times, bazaar households of clean caste divided much earlier than they tend to do nowadays. Because government service was unlikely to result in transfer out of the district, and thus in a need to reconcile the demands of an estate, on the one hand, and a post away from home, on the other, there would have been little incentive for sons to remain with their parents following marriage. If this is so, and there is a greater concern at present than in the past to delay the partition of domestic groups, it could be seen in part as a response to the growing commitment of townsmen to the new bureaucracy.

Notes to Chapter 4

1 Largely due to the difficulties of finding employment in the Nepalese administration, 17 untouchables (16·3 per cent of adult males) have been or are
 currently in some salaried full-time job in India, including the 'Gurkha'
 regiments of the Indian or British armies.

2 In the remainder of this book, there are a number of references to Duari, a
 village some two miles north of the bazaar, which is the focus of Patricia
 Caplan's study (1972). To avoid unnecessary repetition, all further allusions
 to this settlement will not be accompanied by the usual bibliographical
 citation, save where specific points or passages are noted.

3 See McDougal (1968) for a comparison of prices in terai and hill markets
 (especially Table 16 on p. 41).

4 Because of the isolation of the extreme northern mountain regions of far
 western Nepal, school facilities there have developed even more slowly than
 in the rest of the country, including Belaspur. For example, two of the three
 districts making up one zone north of Belaspur are without high schools.
 Thus, there is a shortage of local men with sufficient education to fill senior
 posts in these district administrations, and because Belaspur is comparatively
 near these areas, inhabitants of the district are, not infrequently, posted to
 the north and, indeed, sometimes are accepted into the bureaucracy specifically to fill vacancies in these northern district administrations. Belaspuris put
 up with the hardships partly because of the good salaries, where these can be
 saved, and partly in the hope that after an initial period they will be posted
 elsewhere.

5 See below for a discussion of households.

6 In Kathmandu, it is mainly the need to meet informally with westerners
 which has compelled Nepalese bureaucrats to alter traditional attitudes about
 the role of women in these matters.

7 Persons 35 years of age and over are not eligible for recruitment to the civil
 service.

8 This is difficult to quantify, but genealogies of untouchables resident in the
 town suggest that a great many men begin as temporary migrants and if they
 are successful in obtaining good employment, sever links with home after a
 few years. This is probably due to the general impoverishment of untouchables and the fact that opportunities for their advancement are limited in the

hills of western Nepal. Many, however, have been able to exploit their monopoly of traditional crafts (see Chapter 5).

9 A divorced man living alone who I have counted as a single person, and the eldest brother among a group of (unmarried) orphaned siblings.

10 I find it useful to utilize the familiar term 'family of orientation' (or procreation) to indicate the nature of a household from the vantage point of a particular individual.

11 Since all but two households rely on some source of income in addition to government service, the household affairs for which responsibility may have to be assumed could include the management of land or a shop or both (see Chapter 6).

12 Gazetted officers are required, under the Civil Service Act, to be transferred at least every three years.

5

Craft specialization

THERE has been a dramatic increase in the overall impact of administration on the district during the two decades since the end of Rana rule. This is manifested both in terms of the expanded opportunities for employment which it provides, and the wider role played by the bureaucracy in stimulating the economy. Whereas the Ranas sought, at the very least, to limit their expenditures so as not to exceed income from local taxes, the new regime (with the help of generous foreign aid) has injected large amounts of cash into the district, far outstripping tax revenues. This money has entered the area through, as we have seen, salaries and other costs of administration, and, in recent years, grants for development projects. This, added to more 'traditional' sources of external earnings such as butter exports and wage labour abroad has led to greater monetization in the district as a whole, and, of special interest here, stimulated the growth of Belaspur Bazaar as a commercial centre.

The next two chapters examine the significance of these changes for bazaar inhabitants. This chapter considers their effects on the traditional occupations of untouchables, and on the latters' links with their clients. Chapter 6 then traces the development of retail trade and its contemporary significance for resident shopkeepers who are, in the main, members of clean castes. The chapter concludes with a discussion of the growth of landownership among bazaariyas.

Occupational groups

One of the characteristics which is said to define a system of castes is the organic or inter-dependent nature of their relations, inasmuch as each group monopolizes a specific occupation (see Leach 1962; Bailey 1963). In the far western hills of Nepal, among the clean castes today, it is only the Brahmins who are identified in this way with a particular occupational role, based on their religious functions as household priests (*purohit*), although of course, not all Brahmins practice as such. Those who do, serve only members of clean castes and refer to their clients as *jajman*. The relationship between them is usually regarded as permanent, with sons inheriting the priests or clients of their fathers.

Those ranked below the clean castes are all, by historical association, craft specialists, and it is the polluting nature of these crafts which renders 'untouchable' those who were and are associated with them. Three of the four untouchable groups in the town live mainly by practising their caste occupations. Only the Butchers no longer do so, and it is unlikely that they have done since their arrival in the town. Still, despite the fact that they pursue a variety of 'neutral' occupations—cultivating, government service, shopkeeping—they are considered by the clean castes as no less polluted and polluting than other untouchables because of their traditional craft. The three remaining unclean castes—Tailors, Cobblers and Smiths—are discussed in turn.

Tailors

Due largely to the small proportion of Tailors in the district—they are five per cent of the population—the services of members of this caste are in constant demand. Those in the bazaar make clothes not only for other townsmen, but for inhabitants of nearby villages as well. On the whole, they tend to exchange services with other untouchable craftsmen; relations with members of clean castes, however, are founded on different forms of reciprocity. Two main kinds can be identified.

In one, the Tailor provides his services to a client (*bista*) in the context of a long-standing, heritable relationship. The service is reciprocated by a fixed annual payment of grain (*bali*, lit. harvest) which reflects both the amount of work to be done, on the basis of the numbers in the client's household, and the wealth of the client. This figure may be adjusted from time to time, and is usually supplemented by small cash payments to the Tailor on specific occasions when work is carried out. This work is done either at the Tailor's own dwelling or, more frequently, at the client's home. Since Tailors generally have several clients in a single village or village cluster they spend several days at a time in a specific area visiting each client in turn.

All but four of the 29 Tailor households in the town have such clients: two households contain widows living alone, who are unable to engage in this work; two others have chosen not to make such arrangements. Individual households have from four to 46 clients, resident both in the bazaar and surrounding villages, an average of just under 15 per Tailor household. Clients who reciprocate these services in kind, mainly villagers, pay an average of 10 *pathi* of edible grain.[1]

A small minority of clean caste households in the town (eight out of 75) also make fixed payments in grain to their Tailors. These are households with either substantial land holdings or no sources of income other than land (see Chapter 6). The majority (38 households), however, provide set annual cash payments, which are also generally referred to as *bali*. They range from rs 6–40, averaging rs 22 per client family. This figure is somewhat less than the cash value, based on exchange rates prevailing in the district, of grain payments made by village clients. Because bazaar clients are near at hand, and because relationships between the latter and their craftsmen are more 'multiplex' in nature than those between villagers and craftsmen (who are not members of the same local community), the Tailors receive other non-specific benefits, and so are not dissatisfied with this differential. In any case, the cash given by bazaar clients can be utilized in a greater variety of contexts, including the purchase of cheap grain outside the district (see note 5). What is important to note here is that households offering cash *bali*, which include the wealthiest in the bazaar, are regarded by the Tailors as their clients (*bista*) no less than are those who provide grains.

It is apparent that such an arrangement is not a recent development, but has been followed for as long as the residents of Belaspur Bazaar have earned an almost exclusively cash income. Indeed, it is only the relatively recent growth of land ownership among town-dwellers that has enabled a few to provide grain to their Tailors.

A wholly different form of reciprocity may exist between members of clean castes and Tailors, namely, one in which the services of these craftsmen are paid for in cash on a piece-work basis. Such an arrangement avoids any long-term commitment on either side, and each exchange becomes, in effect, akin to a market transaction. Twenty-seven bazaar households, generally the least well-to-do among the clean castes, acquire the services of Tailors in this way. The distinction between payments given by a client and those given by a transient customer is maintained in terminology. The former pays *bali*, the latter *jhela*, the same term used for payments to agricultural labourers hired on a daily basis.

Informants suggest that the practice of paying *jhela* represents a growing trend among townspeople; similarly, as the surrounding countryside has become more monetized, poorer villagers especially are turning increasingly to this form of exchange.

Bazaar Tailors, for their part, while somewhat reluctant to sever their links to clients—two in five households earn just about enough from this source alone to feed their members—nevertheless find such links of dwindling attraction as increased opportunities arise for the 'commercialization' of their skills. One Tailor reckons that he gets a larger income from piece-work than from his 46 clients (the largest number of clients of any single Tailor household). He explains: 'Many of us want to drop our clients, but (men like) my father'—with whom he shares a joint household—'thinks clients mean security and refuses to give them up. So he and my mother and wife do the work for clients, and I do the piece-work'. Every practising Tailor in the bazaar has an Indian-made machine, invariably purchased in the terai. Women work alongside the men, but sew only by hand.

There are now five tailoring workshops located along the main street in the town. Two of these have been established in buildings purchased by Tailors in the past few years and are open on a permanent basis. A third is in rented premises while two others are located in dwellings owned by bazaar clients, who provide the accomodation free of charge in return for the services of their Tailors. These latter three workshops are open only during the few weeks in the autumn before the festivals of Dasein and Tiwar, when most families in the area require the bulk of their annual tailoring needs. The transactions in these workshops are entirely with transient customers on a cash-for-work basis.

The profits from such commerce can be substantial. Two brothers-in-law working together reckon on a joint income of rs 5–600 per month, the equivalent of a very senior bureaucrat's salary. Admitedly, this is the most successful enterprise of its kind, but for a handful of workshops to earn anything like this level of income suggests a substantial demand for 'free-lance' tailoring services. This is forthcoming partly because of the contraction of traditional Tailor-client links, as I have indicated, and because of the continuous growth of the administration which has brought more outside bureaucrats to live for extended periods in the town. The younger among them generally favour a 'western' style of clothing, and are increasingly emulated in this by the 'modern' young men of the district. To make the trousers and jackets such customers demand—only shirts and socks are sold ready-made in the bazaar—requires certain skills which village Tailors, who make mainly the traditional hill costumes,[2] do not possess, but which a number of bazaar craftsmen, alone in the district, have acquired. These skills have been learned during the course of annual migrations to the plains over a period of years.

Most Tailors resident in the town spend the winter months (January–February) in one of the large towns in the terai. This is the season when there is little work to do at home, and the men attempt to earn some extra cash. No one knows for certain when the practice began, but the older men report that their fathers before them did the same. In 1969, 18 men from 15 of the 29 Tailor households spent at least part of the winter in the plains. It is unlikely that as large a proportion went south in the past as do at present since the military band required about a dozen men at any one time, and most of them were recruited from the local Tailor population.

Men migrate (along with their machines) in teams of two or three closely related kinsmen or neighbours. In addition, they usually bring along an adolescent boy who is still learning his craft. He purchases food and runs errands for the others, cooks for them and may attempt to solicit trade. They either rent a small workshop in the main commercial centre, or find an open space along the main street where they erect a temporary shelter: since the weather is dry and pleasant in the terai at this time of year they require only minimal protection. All income is kept in a common fund from which the team's expenses are met. At the end of the season the net proceeds are divided equally, although the young apprentice may receive a slightly smaller share than the others.

Without taking into account the earnings of one man who became ill shortly after arrival in the plains and had to return home, net income for the winter of 1969 averaged approximately rs 100 per migrant. The latter do not regard such amounts as particularly impressive, but they point out that by spending the winter months away 'there are fewer mouths to feed at home', that they can, at least, cover their own subsistence expenses while in the terai, and purchase a few necessities such as cloth or salt at the same time.

The siting of most of the country's zonal capitals in the plains[3] has attracted large and heterogeneous populations to these centres, facilitated by favourable road, rail and (now) air communications. For the Tailors from Belaspur Bazaar this has meant that to compete for business they have had to learn how to make the western-style clothes worn by large segments of this relatively sophisticated populace. Such talents, as I have indicated, have given them certain advantages in their own district. It has also enabled them to exploit new opportunities in areas north of Belaspur district, particularly the demand for skilled Tailors which has arisen during the past decade in Kalanga, a zonal capital some six days' walk away.

According to one Tailor: 'There are a lot of Nepalese (i.e. administrators from Kathmandu) in Kalanga and they have plenty of money. They buy only the most expensive cloth in the shops (much of it imported by air) and they are willing to pay plenty for good tailoring. They want Kathmandu-style clothes. Village people also come from miles around to have their clothes made up in Kalanga. There are plenty of local Tailors but they can only make ordinary village dress. Some don't even have machines. But we have learned to make modern clothes in the terai and when we go up there we get plenty of work'.

Migrations to the north take place in the hot season between April and June. Because of the difficult trek and the high cost of living in such areas (see Chapter 4) Tailors travel and work together in teams of between four and six men, rather than in the smaller units which go south. Methods of cooperation are similar, but the earnings are considerably higher. Eleven men spent the hot season of 1969 in the north (six of them after spending the winter in the terai) and none brought home under rs 500 after a two month stay.

Cobblers

The Cobblers of Belaspur Bazaar constitute the largest concentration of members of this caste in the district practising their traditional occupation of leather-working (mainly making shoes).[4] Although many members of high castes are reluctant to wear cow-hide on their feet, and several bazaar shops now sell factory-made canvas and other non-leather shoes and sandals, Cobblers continue to rely almost exclusively on their craft for a livelihood.

At one time, Cobblers from the bazaar, like the Tailors, spent part of the winter months in the terai, but increased competition and a host of special taxes on leather imposed by the terai municipalities rendered this migration less than worthwhile, and it is no longer undertaken. A few Cobblers, however, go north during the summer months. Four of the 30 Cobbler households in the town each sent one of its members to Kalanga in 1969, and another seven had done so at some time during the preceding three year period. But despite the high financial rewards no Cobbler household regards such migration as an essential part of its annual economic activities.

There are several reasons for this. Firstly, the journey to and from and the living conditions in Kalanga are, as I have pointed out, very difficult. Second, bazaar Cobblers have no monopoly of knowledge or techniques, such as the Tailors have, which local Kalanga leather craftsmen do not possess, although the former have acquired something of a national reputation for the quality of their work. Third, women play only a marginal and limited role in the shoe-making process, so that a Cobbler's production is determined wholly by his own skills and speed. Since all work is by hand—only one household has a stitching machine—a Cobbler can only make 10–15 pairs of shoes in a month, an amount he has no difficulty selling in the bazaar.

The main advantage of going north relates to the higher prices he can get for his product, an average of rs 20 for a pair of shoes, or just under double the bazaar price. Such a journey, therefore, is usually undertaken to meet a specific and urgent need for cash, to make up for a bad year at home, repay a pressing debt, pay bridewealth or compensation for taking another man's wife, and so on. When he goes, the Cobbler may stay in Kalanga for the whole of the hot season and make shoes to order, with leather he brings from Belaspur, or, at much greater expense, purchases locally. Alternatively, he may make the shoes at home and transport them north for sale. In the latter case, he probably spends only a few weeks in Kalanga, returning home as soon as his stock is exhausted. On average a Cobbler can expect to return home with rs 150 for each month spent in the north.

Except for three households without adult males, and another two whose men are in the Indian army, all Cobbler households engage in shoe-making. Only one household has purchased a small building in the main street of Old Bazaar which serves as a workshop for its men; the majority work at home in the sheltered verandahs at the front of their dwellings.

Five of the 30 Cobbler households still have hereditary clients (also called *bista*) in nearby villages—an average of four clients each—and this is also explained in terms of the elders' reluctance to abandon the security which such clients represent. But although bazaar Cobblers have severed ties with the majority of their clients over the past generation, there is no evidence to suggest that the number of these links was at all significant in the past. Many villagers wore no shoes and those who did, mainly for appearances in the town, generally could barter grain for a new pair annually. Families who preferred to receive a Cobbler's service in the context of a heritable, long-standing tie, did so primarily for status considerations.

The Cobblers entered such relationships in the past mainly to secure a reliable source of grain in the villages. Nowadays, they are in a stronger position to refuse clients, partly because they have begun to cultivate land themselves (see Chapter 6), but primarily because there are cheaper and more reliable grain supplies in recently developed, highly productive surplus areas south of the district, which can be purchased for cash.[5] But even those who retain and are retained by clients make shoes, like the majority of Cobbler households, for sale to villagers and townsmen, administrators and a variety of people passing through Belaspur Bazaar on their way to the plains or areas in the north.

There is still some barter exchange carried on by Cobblers: for grain from villagers, and for salt brought up from the terai by transhumant shepherds on their homeward journey north for the hot months. But the overwhelming majority of their transactions now involve cash.

Smiths

The Smiths constitute the largest untouchable caste in the district, forming approximately 19 per cent of its population. They are divided into a number of sub-groups based on type of craft specialization. The largest section, the iron Smiths (Kami) mainly fabricate and repair agricultural implements. Another section, the Tamata, makes brass and occasionally other metal cooking utensils. The Smiths resident in the bazaar belong to a third sub-group who work in precious metals.[6] Sunar, as they are called, make the gold and silver ornaments worn by Nepalese women: these are received from their natal families as dowries, and from their husbands as wedding presents or gifts on subsequent occasions.

Seven of the nine Smith households in the town engage in this kind of work. In one of the two which do not there is a woman living alone, and the only male in the other is in the police. Relationships with customers are based on cash payment for particular jobs: there is no tradition of any heritable and long-standing link between gold/silver Smith and client, although in the past services were more frequently provided in return for payment in grain.

With the growth of the district capital, Smiths find more work among both the permanent and temporary inhabitants of the town than in the past, but still make regular tours of villages in the district, in each of which they may remain for several days at a time. In this way, a man may earn perhaps rs 60 per month; the bazaar's most skilled craftsman counts on a monthly income of rs 200. Generally, however, the economic position of Smiths, who cannot benefit from temporary migrations to the plains or the far north, and whose skills are not in great demand because of a fairly large population of gold/silver craftsmen in the district at large, is considerably more precarious than that of either Tailors or Cobblers.

Marriages of untouchables

A concern to preserve a respectable standing within the wider untouchable community conferred by their favourable economic position, may help to explain the strong preference for intra-bazaar marriages among the Tailors and Cobblers. Over half of the marriages made by men in these two groups have been with towns-women, while approximately one-third of the marriages of male Butchers have been within the bazaar; by contrast, with one exception, all Smith men have made affinal links outside the district capital (see Table 17).

TABLE 17

Marriages of untouchable males

| | Within bazaar | | Outside bazaar | | *Total (100%)* |
	No.	*%*	*No.*	*%*	*No.*
Cobbler	32	57·2	24	42·8	56
Tailor	27	54·0	23	46·0	50
Butcher	7	35·0	13	65·0	20
Smith	1	6·7	14	93·3	15
	67	47·6	74	52·4	141

Employing a different measure, 19 of 36 Tailor women, and 24 of 38 Cobbler women living virilocally[7] in the bazaar were born and brought up in the district capital. By contrast, 10 out of 25 Butcher women and only one out of 11 Smith women so married are living next door to their natal households (see Table 18).

TABLE 18

Natal homes of untouchable married women living in the town

	In bazaar		Outside bazaar		Total (100%)
	No.	%	No.	%	No.
Cobbler	24	63·1	14	26·9	38
Tailor	19	52·8	17	47·2	36
Butcher	10	40·0	15	60·0	25
Smith	1	8·2	11	91·8	12
	54	48·7	57	51·3	111

The low rate of intra-bazaar marriage among the Smiths is largely attributable to demographic factors. Their members in the town are few, so that spouses must be sought outside the community. On the whole, these are found within nearby villages of the district. The Butchers, with similar numbers, nevertheless seek, wherever possible, to marry in the town, because the alternative is marriage out of the district. Since no other members of this caste are to be found in the villages of Belaspur, they are forced to seek partners in other distant administrative centres where similar communities have been established. Despite a small population therefore, they do frequently arrange intra-bazaar unions, and are able to do this because, lacking identifiable unilineal descent groups, there are few prohibitions on genealogically close unions.

The Tailors and Cobblers, on the other hand, are relatively populous in the town and can, without too much difficulty, find marriage partners locally, yet outside their clan units, if they choose to do so.

The particularly strong tendency for Cobbler intra-bazaar marriage is due not only to favourable demographic conditions, but to occupational differences and, ultimately, distinctions of standing between themselves and other Cobbler communities in the district. For the majority of the latter have abandoned their traditional craft and have become an extremely impoverished segment of rural society. Bazaar Cobblers are aware of their own position as a comparatively well-off and self-sufficient community. They are anxious to point out that they do not porter other people's loads, nor carry palanquins (*doli*) in which the brides of high castes commence their journeys to their new husbands' homes, nor are they tied to these castes as plough-servants or dependent on them for menial work in the fields. These are all references to the demeaning nature of the tasks which are the lot of most Cobblers outside the town, and they are cited as the reasons for the bazaariyas' reluctance to create marriage ties with, for example, the large population of caste fellows in the nearby village of Duari.

These distinctions based on occupation and wealth are sometimes expressed in terms of distinctive myths of origin or even different rank. I have heard it said that only Cobblers who originated, like those in the town, from certain areas to the east, are 'real' Cobblers. One member of the community in the bazaar put it this way: 'There are two kinds of Bahun (the generic term for both Brahmin and Jaisi) and two kinds of Cobbler. The Brahmin does not marry the Jaisi, and we do not marry these other Cobblers. We do not even eat their cooked rice'. Cobbler marriages outside the town tend to be concentrated in a few settlements where there are fellow caste members practising their traditional craft, and economically in a similar position.

The Tailors, concerned as are the Cobblers to maintain both their favoured occupational position and their status, are nevertheless not quite so anxious about marriages outside the locality. This is due mainly to the existence of a number of Tailor groups in the district who continue to practice their craft and have attained relatively comfortable economic circumstances. Members of this caste in Duari, for example, earn an adequate living by tailoring.

Finally, it might be noted that on the whole, the marriage choices of untouchables indicate a strong preference for caste endogamy. Of the 141 marriages made by untouchable men resident in the town, only six are across caste lines. One gold/silver Smith is married to a Muslim woman, regarded as untouchable, from a nearby village. Another Smith is married to a Cobbler woman from the bazaar, while one Cobbler and three Butchers eloped with women of clean castes, three Chetris and a Magar, from villages in other districts, who now live with them in the town.

Conclusion: jajmani ties

In the foregoing paragraphs I have tried to indicate that the stimulus given the district economy by the growth of administration has, on balance, had a substantial impact on the bazaar's untouchables but that it has not affected the various groups among them in the same way. For the Smiths and Cobblers it has meant, in particular, an increase in cash transactions and a corresponding diminution of other forms of exchange. Increasing monetization has stimulated the tendency for traditional, hereditary links with clients to be replaced by more impersonal, market transactions between, especially, Tailors and those for whom they provide services. This arises from a desire to be free of what the young men regard as onerous obligations in order better to exploit a variety of economic opportunities both within and outside the district which have developed during the past two decades.

This raises the question of whether a displacement of grain by cash payments, and of long-standing ties by more casual ones signifies a decline in the *jajmani* system prevailing in this part of Nepal. This is arguable, of course, if such a system is defined essentially in terms of the medium of payment for services, and the permanence of the links between client and craftsman (see Harper 1959). I have suggested, however, that bazaar-resident clients, relying for their incomes mainly on government service and shop-keeping have all along made cash payments to the Tailors with whom they nevertheless had hereditary ties, and alternatively, that villagers who occasionally required the services of silver/gold Smiths or Cobblers, usually acquired these in exchange for grain, which custom did not, however, necessarily imply enduring links. It is also evident that only the Tailors have traditionally maintained lasting relationships with their clients, but that most Cobblers and all silver/gold Smiths established more tenuous bonds with those who engaged their services.

Unless we are to conclude that (leaving aside priestly services provided by Brahmins) the *jajmani* system in this area embraced only the Tailors and their clients, the principles underlying such a system must be seen to be based on something other than the specific content of the relationship between client and craftsman. They must be based, rather, on the kinds of services the latter provide and the former require to be provided with in order to retain their ritual status. For, as Pocock argues, 'whether the payment is in cash or kind and however casual the relationship may appear, there are certain services the need for which derives directly from the structure of the caste system' (1962:83–4). These untouchables are 'religious specialists' whose 'business it is to cope with the impurities arising from the natural course of life' (ibid:85).[8]

Since these services are still required and, more importantly, continue to be offered by specialists, it is necessary to conclude that in the most fundamental sense, the *jajmani* system persists, despite certain organizational changes described above.

To date, there have been no developments such as the replacement of hand-made by manufactured products which could threaten the demand for the services of craft specialists in the hills of western Nepal. Clearly, a situation in which untouchables were compelled to abandon their traditional occupations would no longer warrant being termed a *jajmani* system even if untouchability by traditional occupational association were to continue (as in the case of the Butchers). The demise of *jajmani* could also come about, as Elder has suggested (1970) by the concerted refusal of untouchables to practice their polluting crafts despite continuing demand. It is sometimes argued that growing educational opportunities would lead to such action. This prediction is not borne out by developments in Belaspur.

Although a growing number of untouchable children are now receiving an education (there are ten in primary schools within the bazaar) there is no indication that this is likely to have an immediate effect on the occupational patterns of these castes. The few young men who attended school have taken up their traditional crafts. This is partly explicable by the lack of job opportunities locally, and the difficulties facing an untouchable applicant for a scarce administrative post. There are no places reserved for members of such castes in Nepal. But it must also be seen as a rational decision to exploit an economic 'niche' which provides craft specialists with a comparatively secure living. The best educated untouchable, a young man who recently completed middle school, inherited, and now runs with his younger brother, who completed primary school, the most successful leather workshop in the town. It is perhaps no coincidence that the untouchables who have for many years enjoyed some success in obtaining non-caste linked government posts are the Butchers who long ago abandoned their traditional occupation. Of the four bazaar untouchables currently in government employment, three are members of this caste.

Notes to Chapter 5

1 There are eight *mana* in a *pathi*. One *mana* is equal to approximately one pound (see also Appendix B).

2 Most men in the area wear the traditional Nepalese costume consisting of a double-breasted upper garment which falls below the waist, and a pair of jodhpurs loose at the waist but tapering gradually so that they are tight-fitting from the knees down. Women wear a blouse and a *sari* as a lower garment, with a length of material wrapped round the waist. None of the changes in style mentioned here affect the dress of women. The only perceptible development is that a few women in the bazaar have taken to copying the wives of senior administrators from outside the district who wear their *sari* in the manner of Indian women, i.e., with the end piece thrown back over the shoulder.

3 The capitals of 10 of the country's 14 zones are in the terai.

4 There are a few places in the district where Cobblers still practice their traditional craft, but most, like those in the village of Duari, have long since given this up.

5 With the eradication of malaria in the valley of Lakandra, two days' walk from Belaspur Bazaar, there has been an enormous expansion of paddy cultivation, and the prices there are lower than in Belaspur.

6 This does not purport to be an exhaustive breakdown of the Smiths.

7 This excludes a few married women who for one reason or another are living in their natal homes in the town.

8 Pocock distinguishes between specialists who provide a 'religious' service (and whose ties to clients therefore fall within a *jajmani* context) and those who provide a commodity and 'are correctly described as artisans'. The specialization of the latter type of group 'is not a direct result of the exigencies of the caste system' and therefore, strictly speaking, falls outside the *jajmani* system' (1962:85). He also identifies a third category of specialists working in metal, stone and wood (Visvakarma castes). The division he draws is difficult to apply in the Nepalese context, where no distinction in status is recognized between various craft specialists, so that each serves all the others. Moreover, all groups provide both services and commodities, which render them untouchable and so are essential to the status maintenance of the higher castes. In this sense, therefore, all may be regarded as 'religious' in nature.

6

Shopkeepers and Landowners

The town as trading centre

EVER since its establishment as a district capital, Belaspur Bazaar
has been not only the administrative but the trading centre of the
area as well. Lying mid-way between the terai and the northern
border, the town was conveniently placed for shepherds and traders
on their way south to barter some of their Tibetan salt for rice or
other goods and services produced by local inhabitants, and on their
return journey dispose, if necessary, of goods they had purchased in
the plains. But the trade was sporadic and by all accounts not
extensive, and in this respect the town was of only minor importance.

Nor, until a generation ago, was the bazaar regarded as a commercial centre of any real significance by the district population.
Before 1951, shopkeeping developed hardly at all, for a variety of
reasons. Until the turn of the century, land in the district was in
ample supply and most peasants were reasonably self-sufficient
producers, exchanging directly their 'surpluses' for goods and
services they lacked, without the need for middlemen. Even as
lands became scarce and many turned to migrant labour to make up
their grain shortages, food imports and exchanges were conducted
without the benefit of intermediaries. Bazaar merchants, in short,
never became large-scale traders in grain. Moreover, non-resident
administrators, whose provisioning might have provided local
merchants with opportunities to expand their enterprises, did not, in
fact, depend on shopkeepers for their food requirements. Many of
their day-to-day needs materialized in the form of offerings from
members of the public seeking favours of one kind or another (see
Chapter 3). But for the most part, they relied, in the early Rana days
on revenues from village lands (*jagir*) assigned senior officials (see
p. 32) and, subsequently, on a system (called *jakheda*), of requisitioning supplies from the villages. The latter took turns in providing
the necessary goods which were paid for in cash.[1]

It is not certain if this system extended to the provisioning of the

military garrison—militia men were fed and housed in barracks—
and the jail as well, or whether the method used at present was also
employed in Rana times. This involves an annual auction for the
right to supply the garrison and the prisoners with a stipulated
quantity of grains, cooking oil, vegetables, spices, etc. To bid for
such a contract (*teka*) requires a substantial agricultural holding of
one's own and fairly wide-ranging personal contacts within the
villages to ensure a steady, reliable flow of foodstuffs by a system of
sub-contracting. The likelihood of a bazaar shopkeeper entering a
bid was therefore slim, but even if one did and was successful, it
would have had little bearing on the development of a viable
merchant community in the town.

It was only on the supply of goods produced outside the district
that expansion of commercial activities in Belaspur Bazaar could be
(and eventually came to be) based, but even here town merchants
had problems to overcome. Until only the last few decades, district
residents made few demands for goods they did not themselves
produce. Moreover, the style of life found among senior officials
from Kathmandu was, on the whole, the same as their own, and so
stimulated no new wants among the local people. Only a few spices,
some religious articles and, in the main, cloth, were regularly
imported into the district. Most peasant families, however, rather
than rely on merchants for these needs, went annually to the terai to
purchase them, at prices vastly below those prevailing in the town.
These were paid for (and their taxes raised at the same time) by
selling the clarified butter (*ghiu*) they had accumulated during the
year.

Local commerce, therefore, until very near the end of the Rana
period, existed mainly to provide a few administrators from outside
the district with a limited range of imports, and to supply those
peasants who, for reasons of age, illness or temporary shortage of
cash or butter, were unable to make an annual journey to the terai.
But even these restricted opportunities had to be shared for many
years (until about 1940) with traders from Doti, a district to the west
of Belaspur, who brought goods in by horse caravans. These men
had the advantage, not only of a comparatively inexpensive means of
transport, but of a short trip from their homes to their sources of
supply in the plains.[2] Belaspur merchants, by contrast, had a long
(seven day) journey to their nearest terai market and had to rely on
porters to carry the goods back to the district capital.

The growth of commercial enterprises in the bazaar was therefore inhibited by factors such as a self-sufficient peasant agriculture, systems of gift-giving and of requisitioning which ensured that the administration was supplied directly by the peasants, a virtual absence of demand for consumer goods, a custom of individual household import, and, for a time, competition from outside traders.

During the two decades following the end of the Rana period the prospects for commerce in Belaspur Bazaar have brightened considerably. The enlargement of the administration, coupled with the abolition of the *jakheda* system and the disappearance of *chakari* practices, have created a reservoir of potential customers among government servants. Non-resident bureaucrats have been among the first to introduce into the area a host of new consumer products which have become available for the first time in other parts of Nepal as a result of the country's exposure to the outside world. Increasingly, too, locally resident employees of the bureaucracy, educated in the new secular schools, influenced by their colleagues from outside the district, and able to travel and see for themselves the manufactured products available in Kathmandu and the terai, have developed new consumer habits. They demand cigarettes in place of home grown tobacco smoked in locally made clay pipes (*sulpa*); kerosene lamps instead of tiny oil-lit wicks which still provide the only light in most village homes; and western-style jackets, trousers and shirts in place of the customary Nepalese dress, as already pointed out. They have introduced radios and wrist-watches, batteries and torches, western medicines, and a host of other goods never before seen in the district.

At the same time, population pressures on scarce land, which were resulting in a diminution of the district's forests (from whose products peasants feed their cattle), especially in areas surrounding the district capital, have led to a steady decrease in dairy production and so in the amount of butter peasants have for sale. This is to some extent offset by other sources of cash income, but these are earned piecemeal and not in a lump sum, and have resulted in a lessening of the tendency among many villagers to journey to the terai. They too, have gradually turned to local merchants for their cloth and other consumer needs.

Whereas in 1951, there were perhaps a dozen retail businesses in the bazaar, there are at present seventy, not counting the tailoring and other craft workshops run by untouchables (see Chapter 5). About six of these are dry-weather enterprises, consisting of a ground sheet set up on the public green near the court, on which the merchant sits alongside his display of miscellaneous goods, which are packed away in a small trunk at the end of the day and taken home with him. Most retail businesses in the town, however, are housed in permanent dwellings. When I first made a count of these businesses at the beginning of January, 1969 there were 63 shops of this kind in the bazaar. The discussion which follows refers only to these shops even though during the course of fieldwork several were abandoned or temporarily discontinued while a few new ones were established. The dry-weather businesses on the public green are omitted here, although their operations do not differ substantially from those of the more permanent shops. One community-sponsored Ayurvedic clinic, opened in 1969, is also omitted from this discussion.

Shops in Belaspur Bazaar

Shops open just before ten o'clock in the morning and remain open until dusk, although many, especially those owned by permanent residents of the town, do not cease trading until well after dark. Like government offices they remain closed on Saturdays and national holidays. During July and August, moreover, merchants with paddy fields may shut down their businesses for a few days or even weeks for the crucial phase of planting.

There are three main categories of shop, distributed haphazardly along the bazaar's main street (unlike the situation in many Indian bazaars where particular types of businesses tend to congregate in one area (Fox 1969)): those selling principally (a) cloth; (b) a variety of goods other than cloth; and (c) tea (see Map 5). Two other shops fall into none of these categories. One has the 'agency' to sell primary school textbooks, and supplements this by selling stationery supplies and western medicines. A second is run by a private Ayurvedic physician (*baidye*) who prepares and sells his own remedies.

Cloth shops

There are 21 cloth (*kapda*) shops in the district capital, representing an annual investment in stock of approximately rs 2,000 for the smallest and rs 80,000 for the largest. Nine shops invest under rs 5,000, five over rs 20,000, while the remaining seven invest something between these two figures.

The cloth they sell is manufactured in India and imported by retail shopkeepers in the terai, a handful of whom, in the town of Balnagar, are the main suppliers of bazaar merchants. The latter journey to the plains at least once a year in the late autumn or early winter to make their purchases. They travel in small groups and, increasingly nowadays, the wealthier among them go by plane between Lakandra and Balnagar, a twenty-minute air trip (but a four or five day walk).

Suppliers in Balnagar are mostly members of Indian merchant castes (*baniya*), long-settled in the Nepalese terai, and as such have no kin or other close connection with shopkeepers in Belaspur. Nevertheless, after years of trading together, relationships of trust develop and many bazaar merchants can expect to obtain credit for up to 75 per cent of the value of the merchandise they buy. Credit transactions carry interest of 10 per cent per annum, and six months are generally allowed for repayment. The less well established businessmen must pay for a greater proportion of their purchases in cash, although other sources of credit are available within the district. These are of two kinds: loans given by rich men (sometimes wealthier shopkeepers) and bank loans. The former are secured by mortgaging land, jewellery, cattle or merchandise, and carry interest of 15–20 per cent. Since interest rates are now pegged by the government at 10 per cent, such agreements can only be unofficial, and creditors are increasingly reluctant to offer loans because of the risks involved. For the borrower, despite the high interest, such loans have the advantage of flexibility over repayment: a local creditor will usually be content if the interest payments are forthcoming with some regularity and will seldom call in a loan.

The bank, first established in Belaspur in 1966, grants shop-keepers credit at 9·5 per cent interest per year, but only against certain forms of collateral which can be easily realized. Thus, it lends up to 60 per cent of the market value of gold and silver, and up to 75 per cent of the value of most other goods. Loans on gold and silver must be repaid within a twelve month period; on durables, such as cloth, within six months; and on perishables, such as sugar, within three months. This arrangement tends naturally to favour the already well-to-do borrower with considerable assets. But it does provide a reliable and substantial fund of comparatively inexpensive credit; merchants are turning more and more to this source for their loans. Since the bank opened in the district the amount loaned for purposes of shopkeeping has doubled, amounting, in the last fiscal year, to over rs 35,000.

Once established in business, a shopkeeper is able to tap both the bank and his terai suppliers for credit. Thus, he may deposit with the bank stock worth, say, rs 7,000 to secure a loan of rs 5,000. With such a down payment, he then obtains rs 20,000 worth of new stock in Balnagar. A newcomer to shopkeeping, if unable to obtain credit from any source, relies on his own savings from cash employment (usually in government service) or the sale of household assets to make his first purchases of stock.

Goods bought in the terai must be transported back to Belaspur, and almost without exception, merchants employ porters for the job, at the rate of about rs 50 for the week-long trip during the winter months, each carrying a load of 80 pounds (one *maund*). Not infrequently, merchants bring porters with them from the district, mainly untouchables living in a few villages near the bazaar.

Unlike the practice in some bazaars where prices are set by haggling (Mines 1972:49), merchants in Belaspur mark up their merchandise at least 50 per cent above the cost price in the terai. After allowing for porterage and interest charges, business licences,[3] and, in some cases, rent—four of the 21 cloth shops operate in rented premises—the shopkeeper expects a profit of approximately 25 per cent on his gross sales.

Most cloth shops also carry a few of the various items which are the mainstay of the second category of businesses found in the bazaar.

General shops

General (*besat-khana*) shops, of which there are fifteen, sell a wide range of goods other than cloth: cigarettes, bidis, matches, kerosene, sugar, soap, stationery supplies, sweets, sandals, torches, batteries, biscuits, religious articles (e.g. incense), and so on.[4] The largest makes an annual investment in stock of rs 10,000, while the smallest spends barely rs 200. Most (11 out of 15) represent an annual investment of rs 500–3,000.

In the past, they were supplied in much the same way as are cloth businesses, through retail merchants in Balnagar. For the past ten years, however, general shops have been relying to an increasing degree on a number of traders from an area known as Jorbaj in the south of Belaspur district, about midway between the bazaar and the plains (see Map 2). These 'Jorbajis' purchase goods in the terai and porter them on their own backs to the bazaar and, occasionally, as far north as Kalanga. They trade from November to March, during which time they average two round trips a month. The prices at which they sell their goods to bazaar merchants are necessarily higher than those obtainable in the terai, but are still advantageous to local shopkeepers if the costs of the journey to and from the plains, of bringing the goods back to the district, and of the interest charges on credit are taken into account. Although cash must be paid, local merchants are able to buy in small quantities over an extended period, and they need take none of the risks of theft and damage involved in hiring their own porters.

Only the very largest general shopkeepers, who require a wider selection of goods than that brought in to the town by these traders, and cloth merchants, still go regularly to the plains for their supplies, and even they supplement their general stocks by purchases from the Jorbajis. General shops supplied by the latter take a slightly lower mark-up on their goods than those who obtain supplies in the terai in order to keep their prices competitive, although on the whole the profit margins of all general shops are similar to those enjoyed by cloth shops.

Men anxious to set up cloth businesses, but wary of the financial risks involved, often test their commercial skills first in this type of enterprise and, if successful, expand to include cloth as well. Over half the cloth shops in the bazaar began as businesses selling only general merchandise.

Tea shops

The first tea (*ciya*) shop in Belaspur Bazaar was opened in 1953 by a local resident recently returned from a four year stay in India. Until that time, tea, or the drinking of it in public, was regarded as somewhat impure (*jhutto*). Ex-servicemen and others who had spent time in India welcomed its introduction into the bazaar, and before long tea drinking had become a popular habit. Today, there are 25 tea shops in the town. The main requirements needed to establish such a business are a few glasses, a kettle, firewood, and the ingredients for making tea. Milk is obtained from households in a few nearby villages which have adequate herds of cattle; packages of tea and sugar—Nepalese tea is made extremely sweet—are obtained from Jorbaji traders.

All tea shops also carry a few other goods, such as cigarettes and kerosene, representing an annual investment of rs 25–500 which are also purchased from the itinerant traders. The shops occasionally serve meals to government servants from outside the district who do not have their wives with them in Belaspur, and even to occasional visitors spending a few days in the town. But despite frequent references to these shops by the English term 'hotel', none offers overnight accommodation.

Six tea shop owners have licences to sell spirits (*daru*), for which they pay a fee of rs 50 each. Manufactured in a distillery beside one of the district's largest rivers, by a private concern granted a contract by the administration, it is made from *mauwa*, the flower of the Engelhardtia tree (Turner 1931). Three businesses, referred to here as 'tea' shops, in fact sell little else but spirits, and might be considered a separate category of enterprise. The more popular but illegal 'home made' liquor is distilled from grains, mainly millet, and sold clandestinely in a number of other tea shops after dark.

Profits from tea sales alone can be as high as 40 per cent of the price of a glass (which is uniform throughout the bazaar) and differing degrees of success depend on several factors. The first is location: it helps especially to be near a government office, since according to shopkeepers, administrative employees drink plenty of tea. Also those who work or otherwise spend their days in the town usually congregate for a brief period after office hours to chat, gossip or merely exchange greetings before darkness sends them back to their homes. They tend to gravitate towards a few key spots in both the old and new bazaars, and a tea shop owner near any of these locations usually benefits from such gatherings. A second asset for a tea shop is adequate accommodation for a reasonably large number of people. Unlike cloth and general shops, which are designed so that customers remain outside the premises and the proprietor inside—a knee-high wooden partition dividing them—tea shops must provide seating arrangements (usually inside) for their customers. Untouchables, however, are required to remain outside and even to wash their own glasses. Third, the personality of the proprietor is of some consequence; a sullen or argumentative disposition will drive customers away, while a friendly and sympathetic one will attract and keep them. Finally, a tea shop owner's success in business, like that of any shopkeeper, will depend to some extent on the way he manages his credit sales.

Credit

It was not possible to obtain full documentation about the extent of credit given by all merchants in the bazaar, but an examination of the current credit lists of 19 shops (i.e. about 30 per cent of retail businesses)[5] suggests certain distinctive patterns of credit policy.

Firstly, credit sales constitute on average about 10 per cent of the total volume of a shop's sales.

Second, at any one time, merchants extend credit to a relatively small number of customers. Cloth merchants, with one notable exception (see below), have between 17 and 58 such customers on their lists, or an average of 42 persons per shop. General merchants have between 9 and 49 (an average of 29) persons, while tea shops have between 6 and 27 (an average of 17) credit customers on their current books. These figures, it should be emphasized, do not indicate the total number of customers given credit facilities by bazaar merchants, but merely the way in which the latter seek to keep within manageable bounds the numbers and magnitude of their outstanding accounts.

Third, the amount of credit allowed per customer is similarly controlled. Cloth shops, as would be expected, allow the most, an average of rs 31 per customer, the lowest average figure for a shop being rs 4 and the highest rs 76. General shops allow an average of only rs 11, ranging from rs 4 to rs 18. The average for tea shops (rs 15) is distorted (upwards) by the fact that one of the four shops examined sells mostly liquor, and has a high customer average of rs 32. The other tea shops together average only rs 10 per customer.

A fourth point revealed by an examination of credit lists is that customers benefiting most from this privilege (no interest is charged on credit sales) represent, on the whole, a very selective segment of the buying public. They may be divided into three principal, but not exclusive categories. The first consists of customers who reside in the same settlement as the shopkeeper, and thus are linked to him in a variety of ways—as neighbours, kinsmen, tenants, priests, family tailors or cobblers, agricultural labourers and so on. The extension of credit to such persons is explicable essentially in terms of a complex of relationships inside the merchant's local community, of which the credit transaction may be only a small part. In other words, merchants need not be embarrassed by demands for credit from such persons, but may employ this very avenue as a means to improve their position in the community (see L. Caplan 1972).

Another category consists of customers resident in settlements other than the shopkeeper's own. Those belonging to this category, however, still tend to live in the surrounding area, and indeed are often related to him as affines or linked in some of the ways mentioned above. The point is that far from being strangers, these customers are well known to the shopkeeper, even if not an intimate or active part of his social network. This tends to support Ward's observation that in the absence of formal credit machinery, shopkeepers are limited or limit themselves in extending credit to those about whose circumstances they have personal knowledge (1960). A similar point is made by Hazlehurst about bazaar economies of 'middle range' cities, where shopkeepers' knowledge of the creditworthiness of clients is only possible because of their close identification with the region (1968:547).

Such limitations imposed on the granting of credit means that a large proportion of the district population is excluded from utilizing these benefits. This is because all but five of the bazaar's shopkeepers are men resident in the district capital or within a half-hour walk of it. The population of and in the area immediately surrounding the town, therefore, through its close ties to merchants, virtually monopolizes the limited credit facilities that are available. Alternatively, people living at some distance from the town have few opportunities and less inclination to visit the shops in Belaspur Bazaar and limited chances to obtain credit when they do. Moreover, those living at some remove from the town are more likely to be in areas which are still relatively well-forested, which means they can raise larger herds of cattle and so engage in dairy farming. Peasants in such areas still purchase many of their consumer requirements directly in the terai when they go to sell their butter stocks.

But this does not mean that increased purchases would not be made in the district capital if credit were available to those living outside its immediate environs. This is suggested by the somewhat atypical credit dealings of the only large cloth shop in the town run by a resident of a village situated a long way (5–6 hours on foot) from the bazaar. The numbers to whom he affords credit (237 outstanding accounts) bear no comparison with those of his retail competitors (although the average amount he grants each customer is almost the same). He admits to the difficulties of denying credit to people resident in his own and neighbouring villages who are unable to obtain it elsewhere in the bazaar.

A third category of customer, and the one most favoured by shopkeepers to receive credit, is that of government servants. As Table 19 shows, employees of the district administration constitute an extremely high proportion of those found on the current credit lists of bazaar shopkeepers.

TABLE 19

*Credit Customers**

		Non-government employees		
	Average no. of	*Co-residents*	*Residents of*	*Gov't*
Type of shop	*credit customers*	*of merchant*	*other settlements*	*empl.*
Cloth	42	11	17	14
General	29	8	7	14
Tea	17	2	5	10

* These categories are not exclusive, since most government employees live in the district, and could be listed as co-residents of the merchant or residents of other settlements.

Although there are only 264 members of the administration employed in the district capital, their names appear consistently and with prominence in the credit lists of bazaar merchants. Some are included in more than one list. That members of the district administration are major recipients of credit is undoubtedly due in part to the fact that most live permanently in nearby settlements. But this would not account fully for the disproportionately high numbers granted credit nor for the fact that non-resident government servants are particularly favoured. It may be, of course, that bureaucrats with a reliable and regular cash income are regarded as good risks, so that merchants feel no reluctance in offering them generous credit terms. But such an argument must be balanced against the knowledge shared by all shopkeepers that government servants do occasionally run up as large a balance with as many shops as they can and then, on being transferred out of the district, leave without paying all they owe. Since there are no formal channels through which bazaar merchants exchange information about credit customers, men who exhaust their privileges in one shop may go elsewhere and remain undetected by their new creditors, at least for a time. Most bad debts, which have eventually to be written off, are those incurred by employees of the bureaucracy. The majority of them are either young men in the lower echelons of senior ranks whose homes are outside the district[6], or men in menial posts (usually soldiers or policemen) who are not normally a part of the merchant's social network.

The apparent readiness of merchants to meet the requests for credit from government employees must be explained, therefore, at least partly by reference to the nature of the relationship between shopkeepers and the district administration. All shops must pay a business tax which is based on a rough estimate (arrived at by a committee of government employees) of the shop's stock. Tea-shop owners who need large amounts of firewood must request permits (*purji*) to cut down trees; while those wishing to sell liquor have first to be approved by the district authorities. In addition, the administration sets maximum prices on most goods which are sold in the shops and can fine merchants for exceeding these limits. Shopkeepers are particularly vulnerable to administrative arbitrariness. They express resentment at the readiness of many administrative employees to threaten the use of these powers to ring concessions from them. 'Shopkeepers are helpless against government servants, because if we refuse them credit, they can cause trouble' was how one businessman explained the dilemma.

Through personal links to members of the administration, merchants are frequently able to mitigate the severity of what they regard as 'blackmail', but because each government branch increasingly guards its own prerogatives jealously (see Chapter 10), there is a limit to what employees of one office can do to influence the behaviour of those in another. A general merchant was recently fined rs 50 by the district headquarters for selling writing paper above the official price; the customer who accused and arrested him was a policeman, who, according to the merchant, had just been refused an extension of his already generous credit account. The shopkeeper's father, an employee of the court, sought, through the judge, to intervene with the police commander and officials of the district headquarters, but to no avail. But it would be inaccurate to interpret the large amount of credit given government employees as simply a response to threats. Since most shopkeepers are almost continuously in breach of some rule, they feel obliged to avoid giving those in a position to enforce the law a pretext for doing so. And they regard credit as the least costly and most effective way of doing this.

Although official policy is to discourage links based on credit between bureaucrats and shopkeepers the practice continues.[7]

It is the inability to cope adequately with their credit operations—not only pertaining to government employees, but to customers generally—which, more than any other single factor, is cited by former merchants as the reason for failure in business. Still, most appear to manage well enough and to turn a small but satisfactory profit. The following section will examine the importance of shop-keeping for residents of the district capital.

Town-resident merchants

Thirty-one of the 63 retail businesses in the bazaar are owned and run by residents of Belaspur Bazaar (see Map 5). Newars were the first to establish shops, and were followed by members of other castes as they came to live in the town. Today, 16 Newars, 8 Chetris, 4 Thakuris (one of whom runs two shops), 1 Jaisi and 1 untouchable (Butcher) constitute the resident merchant community. Thus, although clean castes constitute barely half the bazaar's population, they provide virtually all its merchants. The Newars, not surprisingly, are the most 'over-represented' group among the merchant community. Over 50 per cent of town-resident shopkeepers belong to this group, which comprises only 28·4 per cent of the population. Table 20 gives the breakdown of shop ownership by caste.

TABLE 20

Town-resident merchants, by caste

Type of shop	Newar	Chetri	Thakuri*	Jaisi	Butcher	Total
Cloth	2	4	3	–	–	9
General	3	–	–	1	1	5
Tea	11	3	2	–	–	16
Other	–	1	–	–	–	1
	16	8	5	1	1	31

* One Thakuri merchant runs both a cloth and a tea shop. There are thus 30 shop-keepers and 31 shops.

Although shopkeeping has been the occupation of generations of bazaariyas, there are only a handful of shops which have been in operation for an uninterrupted period of more than a score of years. Eighteen of the 31 businesses owned by townsmen were established after 1960, five between 1951 and 1960, and eight prior to 1951. But only six of the latter shops, four of them belonging to Newars, have been running continuously through at least two generations, i.e., have passed from father to son (the present proprietor) without a break in operation. The fathers of another eight resident merchants had been shopkeepers for a time, from three months to 30 years, but their shops had not been inherited by their son(s). Rather, the businesses had been allowed to lapse and the sons had made a fresh start, at a much later date, often in a different type of business and occasionally in another location in the bazaar.

In addition, some 25 male household heads of clean caste whose fathers were shopkeepers, are not now and have never been merchants themselves. Another 10 household heads have at some time in their lives run shops, but are no longer so engaged. It would seem, then, that bazaar inhabitants, on the whole, neither operate businesses for long periods of time, i.e. spend their entire adult lives in commerce, nor pass their shops on intact to the next generation.[8]

There are several reasons for this absence of continuity. One is, undoubtedly, the limited opportunities for shopkeeping and the variety of obstacles to a successful career as merchant which existed until the end of the Rana period, and to some extent still exist today, as I have noted above. Second, the minimal investment required to become a merchant certainly encourages a surfeit of would-be retailers, and given only an average failure rate, results inevitably in a high turnover of shopkeepers. Third, because of the smallness of scale of most businesses, when proprietors die or become incapable of running their shops, and if patrilineal heirs are either too young or, for reasons which will be made clear, unwilling to assume control, it is usually simpler to allow the shops to run down than attempt to reorganize the households' activities and personnel to maintain their existence. It is only when a business becomes large and successful, so that a cessation of operations would lead to substantial financial sacrifices, that efforts to ensure its continuity may be made. The shops which have been in operation for at least two generations are certainly among the most profitable ones owned by residents of the town.

A fourth, and perhaps more important reason, itself partly an outgrowth of the previous three, is that most bazaar residents of clean caste have traditionally regarded shopkeeping as an appropriate occupation to pursue when careers in the administration are temporarily interrupted or when government service is finally abandoned. In Chapter 3 it was shown how during Rana times and for some years after the revolution of 1951 procedures relating to recruitment and promotion in the civil service led to frequent, sometimes prolonged breaks in employment. At such times, a bazaar resident was likely to set up a small general or tea shop which would be relinquished as soon as another administrative appointment was obtained. Five of the 10 bazaariyas who were, but are no longer in business, only established their businesses for this reason, and spent between six months and two years as merchants before being able to return to a post in the administration. Certainly the attitude held by inhabitants of the bazaar to these two modes of livelihood is very different from that recorded by Pocock among Gujerati immigrants to East Africa. He notes how government service 'has always been regarded as a temporary expedient to be thrown aside as soon as a man can set up shop. . . .' (1957:292).

Townspeople who have no hopes or plans of returning to the civil service, i.e. those who reach retirement age or are too old to be recruited again, who resign their posts rather than accept transfer out of the district, or are ignominiously dismissed from their jobs, frequently turn to shopkeeping. The histories of merchants who have established shops in their own lifetimes reveal that the majority (16 out of 24) did so after leaving government service—12 of them having served for over five years. A few examples will illustrate the pattern.

a. A Newar whose father had started a cloth shop after completing 15 years in administrative employment, and had run it for four years until his death in 1941, himself qualified for a service pension in 1962, at which time he established a tea shop.

b. One of the largest cloth shops in the town belongs to a Thakuri whose father had come to Belaspur Bazaar with the militia. The son spent a total of 10 years in government employment and finally left 33 years ago to set up his business.

c. A Chetri, who was dismissed from his administrative post on a bribery charge, after 18 years in service, established a cloth shop.

d. A Newar merchant came originally to the district capital in 1942 as an NCO in the militia. After eight years of service locally he left the army rather than accept a transfer out of the district, married in the bazaar, and opened a tea shop.

The family histories of three of the six merchants who inherited their shops reveal a similar configuration: their fathers had been administrative employees who turned to business on leaving government service.

Occasionally, a government employee, anticipating his retirement, establishes a shop while still a member of the civil service. One Thakuri, in his seventeenth year in service, took extended leave of six months to launch a cloth business, and left his father to look after it when he returned to his post outside the district.

Two other bazaar residents, currently members of the district administration, run (general and tea) shops out of office hours.[9] Transfer away from the district, a possibility in both cases, would probably necessitate closing the shops since there are no other persons at home to assume the responsibility for managing them.

The management of shops

Shopkeeping is, on the whole, regarded as a man's occupation. Women do occasionally work alongside their husbands or sons in tea shops and two such enterprises are in fact run entirely by widows. But on the whole they play little part in business. There are no ritual or other formal prohibitions on their engaging in these activities, although a number of disabilities conspire to make it difficult for them to do so. Women have little experience of and so are usually not adept at handling cash; because they have traditionally been denied the benefits of education, virtually all women are illiterate, which means they are unable to keep written accounts or cope with the complexities of stock purchases, credit dealings and the like. Moreover, as I have noted, women are assigned manifold responsibilities for cultivation as well as various household tasks which leave them little time for anything else.

Of special importance, shopkeeping is monopolized by men because it is a pleasurable and prestigious occupation which enables them to spend their days in the town in regular contact with both the administration and district political affairs, and so with developments which touch the lives of everyone in the area, not least of all those with political ambitions. It is no coincidence that many of the most important political figures in the district at present run shops in Belaspur Bazaar.

Shop management is, in a literal sense, a 'one-man operation'. Although the households of 13 merchants resident in the town contain not only wives but two or more adult males, in only one instance is the full attention of more than a single individual required to run the business;[10] to operate most enterprises not even this amount of time is required. Thus, the great majority of shops close when merchants travel to the terai to replenish their stocks.

That a shop can be managed by a single individual reflects the smallness of scale as well as the modest profits of the vast majority of businesses owned by bazaariyas, as Table 21 shows.[11]

TABLE 21

*Estimated annual net profits of shops owned by townsmen**

	Over 5,000 rs	5,000– 1,001 rs	1,000–500 rs	Under 500 rs	Total
Cloth	1	5	3	–	9
General	–	1	2	2	5
Tea	–	–	9	7	16
Other	–	–	1	–	1
	1	6	15	9	31

* See Appendix C on the profits of shopkeeping.

These figures help to explain the pattern of shop inheritance. I have already indicated the somewhat cavalier manner in which most business ventures are allowed to expire when merchants die or become incapable of operating them. When it is noted that the average annual net profits earned by the great majority of shops do not exceed the salary of a clerk in the administration and, with a single exception, the most profitable enterprises barely achieve the income of a senior official, it is hardly surprising that a potential heir, in government service at the time of his father's death or retirement, is reluctant to abandon his employment to assume the management of a shop. A man would prefer to allow a brother to inherit a business on which he might have a prior claim, or, in the absence of a male sibling, let the business expire altogether, rather than give up a satisfying and lucrative career in administration. Only when a shop is relatively profitable is there an attempt to ensure continuity, provided there is someone able directly to assume its management. In such cases, shops, like all household property, are transferred in the male line, although which son inherits will depend on a combination of circumstances. If the household is still not divided and all sons are at home when their merchant father dies or gives up active management, it is likely that the eldest son will take up the running of the business, and it will become his property when the household estate is finally partitioned. If, on the other hand, as often happens, older sons initiate the process of separation from their father's household while the latter is still alive, a younger brother, who has remained at home to aid and support his parents in their old age, will inherit the shop, along with the household's main dwelling (*mul ghar*) where the business is probably situated. Of the six bazaar residents who inherited the shops they now run, three are eldest sons, two are youngest sons, and one is an only son.

Whereas a dwelling can be and occasionally is divided among a man's sons when the household estate is partitioned (thus, several bazaar households occupy a single dwelling) the business remains intact and, moreover, is not jointly inherited by members of two separate households. Those who do not inherit shops but nevertheless desire to become businessmen are expected to establish wholly separate enterprises. In two instances where sons took over their fathers' shops, non-inheriting brothers established new businesses in other dwellings. In one case the dwelling was already owned by the household and in the other it was purchased by the aspiring merchant with part of his equal but distinct inheritance.[12]

The mode of shop inheritance is thus related to the limited requirements of capital, time and skills demanded to set up and operate a retail enterprise in the town, and the petty profits obtainable from it. At the same time, such an inheritance pattern will help to ensure that a shop is unable to grow much beyond its existing size. The profitability of a bazaar business is, to a large extent, circumscribed by the limited 'inputs' of a lone businessman, and by no means constitutes an objective measure of the potential of the enterprise. All residents of the district capital are aware of the growth of commerce over the years, especially since 1951, and a few shops have expanded their operations and profits in this period. The bazaar's most successful merchant (a Newar) inherited a modest cloth shop from his father and transformed it within two decades into a business showing an annual profit of some rs 20,000 (see Chapter 8). The largest general shop was established only ten years ago, also by a resident Newar, with the aid of a rs 200 loan from his father, a government servant, and today it has an annual sales volume of approximately rs 15,000.

But by and large growth has taken the form of a proliferation of new, small shops, rather than the emergence of a few large-scale businesses from an already established merchant community. Why, we might ask, do existing shopkeepers not take advantage of the new opportunities for expansion? More precisely, why is it not thought feasible or desirable for several male members of even a single domestic group to pool their efforts in an attempt to break out of the limitations of one-man enterprises? For although a relatively successful shop may encourage the members of a household to remain together for a greater than average period of time—four of the seven most profitable shops owned by townsmen are run by the heads of joint households—it does not apparently stimulate cooperative effort to expand the business. Where there are two or more adult males in a household only one manages the shop, while the rest pursue other occupations.

The explanation must be sought partly in the history of commercial enterprise in Belaspur Bazaar. Until recently, as I have pointed out, even the pettiest shopkeeping was fraught with risks while the possibilities for large-scale business ventures were exceedingly limited. Since 1951, increased opportunities have to some extent been neutralized by enhanced competition, much of it from nearby villagers, and by the fact that townsmen were prevented from moving into a recently established commercial area in the northern part of the town, i.e. New Bazaar (see Chapters 7 and 9). This has given rise to what Fox calls a 'subsistence' ideology of commercial enterprise. In Tezibazar, the north Indian market town he studied 'if his family is fed and his desire for savings appeased, the typical merchant is satisfied and neither asks nor expects any more from his business. Because most shops are small and capital is limited, the businessman is extremely wary of further investment' (1969: 144).

In Belaspur, merchants tend to regard the main aim of their businesses as providing a 'little extra cash' for paying taxes or school fees, purchasing a few consumer goods or some measures of grain to make up a small deficit, etc. One outcome is that townsmen, whatever their practical commitment to shopkeeping, view it as a peripheral activity. In consequence, the personnel of a domestic unit, as well as the energies of its (merchant) head are dispersed among a variety of activities. The household of only one merchant has no other income than that provided by his shop. In pursuance of this policy of dispersal, and risk-spreading, a substantial amount of capital, much of it the profits of shopkeeping, which might otherwise serve to expand business operations, is directed instead to what are regarded as more worthwhile economic activities. Merchants have increasingly invested in buildings, money-lending and (with a view to administrative careers) education for their children. But by far the greatest proportion of money has been invested in land.

Townsmen as landowners

The first generations of immigrants to the bazaar were, on the whole, landless, and thus forced to rely on sources of livelihood other than agriculture. Untouchables practised their traditional crafts and, in particular, the Tailors, who are musicians, served in the local militia. Those unable to do either worked as agricultural labourers for nearby villagers. Settlers belonging to clean castes, to avoid the latter alternative, had either to secure jobs in the administration or engage in some form of commerce.

A number of factors contributed to the townspeople's divorce from the land. Firstly, many of the earliest Newar settlers were from non-farming castes in Kathmandu Valley and probably had little experience of or interest in agriculture. Second, although both commerce and administrative employment were fraught with uncertainties, on the whole, bazaar residents of clean caste, for reasons already noted, managed to do comparatively well out of both, and, in addition, relied on a variety of other, supplementary sources of income which they, in particular, were conveniently placed to exploit (see Table 23 p. 117). Third, lack of sufficient capital contributed to keep many bazaar inhabitants, especially untouchables, from becoming landowners. It is only in recent decades that they have acquired the financial means to make substantial purchases of agricultural plots. The expansion of the administration after 1951 contributed, as I have shown, to an upsurge of commerce in the town. At the same time, alterations in administrative practices in the post-Rana period provided greater security for government servants and increased their chances of rising in the bureaucratic hierarchy. These changes have resulted in greater incomes and opportunities for bazaar residents to accumulate the sums needed for investment in land.

Moreover, it is only in recent decades that increasing competition from villagers for administrative posts as well as in commerce (see Chapter 7) has rendered the traditional occupational preserves of townsmen less certain than in the past, heightened their awareness of the risks inherent in an exclusive reliance on these sources of livelihood, and made more attractive the security conferred by land ownership. Whereas until very near the end of the Rana period only a small minority of bazaar households earned income from the possession of agricultural fields, today the vast majority have some commitment to this source of earnings.

Just over half of the total current income of grain (paddy, maize, millet and wheat) from their fields is produced on lands purchased in their own lifetimes, mainly after 1951, by contemporary residents of the bazaar.[13] In all, 36 of the 75 clean caste households have bought land, and sixteen of these have no other fields but those they have themselves purchased. In four cases household heads immigrated to the town in recent times from within the district, and merely sold their village lands, inherited from their fathers, to buy others nearer the town. The rest, however, had inherited no fields from the previous generation. For the untouchables, 22 of their 77 households have purchased plots for cultivation; 14 of them have no other (i.e. inherited) land.[14]

The failure to receive land from a preceding generation is no proof that the latter possessed no land, for the fortunes of any particular household rise and fall during the course of its lifetime. But the fact that one-quarter of all land-owning households in the district capital received no inheritance of land, as well as the testimony both of land records and family biographies, suggests a definite trend in the direction of increased land ownership by the present generation of bazaar dwellers. By this I mean not merely an attempt to keep pace with a growing population, but an expansion of land holdings in an absolute sense.

During the past decade in particular, wealthier townspeople have begun buying fields outside the district, mainly in Lakandra valley and, to a lesser extent, in the terai. Lands in these areas are expensive, but by comparison with those in the hills of Belaspur, considerably more productive and apparently worthwhile despite having to share the crop with local tenants.[15] The eradication of malaria in these areas and the recent improvement in communications between the hills and the terai during the past few years have made it possible for owners to visit these lands more frequently and, in a few instances, to spend prolonged periods of time there, actually supervising cultivation themselves. In such cases they employ local agricultural labourers and thereby eliminate the need to rely on tenants (most of whom are indigenous Tharu). Twelve bazaar households—seven Chetri, two Thakuri, two Newar and one Tailor—have bought lands in these areas whose current value is estimated at rs 130,000. These fields together provide just under half of the grain income from all lands purchased by living bazaar residents.

It is not too difficult to identify the sources of the funds which residents of the district capital have invested in land. If the 22 untouchable households which have bought fields are examined, we note that with only two exceptions all have been able to become landowners, if on a comparatively modest scale, because of their success in commercializing traditional crafts (see Chapter 5). Although for seven untouchable households government employment is or has been important, in only one has it been the dominant spring of cash earnings. In another household shopkeeping has provided the bulk of the funds for land purchases.

Among the households of clean caste, however, administration and commerce are clearly of paramount importance as investment sources. Twenty of the 36 domestic units which have bought fields rely or have relied mainly on government service for their regular cash earnings; another ten have depended on shopkeeping for the major portion of their cash incomes. The significance of these two principal sources of capital accumulation for members of clean castes becomes even more apparent when it is noted that lands bought with earnings from government service provide just over half, and those bought with the profits of shopkeeping just under 40 per cent, of all grain income from lands purchased by members of clean castes living in the town.

This trend towards investment in agricultural plots has resulted in a situation where today approximately 80 per cent of all households (93 per cent of clean caste and 66 per cent of untouchable domestic groups) in the bazaar own some cultivating land. Fields belonging to untouchables, however, produce only a fifth of the total grain income from all the lands of townsmen.

The significance of land ownership for town residents can be at least partly gauged by the degree to which these lands produce the grain needed to meet immediate food requirements. The fields of bazaar inhabitants produce in toto just under the 33,810 units of grain needed in a year to feed the town's present population (see Appendix B). But whereas the lands belonging to members of clean castes supply well over one and a half times their food requirements, those of untouchables provide barely a third of theirs.

If bazaar households are categorized into those whose fields produce sufficient or more than sufficient to meet food requirements and those which do not, the pattern summarized in Table 22 emerges.

TABLE 22

Grain production of town households

| | Households with land | | | Households without land | Total no. of households |
	Total	Suff. prod.	Insuff. prod.		
Clean castes	70	47	23	5	75
Untouchables	51	12	39	26	77
All	121	59	62	31	152

The two broad categories of 'sufficient' and 'insufficient' production, of course, mask a wide range of differences as between, for example, a dozen (untouchable) households which produce under 10 per cent of their food demands, and another ten (clean caste) domestic units whose lands provide over three times, and in two cases, six times, their food requirements.

It will be noted that approximately two in every five clean caste households (37·3 per cent) still do not produce enough grain to feed their members. Nevertheless, the growth of land ownership among these townsmen has altered the previous pattern of income distribution which had been overwhelmingly dominated by government service and shopkeeping. Earnings from their fields now amount to approximately rs 103,900 per annum, or just under a third of their total income.[16] The average income from its fields of a landowning household is about rs 1500. This is to be compared with earnings from government service which amount roughly to rs 116,800 or rs 2650 per household with one or more members in administrative service, and with income from shopkeeping which amounts annually to just over rs 60,000, i.e., an average of rs 2100 per shopkeeping household of clean caste.[17] Comparative income figures of clean caste households are given in Table 23. This table does not purport to offer a comprehensive summary of *all* income earned by clean caste households in the town, but only to provide a rough indication of the scale and main sources of livelihood.

TABLE 23

Estimated income of clean caste households in town

Source	No. of households with income	Income to nearest 100 rupees	Percentage
Land ownership	70	103,900	32·4
Government service	44	116,800	36·7
Shopkeeping	29	60,000	19·2
Other*	44	37,000	11·6
		318,700	100·0

* This category includes income from:

a. *Rent* Since 1951, the letting of buildings in town has become a profitable source of earnings for bazaariyas. In all, 15 clean caste households earn approximately rs 6,600 a year by renting accommodation to the administration, government servants, or shopkeepers.

b. *Teaching* The dramatic expansion of educational facilities during the past two decades has created a widespread demand for primary school teachers. Five residents of the town work in district schools and earn about rs 6,400 per year.

c. *Document-writing* Most dealings with the administration require members of the public to submit written documents. Whereas the majority of people are content to rely on local village specialists to compose these, many, especially those involved in court litigation (see Chapter 8) prefer to seek the services of scribes (*lekhendas* or *lekhapardi*) practising in the town, in the belief that they possess, by virtue of their proximity to the administration (in particular the district court), greater knowledge of its workings. These document writers charge on the basis of the amount of time spent on a paper, the capacity of the client to pay, and the nature of the relationship between the two men. Three townsmen practice as part-time scribes, and earn perhaps an average of rs 300 per annum each.

d. *Miscellaneous sources* There are a variety of miscellaneous sources to which a few households have occasional access. Thus, two men earn cash by carpentry, which is not caste-specific work in the hills of Nepal. One household of Joggis has a small income from begging and from temple duties. One bazaar resident has a government monopoly to distil spirits in the district which he then sells to licensed retail shops, while another has a contract to provision the army garrison. Three men currently serving in the Gurkha regiments of the Indian army remit a part of their salaries, while four others—two ex-Gurkhas and two former government servants—receive pensions. Six households have regular income from interest on loans, while eight of the poorest domestic groups provide agricultural labour to other townsmen and villagers. Leaving aside earnings from the latter kind of work which I was unable to estimate, income from these miscellaneous economic activities amounts to approximately rs 23,100 in a year.

Occupational diversity

These are aggregate figures, and individual households, of course, have different patterns of income distribution. Table 24 summarizes the occupational diversity of clean caste households, taking into account only the three principal income sources, viz. shopkeeping, land and government service.

TABLE 24

*Sources of income of clean caste households in town**

Source	Number of households
Land only	10
Government service only	2
Shopkeeping only	3
Land and government service	35
Land and shopkeeping	14
Land, government service and shopkeeping	11
	75

* Other sources discussed above are omitted here.

The great majority of clean caste households (60 out of 75) combine land ownership with either government service or shop-keeping, or both. Examining those households which derive a livelihood from more than one source, we note that of the 35 domestic groups which have income from land and government service, only five earn more from their lands than from employment in the administration; of the 14 with income from land and shop-keeping, half earn more from the former than from the latter, while for the other half the reverse is true. Of the 11 households with income from all three sources, one earns most from land, two earn most from shopkeeping, while eight earn most from government service.

In sum, then, 23 domestic groups of clean caste (31 per cent) derive more income from land than either government service or shopkeeping, 40 units (53 per cent) rely on government service to provide their largest share, while 12 households (16 per cent) count on shopkeeping as their major source of earnings. If all other means of income were taken into account, the pattern would be altered slightly, since only two households derive more income from sources other than land, government service or shopkeeping.

The increase in land ownership among clean castes, which has altered the previous balance of income, compels the household to deploy its manpower on a wider front than was necessary in the past. On the whole, this has not proved too difficult because a significant proportion of land purchases has been outside the district and such lands are still mostly let out to tenants. But even the fields in the hills near the town—most land purchases have been within a narrow radius of the bazaar—which, on the whole, townsmen cultivate themselves, can be managed easily due to the division of labour which assigns to the women the main burden of agricultural tasks. At peak seasons, moreover, to cope better with these duties several households combine their labour to work in large teams on a direct exchange basis (here called *hade-parima*).[18] If necessary, jobs for which men are responsible, such as ploughing, can be devolved on agricultural labourers hired from households in the town or surrounding villages.

Domestic units which combine shopkeeping (the preserve of men) with agriculture have little difficulty meeting the demands of both occupations. In any case, as I have indicated, shops are usually closed for several days at the height of the household's cultivation activities in July/August. In the case of those domestic units with members in administrative employment outside the district, it has already been shown how most men serve while they occupy a subordinate status in the household and, at least up to the present, return home to assume control of a household estate when they succeed to a dominant position in the group. So that generally the senior male (or occasionally a mature woman) remains at home to manage its affairs including the cultivation of land, while more junior members are away in government service. Rao's argument concerning the compatibility of diverse occupations and joint household organization is, if anything, strengthened by the evidence from Belaspur Bazaar (1968). Seven of the 11 households which combine cultivation, shopkeeping and government service are jointly organized. Moreover, the four wealthiest domestic groups in the town have earnings from all three sources.

However, as bazaar residents continue to invest in land, they are, as we might expect, having to expand their participation in farming activities—both at a cultivating and a supervisory level—and, in general, assuming a greater commitment to agriculture, even if they still have a long way to go before they reach the new ceilings on land ownership set by recent land reform regulations (see next chapter). Thus, for example, 38 clean caste households already keep a pair of bullocks for ploughing, and 45 have at least one cow or buffalo, so that time must increasingly be devoted to tending cattle. At the same time, as already noted, townsmen are becoming more reluctant to abandon lucrative and secure careers in the civil service. With these diverse tendencies at work there could develop considerable strains on a household's ability to cope on two or more occupational fronts. But this is still in the future.

Conclusion

This chapter has examined the expansion of commerce and land-ownership among residents of the district capital. Until the middle of this century retail trade was constrained, on the one hand, by a peasantry largely self-sufficient and extremely modest in its demands for goods not produced locally, and, on the other, by an administration which did little to encourage the growth of a merchant community.

Since 1951, all this has changed, due primarily to a dramatic increase of consumer wants and to developments in the district, largely stimulated by the administration, which have encouraged and enabled the peasantry to turn to local shopkeepers for the satisfaction of these new demands.

Commercial growth, however, has proceeded by a proliferation of petty enterprises, rather than a substantial expansion of existing businesses. Townsmen, however much committed to and dependent on shopkeeping, continue to regard it as somehow peripheral to other sources of livelihood, a result of and contributing factor to the petty profits obtainable from these businesses. Thus, shops continue to be run as one-man enterprises and bazaar households prefer to diversify their capital investments, one result of which has been an increase in the ownership of agricultural land.

These trends have been encouraged, furthermore, by the growing involvement during the past decade or so, of village inhabitants in the economy of the town. Indeed, recent developments both within and outside the district which have had so great an impact on the community of bazaar residents, discussed in this and the preceding two chapters, have also had a profound effect on inhabitants of the surrounding countryside and consequently, and more importantly for the present discussion, on the traditional relations between townsmen and villagers. These links form the subject of the remainder of the book.

Notes to Chapter 6

1 According to one study of Chinese bureaucracy, commodities needed by local administrators from outside the area were either requisitioned without payment or bought at an 'official price' which was lower than the market rate (T'ung-Tsu Ch'u 1962:29–30).

2 It is not clear why these Doti traders stopped coming to Belaspur, but undoubtedly part of the reason was the growing competition from local merchants.

3 A fee (rs 2–10), based on the size of a shop's stock, is taken both by the district administration (see below) and the panchayat (see Chapter 9).

4 Merchants who set up businesses on the public green sell a limited range of these 'general' goods.

5 I was able to examine the current credit lists of nine cloth, six general, and four tea shops, one of which relied mainly on liquor sales. In each category, shops were divided equally between those owned by bazaar residents and by villagers.

6 These young men constitute something of a 'delinquent' problem in the bazaar, inasmuch as they spend a great many evenings drinking and, it is said, quarrelling and fighting. Virtually all are unmarried, and complain that there is nothing to do and nowhere to go in the town. Though senior government servants, they have no administrative responsibilities in their offices.

7 I have been told that it is illegal for members of the administration to accept credit from local shopkeepers. This is presumably a reference to Chap. 9, clause 6 of the (revised) Civil Service Regulations (1965) which states: 'No civil employee shall accept loans from or come under the financial obligation of any person having connection with his official duties'. There have been several attempts recently to organize a cooperative shop for government servants, but these have proved unsuccessful.

8 A similar situation apparently obtains in Tezibazar, a market town in north India, where, Fox notes, 'even in the case of the old-time Baniya merchant families a man is rarely found in the same business as was his father and most businessmen have conducted two, three or more different kinds of businesses in their lifetimes' (1969:151).

9 The Civil Service Regulations do not prohibit such activities by employees, but require those above the rank of *kharidar* (a non-gazetted, second-class post) to receive prior permission (see Chap. 9 clause 5).

10 This shop, the largest in the bazaar, is owned by a Newar who is a prominent district politician. Since he spends much of his time away from the town, the business is run by his widowed mother and several unmarried sisters.

11 The profits of shops owned by bazaariyas are similar to those of shops belonging to non-residents.

12 In assessing the worth of a household's estate for purposes of inheritance, only the stock on hand in a shop is taken into account; there is no notion of a business's 'goodwill' value.

13 Lands in this part of the country are held under *raikar* tenure, which means they can be bought and sold more or less freely (see M. C. Regmi 1963).

14 Several household heads who have not purchased lands inherited them from their fathers still alive in the town (and heads of separate households) who did buy them. A few other household heads who have not bought land are recent settlers in the town from nearby villages, where they still cultivate fields.

15 There are two main types of tenancy agreement applicable to lands in the plains and valleys owned by hill-dwellers in this part of Nepal. In one, termed *tirkut*, the tenant takes two-thirds of the main crop (usually paddy), but provides the various 'inputs' himself; in the other (*adyan*) the main crop is shared equally, with the owner usually providing the seeds. The first type was more widespread in the past when tenants were difficult to find because of malarial conditions in these areas.

16 Grain production has been converted into cash at the average annual market rate in the district: thus, the cash price for one *pathi* of wheat, maize and millet is rs 3.00, and for one *pathi* of rice rs 5.00 (or rs 2.50 for one of paddy).

17 These figures are not strictly comparable. That for income from landholding, while excluding the value of grains kept by tenants does not take account of other costs of cultivation. Chief among these are the payments made to agricultural labourers, which I was unable to estimate. The amount earned in government service is also a gross figure. There are various deductions from salaries (such as contributions to employees' health fund) which would have to be made to arrive at net earnings. Moreover, employees serving outside the district who must pay their own maintenance costs are unable to transfer a large proportion of their earnings home, so that the income realized by their households is substantially less than gross earnings. Finally, the figure for earnings from shopkeeping is an estimate of net profits based on merchants' statements of their annual stock purchases, mark-up, transport and other business costs. As noted in Appendix C, it assumes a stock turnover of 100 per cent during the year, achieved by the majority of but obviously not all general and cloth shops in the town.

18 Cooperative labour groups have been noted in various parts of Nepal (see Pignède 1966; Hitchcock 1966; L. Caplan 1970).

Part Three
Townsmen and Villagers

7

Economic Relations

FOR almost two centuries following the incorporation of Belaspur into the kingdom of Nepal, up to the end of the Rana period, relations between villagers and townsmen were essentially organic in character. The former, were, on the whole, self-sufficient cultivators; they took little interest in government service and none in commerce, which were the economic mainstays of the latter. Villagers supplied townspeople with food. The bazaar, in turn, was for some villagers at least, an important source of cash (to obtain which grain was sold), the services of certain craftsmen, and a limited range of consumer goods.

Most people in the countryside looked on Belaspur Bazaar as only the locus of district administration (and to a lesser extent, the commercial hub of the region) which they visited when occasion demanded it. Some had more than a sporadic interest in the town: thus, men employed by government offices or awarded contracts to provision the military garrison or inmates of the jail, or made responsible for the collection of land revenues in a sub-district, spent a fair amount of time in the bazaar. But these villagers, who stood most to gain from the administration were not seen to constitute a threat to the livelihood of the townspeople themselves.

During the past quarter of a century or so the previous structure of relations, based on an interdependence of mainly economic roles and functions, has been gradually eroded, to be replaced by one founded on a growing clash of interests between townsmen and villagers (or, more precisely, certain categories of villager). Briefly, this new pattern of social ties has emerged because changing conditions in the district and country as a whole have encouraged and to some extent compelled villagers to expand their range of activities outside the traditional agricultural sphere. In Belaspur, this has meant encroaching on what had previously been regarded as the economic preserves of bazaar dwellers. This chapter examines the extent of this encroachment, and identifies those categories of the village population most involved in the process.

Villagers in town

Villagers today own 53 of the 217 private dwellings in Belaspur Bazaar (see Map 3). Only six were bought or built on empty plots purchased from townsmen (mostly Newars) prior to 1951. These dwellings, situated at the northern and southern ends of Old Bazaar, were acquired either by relatively important government employees or a few sub-district headmen (see Chapter 8) who thought it politic to have a 'pied-à-terre' in the district capital. Six other dwellings were purchased or erected between 1951–63, partly for the same reasons, although by this time there were other advantages to owning property in the town, as I show below. A major and sudden expansion of village presence in the district capital followed on the opening for development in 1964 of a new area to the north of the old town. Since that time villagers have constructed 35 of the 49 dwellings in New Bazaar at a cost of approximately rs 80,000 and purchased (for an additional rs 15,000) six more in the old part of town. Virtually all this recent investment in property has been directed to two main kinds of enterprise: renting accommodation and shopkeeping. Buildings previously acquired by villagers for other ends are now utilized to these purposes as well.

The rapid growth of the administration during the past two decades has resulted in a situation where half of the 16 government or quasi-government branches and agencies in the district capital are required to rent buildings to serve both as offices and official accommodation for senior personnel. Since all administrative branches established prior to 1951 were housed in government-owned dwellings this kind of enterprise was hitherto unknown to local people. The scale of profit it provides is also outside the range of local experience. One villager who purchased a plot of land containing a small hut in the northern part of Old Bazaar for rs 900 two years ago, and constructed a large two-storey building at a cost of rs 10,000, now receives from the bank an annual rental of rs 2,400, and so can expect to recoup his substantial investment in 4–5 years.

In addition, a number of low and medium-ranking government servants either from outside the district or whose homes inside the district are too distant to allow them to commute daily to work, rent rooms in the town. The expansion of commerce has also brought a number of villagers into the bazaar to establish shops, which process is traced below. Here, it is important to note only that many, either unable or unwilling to purchase their own business premises, rent space from those owning property in the town. Just under two-thirds of the 41 dwellings which are wholly or partly rented to administrative offices, government employees and shopkeepers, are owned by villagers. An even higher proportion of the income from this source (69·3 per cent) is earned by villagers owning property in the town.

The latter are at an advantage over townsmen in the competition to provide accommodation for two main reasons. In the first place, the buildings they own do not have to serve, as do those of most town dwellers, either partly or wholly as their residences, and are therefore more readily available for rental. Secondly, since most of their dwellings have been constructed fairly recently (after 1964) villagers could take greater account of the needs of government offices. Indeed, in a number of instances villagers have all but been 'commissioned' to erect dwellings to the requirements of specific government offices. Thus, one man who purchased a plot in town with the intention of constructing a building on it, was in effect invited by the district council secretariat to provide for certain of its needs on the understanding that the building would be rented for a suitable figure. Townsmen, by contrast, can offer only old and often unsuitable buildings or part-buildings to let. Moreover, they have been prevented from acquiring land and thus from erecting more adequate and rentable dwellings on recently allocated development sites in the northern part of the town. This prohibition arose as a result of growing interest in and movement of villagers into the commercial life of the district capital, which culminated in 1964 in the opening of New Bazaar.

Until the end of Rana rule shopkeeping was all but monopolized by residents of the town. A number of villagers did come to live permanently in the bazaar and thereafter became shopkeepers, but, as I indicated in Chapter 2, it is unlikely that their reasons for settling initially in town were connected solely with an ambition to enter commerce. The dearth of village residents in the ranks of businessmen in the district capital was not due entirely to an absence of business experience. A few villagers spent some time during the dry months of every year on the public green in the bazaar selling, as they still do, a limited range of general merchandise. Then, too, a large village might very well contain a shop carrying a few items required regularly by local households. A handful of Belaspur villagers even operated small shops in the terai or across the border in India during the winter months. Some peasant families in the district, therefore, did have experience of commerce prior to 1951. In any case, considering the minimal skills required to operate a shop in the town, a lack of background would not have prevented men from entering business since it certainly did not do so later on. Nor did villagers refrain from commerce because they were deliberately excluded by townsmen: certainly the latter never conspired to prevent any property sales to non-residents. Moreover, those villagers who owned dwellings in the town prior to 1951 did not utilize them as shops, even though there were no measures to discourage them. The reluctance of peasants to become merchants in the district capital attested, rather, to the traditional adequacy of their lands and the less than attractive prospects of commerce in the town (see Chapter 6).

When the latter outlook altered after the revolution, so too did the earlier attitude towards business in the bazaar on the part of people in the villages. To-day, they operate just over half the shops (32 out of 63) in the district capital. None was established prior to 1960, and only three were begun between 1960–63. By this time, however, villagers' demands for business premises in the town had grown considerably, but could not be satisfied in the bazaar as it existed then. Most prospective merchants wanted to own their own buildings in town, while resident townspeople were understandably more anxious to rent out their own vacant premises, although even these were in short supply at the time. In 1964, the Village panchayat—with jurisdiction over an area much wider than, but encompassing the bazaar, and which was dominated by villagers (see Chapter 9)—decided to extend the main street of the town in a northerly direction, and to sell plots of land for commercial development. The council stipulated that those who already owned a house in the existing bazaar could not apply for a plot in the new area. This ordinance had the (intended) result of enabling villagers to take advantage of new economic opportunities becoming available in the district capital, while at the same time preventing townsmen from expanding their existing property and commercial interests.

Forty-eight plots of roughly equal size were offered for sale. Ninety-six requests were received (only seven were from eligible residents of the town) and the successful applicants were chosen by public draw. All but two of the plots went to villagers,[1] three of whom, however, became permanent residents of the town soon after. Sixteen of the plots subsequently changed hands—the rules about selling these properties were left unclear—and a few more bazaar residents were able to buy buildings and/or land in the development area. But on the whole New Bazaar is regarded as the domain of villagers, who own the great majority of the buildings and run 21 of the 26 shops there. Since 1964 other villagers, some of whom were unable to find premises for business in the new neighbourhood, have bought or (in the main) rented them in Old Bazaar so that 11 of the 37 shops in the original section of town are also run by people resident in the surrounding countryside.

In the space of barely five years since the opening of New Bazaar villagers have become as successful as, if not more so than, the resident merchant community, despite the fact that only eight had had any previous experience of running a shop, and none has any forebears with such a background. They now own more shops, invest more in stock (a reflection of the fact that they run more cloth and general, but fewer tea shops) and thus earn greater profits than the majority of townsmen. Apart from the representation of castes among them (they belong only to twice-born groups, the majority of them Chetri)[2] villager shopkeepers differ from their town-based counterparts in one important respect: with rare exceptions, they are self-sufficient if not well-to-do landowners to whom shopkeeping, by comparison with the main economic mainstay, subsistence agriculture, is financially of little account.

It is impossible to say with the same degree of certainty how villagers have expanded their participation in bureaucratic service although some indication is given by the fact, already noted, that the fathers of only 38 per cent of those now employed in the district administration had been government servants. In the past, wealthy and important villagers sought or already possessed village or sub-district headmanships which were at least as prestigious and financially advantageous, and certainly more secure than administrative service. Those who stood to gain most from government employment belonged to the less privileged sections of the peasantry. Men of little consequence acquired status and prestige in their own settlements through their association with the administration. Moreover, some of the richest men in the district today trace the origins of their wealth to Rana government service, either their own or that of immediate ancestors. The majority of those who spent many years in administrative posts were usually able, during the course of their employment, substantially to improve their economic positions, in one way or another, however menial their work, and insignificant their salaries.

But if these were some of the perks of government service, an important, perhaps the most important, factor encouraging local inhabitants initially to seek these posts was the need to earn cash. Villagers required cash for taxes and to purchase a few essential goods not produced locally. Although a few wealthy peasant households supplied members of the administration from outside the district as well as townsmen with grain supplies in exchange for cash, there was, for the great majority of the people in the district, no means locally to procure any but an income in grains.

The low level of monetization was a contributing factor to, but only partially alleviated by, large-scale service in the Gurkha regiments of the British Army mostly on the part of Magars and Gurungs in Belaspur. Most villagers as already pointed out, had to rely mainly on the export to the terai and thence to India of clarified butter. But from the early part of this century, because of the steady denuding of forests, especially in the area around the bazaar, the numbers of livestock which peasants could raise dwindled, and many found their cash incomes from this source steadily decreasing. More and more villagers were compelled to become seasonal migrants, spending between one and four months of each year working as unskilled labourers in India (see McDougal, 1968).

A post in the district administration was thus a rare opportunity for a Belaspur man to earn a regular cash income locally. But there were relatively few posts available to local people, and all but the most menial required a degree of literacy which few villagers possessed. The overall impression gained from informants and biographical data is that the literate, and therefore wealthy, members of village society who could qualify for the more important administrative posts open to district residents, were content to depend on their lands for economic, and on their headmanships for political, status. They therefore either ignored the administration as a source of employment, or, at most, on occasion sought to derive some specific and temporary advantage from it. But there was in no sense the kind of commitment to this form of livelihood found among residents of the district capital who managed to retain a substantial hold on administrative jobs throughout the Rana period even if, as I showed earlier, no individual enjoyed long-term security in any single appointment.

Although the latter still retain an interest in administrative posts out of proportion to their numbers, the attitude of villagers, especially the wealthy among them, to this form of occupation has altered considerably. In the immediate aftermath of the revolution recruitment to the highest levels in the district civil service was thrown open, and there were, for a time, prospects of unprecedented power and authority available to district residents which brought village leaders into government service, many for the first time (see Chapter 8). This interest in the administration grew, moreover, when headmen's duties began to be circumscribed and were finally abolished altogether under a comprehensive land reform programme introduced in 1964 (see below). The attractiveness of employment in the civil service also increased as the prospects of a secure and financially rewarding career materialized in the post-Rana years.

Since 1956, as already pointed out, only a high school education provides an entrée to the senior ranks of the administrative services. Until the establishment of a high school in the district capital in 1961, young men anxious to go on with their education after completing eighth grade (middle school) had to go either to a school in the terai or in Kathmandu, at considerable cost to their families. Even nowadays, to support a student in high school locally requires a substantial outlay of funds. Monthly fees are rs 6 for the lowest (sixth) grade rising to rs 10 for the highest (tenth) grade. In addition, uniforms as well as books and stationery (which are portered in from the plains and so quite expensive) must be purchased. Students unable to live at home have the added costs of board and accommodation. This means, of course, that only the wealthier village households can afford to send their sons to high school.

The costs of university education, which provides access to the very highest levels (gazetted posts) of administrative service, can reach rs 2,000 a year, since they involve not only fees, but generally maintenance in Kathmandu,[3] and so are beyond the means of all but a handful of families in the district. Nevertheless, villagers are clearly making substantial investments in education and so obtaining the means to compete for senior government jobs. All but twenty of the 153 students in the district's high school are villagers, while five of the seven young men from Belaspur district who have attended or are attending Tribhuvan University are from extremely well-to-do families outside the town.

Increased interest in government service on the part of Belaspur villagers is part of a trend throughout the country which has both accompanied and stimulated the dramatic growth in the rate of literacy. Nowadays, university, high and middle school and, to some extent, even primary school graduates not only aim to secure a white collar job, but are increasingly reluctant to engage in any form of manual—including agricultural—labour, considered the preserve of the illiterate. Moreover, even the sons of wealthy families who, in the past, were content to demonstrate and enhance their enviable status by idleness, nowadays expect and are expected to take respectable jobs in 'service' for at least a part of their adult lives. Until now the escalating demand for such posts has been met partly by the normal expansion of the civil service, and, especially in Kathmandu, by a deliberate inflation of the numbers of bureaucratic personnel (Mihaly 1965).[4] The total absence of alternative white collar employment in Belaspur as in all the far western hills suggests that, as educational opportunities continue to spread, the pressure on places in the district administration is not likely to abate.

To this point I have stressed the inducements which have encouraged villagers to create these interests in the bazaar: mainly the greater opportunities which now exist for financial gain in government service, shopkeeping and the ownership of property in the town. But there is another side to it as well. For in Belaspur, as in most parts of the Nepalese mid-montane region, since the beginning of the century growing pressures on land resources occasioned by a rapidly expanding population and exacerbated by a stagnant agricultural technology have transformed a self-sufficient peasantry into one increasingly dependent on alternative sources to supplement a growing inadequacy of grain production. There is no need to rehearse in detail the familiar pattern of too little land for too many people described for other parts of Nepal by McDougal (1968), L. Caplan (1970) and most recently and thoroughly, Macfarlane (1972).

In her study of Duari village, Patricia Caplan notes that despite the high infant mortality rate, men sire an average of four children who survive to adulthood, which, given a roughly equal proportion of males and females, and an inheritance system which divides a man's land equally among his sons, means that the average household's land must be divided into *at least* two parts in each generation.

She writes: 'A generation ago, the village was probably just sufficient in grain; two generations ago, it may even have produced a surplus. ... Today, the land produces only half the population's grain requirements, and the population appears to be doubling each generation' (1972:24). This observation probably holds true for the whole of Belaspur district.[5]

But land hunger obviously affects various categories of the peasantry differently. Wealthy families are able to offset the effects of population growth and property divisions by expanding their land holdings, generally at the expense of the less fortunate members of the community (or, as in recent years, by purchasing newly reclaimed lands outside the district). Thus, such villagers have remained largely immune from the kinds of land pressures experienced by the majority of the rural population. And since they are the persons who, as I have suggested, are now competing for the choicest government posts, and can most afford to buy property and establish shops in the town, it is not enough to suggest that worsening economic conditions among the peasantry of the district as a whole have stimulated them to turn their attentions to other prospects in the bazaar. It is equally, if not more, likely that the recent introduction of a land reform programme in the country has convinced these villagers that they can no longer rely on their lands alone to provide for the future.

The major provisions of the programme were included in the Lands Act of 1964 which, with subsequent amendments, contained the following:

a. Ceilings were placed on the ownership of land. In the hills outside Kathmandu valley the limit was 80 *ropani* (10·4 acres) per family, with an additional 16 *ropani* (2·1 acres) for a homestead site and 20 *ropani* (2·6 acres) allowed as a tenant holding.[6]
b. Tenants were to be given greater security after cultivating a plot of land for one year.
c. Interest rates were pegged at 10 per cent; a variety of existing credit arrangements were to be examined retroactively and any amount realized by the creditor in excess of the stipulated limit would be deducted from the principal. All further loans were to be channelled through newly created land reform offices.
d. A compulsory savings scheme was inaugurated to provide a source of inexpensive agricultural credit. Every landowner and/or tenant would deposit a fixed amount of grain (later cash) per unit of land cultivated.
e. The traditional system of land revenue collection (see Chapter 8) was

abolished although until new arrangements could be fully introduced, former tax-collectors would continue to be utilized.

This is not the place to assess the full implications of these measures.[7] Here it is only important to point out how they have encouraged wealthy villagers to enter the economy of the town. In this connection it was the establishment of ceilings on land holdings which probably had and is continuing to have the most far-reaching effects. Though setting generous limits within which a household can live in the kind of prosperity which few hill dwellers actually ever attain, this stricture has created a feeling that investment in land is now fraught with uncertainties. These fears, moreover, are compounded by the regulations protecting tenants and share-croppers, who in the normal course of events would be relied upon by large landowning families to cultivate at least a part of their fields. Then, the ceiling on interest rates and the interception of loans has contrived to block or at least render extremely hazardous the only other traditional avenue of investment available to rich peasants. It is not surprising, therefore, that many of them saw in those careers usually associated with townspeople prospects of unfettered advancement and profit which they felt were being denied them in their traditional rural pursuits.[8]

In a word, then, during the last two decades villagers have come to town. Over the last five years alone they have spent an average of rs 25,000 each year to purchase land and construct new dwellings, and now own one-quarter of all private property in the district capital. They run more than half the shops and invest over rs 150,000 annually in merchandise to stock them, earning upwards of rs 50,000 in profits. Finally, villagers in government service are paid just under rs 355,000 a year in salaries by the district administration (see Table 25).

Villagers near town

In the discussion so far I have referred to villagers as an undifferentiated category, save to note that it is the wealthiest among them—belonging, as we might expect, to the highest castes—who can afford the education needed to enter administrative service at senior levels, and the capital required to purchase property, construct dwellings and run shops in the bazaar. But geography, too, has conspired to enable primarily those resident in areas nearest the district capital to exploit these developments. Thus, the great majority of the 190 Belaspur villagers employed by the district administration live within daily commuting distance of the town. Seventy-two per cent can reach their offices in under 30 minutes; five per cent live between 30 and 60 minutes away; 17 per cent between one and three hours away; while only six per cent live beyond a three hour walk (5–6 miles).[9] This means, in effect, that an area more or less coincident with Simta sub-district constitutes the primary fund of recruitment for the district administration (see Map 2).

Being able to live at home and therefore not have to incur extra expenses on daily subsistence, of course, helps to make government service financially worthwhile and generally more appealing. But the predominance in the administration of villagers who live in the area surrounding the town can only be fully understood by reference to other factors as well.

The first is that persons resident near the administrative offices can most easily combine the management of their household affairs with careers in government service (see Chapter 4).

The second is that key educational facilities in Belaspur district were and still are located in the bazaar. The *bhasa* school and later the district's first middle school, which was then expanded to become the high school, were built in the bazaar which means that for the past 50 years, and especially during the crucial 20-year post-Rana period, those resident in villages in the immediate vicinity of the district capital (and, of course, in the town itself) have had far greater opportunities to educate their children than those resident in out-lying areas of the district. Consequently, they have enjoyed a special advantage in the competition for non-menial administrative posts (i.e. those requiring varying degrees of literacy).

Finally, a situation of this kind arises because, as I noted in Chapter 3, those who seek posts in the district administration, confer them directly, or obtain them for others, are involved to a large extent in a series of ongoing exchanges at the village level, i.e. in exchanges which cannot be understood by reference to bureaucratic procedures alone. Villagers in positions of influence within the administration help their kinsmen, neighbours and village clients wherever possible to find jobs in government offices. By this process, which is cumulative, a few settlements, after a time, come to provide a disproportionate number of the employees in certain offices, indeed, almost to monopolize posts (especially of menial and junior rank) in these offices, and ultimately in the district administration as a whole.

Thus, while 45 rural settlements[10] are represented among the 190 Belaspur villagers working in the district administration, 88 employees (46·2 per cent) are from only five settlements (excluding Belaspur Bazaar itself). These settlements are within a half-hour walk of the government offices, which helps to explain their predominance. But there are other settlements only marginally farther away which are much less well represented among government employees of the district bureaucracy. The point is that once residents of a particular settlement gain entry to an office, the tendency is for them to perpetuate their presence: they bring influence to bear on either the office head or a strategically placed official, probably from the same settlement, to fill vacancies with fellow villagers. Villages which provide the earliest recruits to an office are thus able to maintain their presence in that office for a considerable time. Only the transfer or resignation of a key official and his replacement by another from a different settlement can end the dominance of one village and signal the 'rise' of another.

Villages in close proximity to the bazaar also provide the vast majority of rural inhabitants who own property or run businesses in the district capital. Twenty-seven of the 32 shops (85 per cent) and all but four of the 53 dwellings (92 per cent) owned by villagers in the town belong to residents of these settlements. The explanation for this must proceed along somewhat different lines. It is unlikely that such a situation has emerged because villagers resident in areas surrounding the town are necessarily wealthier than those living at some remove. Nor is it a question of one man with business or property interests in the town in any sense 'recruiting' fellow villagers to these pursuits. When plots in New Bazaar were first offered for sale only 10 of the 96 applications came from villagers living beyond a three hour radius of the town.

It is undoubtedly the case (as with civil servants) that villagers living close to the bazaar can more easily combine the organization of a household—nearly all the persons concerned have ample land holdings and therefore must devote a reasonable amount of time to their estates—with shopkeeping and/or property management in the town than those living farther away.

But what is of crucial importance here is that villagers who live in the shadow of the town develop over time an extremely useful information network. Men sit for hours on the public green or in bazaar tea shops exchanging news and opinions about the failures and successes of shopkeepers or the latest property transactions in town. Anyone with half a mind to know in minutest detail the ins and outs of every enterprise has only to appear with some regularity at these gatherings. Even those without specific business in the bazaar spend much of their time there: the wealthier they are the less likely are they to take an active part in cultivation activities in the village and the greater the amount of leisure they have on their hands. The closer to the town they live, the more frequent and prolonged are their visits. Such men, who constitute a kind of reservoir of potential entrepreneurs, accumulate a store of contacts and through these, expert knowledge which gives them a distinct advantage over other villagers less strategically placed to assess the new economic possibilities increasingly available in the district capital and to exploit them when they arise.

Such villagers also cultivate a knowledge of administrative procedures and personnel which not only enables them better to cope with the usual red tape if required to obtain licenses and permits, but through which/whom they keep abreast of new edicts and pro- grammes decreed in the nation's capital which are bound to affect economic or political conditions in the district. And, as I have noted, and will subsequently discuss in more detail, many villagers with new financial interests in the town have established these as much to pursue political as economic goals.

Certainly the most striking example of village encroachment on the town concerns Bhuka, a settlement containing slightly over 1,400 persons, on the western slopes of Simta ridge, just below the district capital (see Map 2). One quarter of the shops run by villagers are in the hands of 'Bhukals', who contribute some 22·5 per cent of the total annual investment in stock by rural inhabitants; they own almost one-half of the bazaar dwellings owned by villagers and receive over 70 per cent of all the income accruing to villagers from the letting of premises in the town; and, finally, Bhuka provides the single largest contingent of employees in the district administration (28 men) and earns 11·6 per cent of all the money paid out in salaries to rural inhabitants, more than any other village community. This settlement, not surprisingly, contains some of the district's wealthiest and most prominent men (see following chapters). Table 25 com- pares the economic interests of all villagers and of Bhukals with those of townspeople in various 'enterprises' discussed above.

TABLE 25

Comparison of interests in various enterprises by townsmen,
all villagers, and Bhukals

	Townspeople	All Villagers	Bhukals only
Private dwellings in town owned by	164	53	25
Shops in town run by	31	32	8
Annual income from rental of dwellings in town (in rupees)	10,200	14,200	10,200
Annual investment in stock (in rupees)	152,700	158,500	35,600
Annual income from employment in district administration (in rupees)	46,700	354,700	41,200

This growing economic competition has, if not created, certainly helped to intensify feelings of hostility between townsmen and villagers generally (Bhukals, in particular, for reasons which will subsequently become apparent). This enmity, many insist, has existed since the creation of the bazaar, and it is 'explained' in terms of certain personality and cultural differences between them. Each believes the other to speak a separate variety of Nepali, and to follow separate customs (*ran san*), although, in fact, the variations in speech and manner between the two categories are no greater than those (minor differences) within each. Townsmen compare their own peaceful natures with the quarrelsomeness of villagers. The latter, for their part, express annoyance at what they characterize as the 'superior air' assumed by townsmen 'because they do not farm' (which, as I have shown, is no longer the case). Furthermore, a theme returned to time and again by villagers when discussing the hostility between themselves and bazaariyas concerns the 'pretensions' of the latter despite, on the whole, a low ritual status. At every opportunity they remind townspeople (the clean castes, especially) of their hybrid origins, a reference to the comparatively high number of inter-caste unions entered into by townspeople.

Marriages of townsmen

The growth of an administrative and commercial centre in the midst of a traditional peasant society presented new settlers in the bazaar, most of whom were men, with difficulties relating to the establishment of affinal ties with members of their own castes in the district. For Newars there was simply a dearth of members of the same caste in the villages of Belaspur district. Early immigrants of other clean caste groups, for different reasons (discussed below) could not find suitable partners in the rural areas. A large proportion of townsmen, therefore, made and have continued to make alliances within the bazaar itself. Approximately 40 per cent of all clean caste marriages (45·5 per cent of men's and 31·6 per cent of women's), and almost one half of Newar unions, about which I have information, have linked together households in the town.

But the possibilities for intra-bazaar unions are necessarily limited by the rule prohibiting marriage in the male line; even Newars, who recognize no named descent groups, do not marry for at least three generations, and generally five. Many townspeople, therefore (again, particularly Newars) have made alliances out of the district, usually in other administrative centres of western Nepal, where enclaves of the same caste, often facing similar problems, can be found.[11] This has led to the creation of marital links as far away as seven days' walk from Belaspur Bazaar. Moreover, about one-fifth of out-of-district unions involve local women (most of them Newars) who have married officials from other parts of the country posted temporarily to the district administration. In addition, a few locally resident government employees have imported wives married while they were serving in other districts. Table 26 summarizes the distribution of marriages made by townspeople of clean caste.

TABLE 26

*Distribution of clean caste marriages**

	No. of marriages	Intra-bazaar %	Outside bazaar %	Marriages outside bazaar: Within district %	Outside district %
Newar	199	97 (48·7)	102 (51·3)	44 (22·1)	58 (29·2)
Chetri	68	17 (25·0)	51 (75·0)	26 (38·2)	25 (36·8)
Thakuri	16	3 (18·7)	13 (81·3)	7 (43·7)	6 (37·6)
Gurung	12	4 (33·3)	8 (66·6)	4 (33·3)	4 (33·3)
Magar	11	1 (9·1)	10 (90·9)	7 (63·6)	3 (27·3)
Joggi	5	– –	5 (100·0)	2 (40·0)	3 (60·0)
All	311	122 (39·2)	189 (60·8)	90 (29·0)	99 (31·8)

* These are crude figures, meant to convey a general pattern.

The marriage pattern summarized above is a spatial one, but the same factors which have led townspeople of clean caste to look for partners mainly inside the bazaar or outside the district have also encouraged unions across caste lines. Over 15 per cent of their unions, 16·6 per cent of men's and 14·0 per cent of women's, have involved partners of different clean castes. Table 27 presents the configuration of these marriages.

TABLE 27

Inter-caste marriages

		Thakuri	Chetri	Newar	Magar	Gurung	Other	Total
Made by:								
Newar	Men	–	4	–	9	2	–	15
	Women	5	6	–	–	–	3*	14
Thakuri	Men	–	1	2	–	–	–	3
	Women	–	–	–	–	1	–	1
Chetri	Men	–	–	6	–	–	–	6
	Women	1	–	3	–	–	–	4
Magar	Men	–	–	–	–	2	1†	3
	Women	–	–	–	–	–	–	–
Gurung	Men	–	–	–	–	–	–	–
	Women	–	1	–	–	–	–	1

* A Brahmin, a Rai (tribal group in eastern Nepal) and a Joggi.
† A Thakali from west-central Nepal.

The numbers of inter-group unions involving Newars would be even higher if account were taken of those marriages within the Newar community itself between persons of different rank, a practice tolerated in the bazaar as long as the barrier of untouchability was not broken. But all Newars who were not already so became 'Shresthas' on or soon after arrival (see p. 25) and no record remains of the precise affiliations of the early settlers. This is apparently a feature of many Newar communities outside Kathmandu Valley (Furer-Haimendorf 1962).

Most inter-caste unions created by Newar men have been with women of marginally lower-status 'tribal' groups, principally Magars. The offspring of these unions are often referred to as 'Nagarkoti', but for all intents and purposes they are regarded as Newars and marriages between them are considered isogamous. Newar women who have married outside their caste have, with a single exception, established hypergamous unions either (as in eight cases) with members of the administration posted temporarily to the district or (as in six cases), with members of the administration from outside the district who settled in the town. But whereas, because of virilocal norms, the majority of unions in the first category found their way out of the area when the men were posted elsewhere, the second kind have had a significant effect on the pattern of relations among members of clean castes within the bazaar. They have also contributed to shaping the links between townsmen and villagers because the origins of these unions can be sought in the attitudes of villagers to marriages with those claiming equal ritual status who settled originally in the town from other parts of the country.

The Brahmins, Thakuris and Chetris of the villages were reluctant to create marriage alliances with these immigrants, both because of their uncertainty about the latters' caste credentials, and their relative poverty.[12] The refusal of twice-born castes in the villages to offer their women to the earliest of their caste fellows from outside the district probably compelled the latter to take women of lower ritual status as wives. The founding settlers—a Brahmin, a Thakuri, and five Chetris—of the seven clan groups of twice-born status in the bazaar which originate outside the district, wed as follows: five married Newar women (one also took as his second wife a Gurung); one married the descendant of a slave;[13] only one married a village woman of 'pure' Chetri status. In the latter instance, the Chetri migrant had come with substantial financial resources and established a business in the bazaar. His rapid success quelled the initial fears about his origins.

The reluctance of high-caste villagers to acknowledge the claims of new bazaar immigrants to equal status exposed the latter to pressures from lower-ranked Newar families—confronted, as already noted, by their own problems resulting from demographic imbalances

—to accept their women as wives. On the whole, these Newars, by this time well settled in the town, offered moderate wealth and the influence which went with near monopoly of those administrative posts open to local residents.

Inter-caste unions, save in the case of those which unite two partners of twice-born status, marrying for the first time, involve no wedding rite, nor any custom of bridewealth or dowry, although it is by no means unusual for some transfer of property to take place at the time of or following the establishment of the union, usually from the bride's family to the bridegroom's, or to the bride herself. The marriage is signified by the couple taking up residence together, and the woman is thereafter referred to as the man's wife (*swasni*) and he as her husband (*logne*). Strictly speaking, then, such marriages are not sanctified by Hindu religious 'authority', but should not, because of this, be considered as instances of concubinage and thereafter as productive of illegitimate children. The marriages are recognized by the community and, indeed, should another man seduce the woman, he is liable to pay compensation to the cuckold.

Such inter-caste unions raise a host of interesting questions, some of which I have discussed elsewhere (1974). Here, only several points might be noted, one of which is that unions involving partners of different caste are not invariably secondary marriages, made possible only after primary, isogamous ones have been forged. Dumont propounds such a view partly on the grounds that 'there must be in the house a woman whose cooking the family can eat before a subsidiary wife can be admitted' (1964:93). The facts of the situation in Belaspur Bazaar belie this reasoning. In the first place all but a handful of the inter-caste marriages noted above are primary or principal unions (indeed, in most cases, they are only unions).

Secondly, the question of cooking and inter-dining in households containing hypergamous unions is less problematical than Dumont would suggest. In a community where such unions are not exceptionable pressures to conform strictly to commensal regulations within the household are light, and there are few husbands who would consistently refuse to eat even ritually important foods prepared by their lower caste wives in the privacy of their kitchens. Still, as Furer-Haimendorf notes, some men who are of higher status than their spouses do cook for themselves, and certainly all would claim *publicly* to do so (1964:99). This is surely not so unusual: Yalman reports that in the Ceylonese village he studied persons of high caste occasionally take food prepared by persons of low caste but he remarks that 'this would be vehemently denied in public' (1962:96).

Another point of significance relates to the effects of these unions on inter-caste relations in the town. Almost one in five households of clean caste in the bazaar at present (14 out of 75) contains members of more than one caste who are related to one another. Two of the most 'mixed' domestic units in the town are illustrated in Figure 1.

FIGURE I

Two multi-caste households

Household 'A'

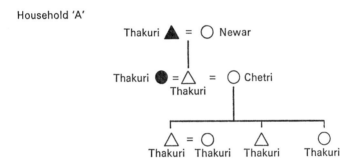

Household 'B'

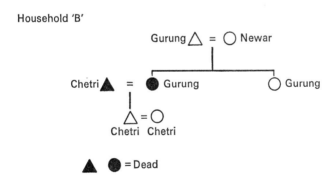

A bald statement of even such a relatively high proportion of multi-caste households fails to convey the full extent of links among townsmen of different groups. There are also various ties between uni-caste households created by multiple marriages. The children of one Chetri government official from outside the district are related through their locally resident mothers (a Gurung, a Newar and a Chetri) to other bazaariyas belonging to these groups, while one Newar woman married first to a Gurung and then to a Thakuri has generated close kinship ties between the households to which her children of different castes are affiliated. The combination of affinal, matri- and patri-lateral ties among members of the same and different castes is therefore exceedingly varied and complex; households are so inter-woven that the vast majority of clean-caste townsmen could, without projecting very far into the past, be located on a single genealogical chart.

There is, moreover, a sense of close attachment between affinally linked households which are expected to cooperate with one another, provide assistance of varying kinds (including loans), and, in political contexts, give support when required. Inter-caste marriages, then, involve more than simply two individuals, although they may not be 'alliances' between sets of kinsmen, if by this we mean that the connection is intended to be perpetuated in the next generation (Yalman 1962:95).

The notion of a uni-caste household must be understood in the context of how caste membership is determined. We would have to regard as uni-caste, for example, a domestic group containing a married pair each of whom is in fact 'half-caste', viz., the Newar husband might be the child of a Gurung mother, and his Newar wife of a Chetri mother, but both are Newars because each had a Newar father (who may himself have been the son of a Magar woman). In other words, despite constant hybridization, caste affiliation is clear and consistent, and based on the principle that the child of a marriage between members of different clean castes, save those involving Brahmin men,[14] assumes the status group of its father.

Discussion: inter-caste marriages

In his introduction to *Aspects of Caste in South India, Ceylon and North-west Pakistan* Leach invites his readers to consider 'just how far a social system can differ from the orthodox Hindu prototype yet still deserve the cultural label "caste"' (1962:2). A crucial feature of the 'orthodox Hindu prototype' would appear to be caste endogamy. According to Leach: 'The kinship peculiarity of caste systems does not lie in the internal structuring of kinship, but in the total absence of kinship as a factor in extra-caste systemic organization . . . kinship relations are exclusively internal' (1962:7). In a different paper he again notes how 'each individual is born into a particular named group which is the same as that of *both* his parents . . . (1967:9) (my emphasis).

Other anthropologists have joined Leach in arguing that endogamy is a fundamental feature of any definition of caste (Berreman 1960; Mandelbaum 1970), while Atal has recently identified intramarriage as the basic or pivotal attribute of the system (1968). Barth is somewhat critical of this approach, arguing that it takes no account of the structural significance of endogamous practices. He suggests that 'Only those intercaste relations which would create ambiguity in the principles of status ascription are incompatible with the structural features of a caste system. It follows logically from this that a pattern of caste endogamy is vital to any system of kinship only where rights and status are transmitted to children from both their parents' (1962:132). In the Pathan case the stress on patrilineality 'serves to make matrilineal and matrilateral kinship irrelevant to status and authority ascription, and thus obviates the need for caste endogamy' (ibid). Pocock, too, has recently pointed out that 'where the paternal side is the valued side in descent . . . violations of endogamy are more common than is often supposed' (1972:55).

This view, which is applicable to the Nepalese situation described above, raises questions about Berreman's stress on the cultural plurality of castes. For him, an important function of endogamy lies in its implications for the distinctiveness of these groups. By restricting intermarriage and interaction generally, he argues, caste systems inhibit the opportunity for shared culture (1967). In Belaspur Bazaar interaction between these groups is clearly anything but restricted and the result is a broadly uniform set of customary practices. All speak Nepali as a first language (including Newars), wear the same dress, celebrate the same festivals and household rites, utilize the same category of ritual specialists, and so on.

Still, despite this uniformity, perhaps because of it, there is a sense in which we may speak of cultural distinctiveness. It is not the fruit of separation, as Berreman suggests, but rather arises from a common belief in and perception of difference imposed by a system founded on hierarchy. Indeed, Berreman makes much the same point when he notes, in a statement seemingly at variance with his other argument, that even 'when interaction between castes is maximal and cultural differences are minimal, the ideal of mutual isolation and distinctiveness is maintained and advertised among those who value the system' (1967:52).

It is assignment at birth to membership of specific castes which confers this difference. And whatever their matrifiliation or their private behaviour within a household, men behave and purport to behave publicly in a manner commensurate with their ritual status. At public gatherings they eat only foods appropriate to their caste, prepared by persons of proper rank and served in an acceptable manner. They follow established mourning procedures normally associated with their ritual status, so that a Thakuri son of a Magar woman mourns his Thakuri brother for 13 days, but his mother for only three. Again, whatever their matri-filiation, men ranked as Thakuris and Chetris wear the sacred thread conferred publicly by Brahmins. Bazaar residents (such as Newars) who rank below the twice-born groups make no attempt to belittle the latter, but if anything acknowledge their ritual superiority (even though they may be the closest of relatives) and accord them the respect which is thought to be their due. There is, then, a dissociation of marriage practice and ritual status. The latter is conferred by patrifiliation and validated by reference to shared values and symbols.

Despite the close unity wrought by kinship and affinity, townsmen regard themselves as composed of distinct caste groups, hierarchically ranked and, by virtue of their ritual differences, culturally distinct. From the vast panorama of Hindu beliefs they select only some through which they symbolize their separate statuses. Villagers, by contrast, choose a more 'orthodox' cultural model against which to measure castes in the bazaar, and denigrate (especially) those claiming ritual equality with themselves, comparing the purity of their own castes which result from endogamous marriages with the counterfeit (*nakali*) groups produced by hybrid unions in the town.

Conclusion

This chapter has focussed on the manner and extent of the encroachment by villagers into what, until the end of the Rana era, were regarded as the traditional economic preserves of bazaar residents. Villagers now own a significant proportion of the buildings and a majority of shops in the bazaar. They also seek, no less avidly than townsmen, to benefit from the enlarged administration and the opportunities now open to local people to enter its higher ranks. Those who have enjoyed the most success are wealthy villagers belonging to the highest castes. Moreover, it is primarily that category of well-to-do villager resident in the immediate environs of the town, for example, Bhuka village, which is best able to exploit these opportunities.

Finally, note was taken of the growing enmity between bazaariyas and villagers, especially those most involved in the competition for these resources. The hostility is encouraged and to some extent expressed by the pattern of townspeople's marriages. The majority are either out-of-district or intra-bazaar (including inter-caste) unions. The outcome is a situation in which a limited number of ties between them and their village neighbours exist which might mitigate this hostility. Alternatively, and perhaps of greater importance, it has allowed a highly inter-connected set of links to develop among clean castes in the bazaar, fostering and abetting their unity and cohesion in the face of the confrontation with villagers. The cleavage has been given an even sharper focus by political events following on the end of Rana rule, discussed in the following three chapters.

Notes to Chapter 7

[1] The two townsmen who were drawn were in the process of effecting a division of property with older brothers and pleaded that they owned no dwellings in Old Bazaar.

[2] Sixteen shops are owned by Chetris, six by Jaisis, five by Thakuris, and three by Brahmins. See Table 20 for the castes of town-resident merchants.

[3] There are a number of colleges in various parts of the country, including the western terai, offering Tribhuvan University's syllabus, and candidates can both prepare for and sit the intermediate or final exams in such centres. But because the level of instruction is understandably lower in these areas than in Kathmandu, the failure rate is much higher, and students try as much as possible to study in the nation's capital.

[4] It is no longer possible for administrative growth in the country as a whole to keep up with the numbers of high school and university graduates. In Kathmandu Valley, 18 per cent of the latter were reported to be unemployed in 1969 (see L. Caplan 1970a).

[5] If unofficial census figures given by Landon (1928) can be relied upon, the population of Belaspur district (prior to the administrative reorganization of 1962) rose from 84,000 in 1920 to 260,000 in 1952, and to 300,000 by 1961.

6 Villagers in the hills are not accustomed to measuring lands in terms of area, in which the new ceilings are set, and often do not know how much land they actually own, although of course they know its productivity. Since dry lands have never been surveyed in the hills, the land reform administration translated the amount of seed sown (which peasants, of course, know) into a rough estimate of the size of these holdings.

7 Patricia Caplan records the reactions of certain groups in the village of Duari to the land reform programme (1972: 37–40).

8 It should be noted that this was one of the aims of the land reform programme. In the preamble to the legislation of 1964 it states: ' . . . . . it is desirable to divert inactive capital and man-power from the land to other sectors of the economy in order to accelerate the pace of development. . . .' Fox notes a similar shift of investment from village to town following zamindari abolition in India (1969:137).

9 Three hours appears to be the maximum time a government servant will spend walking each day to and from work. Those who live farther away generally rent accommodation in the town, and return home only at 'week-ends'.

10 I am referring here to traditional village units and not the new statutory Villages established in 1961 for the purpose of electing panchayats (see Chapter 9).

11 This is similar to the problem faced by the Butchers, who solve it in much the same way (see Chapter 5).

12 Members of these castes who moved to the bazaar from other parts of Belaspur district continued to make affinal alliances in their areas of origin with members of their own castes.

13 Slavery was abolished in Nepal in 1924, and the former slaves granted the sacred thread and the status of Gharti Chetri by government decree.

14 The offspring of hypergamous unions involving Brahmin men belong to groups below that of their fathers, the precise rank depending on the caste of their mothers.

8

Political Relations
Rana and early post-Rana periods

THE division of economic roles between townsmen and villagers which characterized the Rana period was reflected in, and paralleled by, a virtual absence of political interaction between them. There were, in effect, no contexts within which residents of the bazaar, on the one hand, and villages on the other, could compete for power. As I noted in Chapter 3, the Ranas and their appointees from Kathmandu monopolized all senior offices and so kept the comprehensive power and authority vested in the administration out of the reach of all district inhabitants. The less important posts open to local people did provide many of them with the opportunity to enhance their financial positions during their terms of office. Indeed, it would be rare to encounter someone who could not catalogue a host of ways in which government employees at every level used their official positions for personal gain, often at the expense of members of the public. Linked to the financial advantages was the prestige attached to government service so that a reputation could be enhanced and a political following created or enlarged through employment, however menial, in the administration.[1] But in as much as the 'arenas'[2] within which men sought advancement were coincident with single settlements or perhaps a cluster of neighbouring settlements, the benefits of service were, so to speak, 'negotiable' only within limited geographical and social contexts. Moreover, the Rana government, through its machinery of tax collection, not only helped to create and reinforce the traditional boundaries of political activity but defined the rules governing the competition.

Headmen

Since administrative expenses in the district were met wholly out of local revenues, the collection of land taxes was an important if not the dominant concern of district administration during Rana times. Land surveys (*jac*) were conducted periodically, at which time revenue settlements were determined, and these served as the basis of tax assessments until the next survey (see note 25, p. 55). Districts were divided into major revenue units or sub-districts, their boundaries usually corresponding with principal geographical features, and one or more sub-district headmen (*jimmawal*) made responsible for tax-collection in these units.[3] In the old district of Belaspur, i.e. prior to 1962, there were 16 sub-district headmen distributed among nine revenue divisions (called *dara*). These were, in turn, sub-divided into smaller revenue units, generally (but not invariably) coterminous with traditional villages, and each was made the charge of a village headman (*mukhiya*).[4] In 1962, there were 295 such functionaries in the district. They collected taxes from those who owned land in their revenue units and passed these on to the sub-district headman who paid them to the revenue office in the district capital. Neither type of headman had any proprietary rights in the lands for whose taxes he was responsible, but together they could claim up to five days of free labour from each household paying tax (called *raiti*). In addition, village and sub-district headmen were entitled to a commission (2·5 and 5 per cent respectively) on the amount collected. Headmen were also granted the right to hear minor cases and impose limited fines (up to rs 25), although they seldom exercised this latter prerogative; on the whole, tax-payers benefited from the mediation offered by these notables.

In return for their privileges, headmen were held accountable by the government for all revenues, and had to meet them personally if for any reason tax-payers were unable to fulfil their obligations. They were also expected to act as hosts to members of the administration visiting their settlements, recruit villagers to porter loads for the militia as well as for senior civil servants, report the presence of unauthorized strangers in their areas, and assist in the arrest of any villagers wanted by the authorities. In brief, a headman was expected to act as the vehicle of government in his revenue domain and even had the services of a messenger (*katuwale*), who received a small annual payment from each household as well as a larger one from the headman, to carry his instructions to the villagers. In a less official capacity, tax-collectors played some part in helping peasants within their own areas to effect their occasional dealings with the administration and a few sub-district headmen even maintained a residence in the district capital.

Initial appointments to sub-district headmanships were made on three main bases.

Firstly, they were not infrequently granted to scions of the traditional 'aristocracy' in the region. These were members of the Thakuri royal families who had established a number of petty kingdoms throughout western Nepal in the fourteenth century (see Chapter 2). To win the support of these erstwhile rulers the victorious Gorkha monarch allowed many to retain at least some of their traditional privileges in parts of the area over which they had formerly ruled. Although the Ranas, when they took power, abolished many of these prerogatives, a few aristocratic families with whom they made marital alliances, or otherwise maintained amicable relations, were rewarded with sub-district headmanships. This helps to explain why Thakuris, who constitute barely 15 per cent of the district population, held 10 out of 16 such offices in 1962.

Second, they were occasionally conferred on men from outside the region who, after serving in the local administration, decided to settle permanently in the district. Thus, several prominent families in Belaspur, including that of the sub-district headman of the Simta revenue unit, trace their origins in the area to a former senior official in the district administration who had been rewarded in this way.

Third, these offices were granted to prominent residents whose influence and support was sought by the regime.

Not surprisingly, sub-district headmanships came to be associated only with rural families from among the higher castes in the district. Although no specific ruling banned untouchables from holding such office, there is no evidence of any having done so in Belaspur. Indeed, only one of the 16 sub-district headmanships in 1962 was held by a member of a drinking caste, a Magar.

Village headmen were also appointed by the revenue office, frequently in response to an appeal by some of the candidate's more influential followers-cum-prospective taxpayers and/or the recommendation of the relevant sub-district headman. Like the latter, village headmen tended to be members of the highest castes. Thus, in 1962, of the 34 tax-collectors under the jurisdiction of the Simta sub-district headman (a Chetri of Bhuka village) there were 20 Chetris, nine Thakuris, one Brahman and two Jaisis; only two—Magars—were members of drinking castes.

Once approved by the tax office, a headman at either level was secure in his post during his lifetime provided he fulfilled his obligations to both his tax-payers and the administration. Although for some time it was apparently possible to transfer titles and tax collecting privileges by sale (a practice prohibited by the government around the turn of this century) a headmanship tended to remain within the same descent line for generations. Generally, the eldest son succeeded, but competition for the office could and did occur from time to time within the group. The succession might be disputed if the incumbent died without male issue or if the rightful successor had as opponent a near agnate who thought himself more competent and deserving.

Not infrequently, such challenges went by default if the superior wealth, influence and support (among tax-payers) of the challenger was recognized and in such cases the lawful claimant would probably endorse the request of the other to be granted the title. Thus, the history of succession to headmanship in Simta sub-district over the past three generations reveals that in no case did the eldest son actually assume the title, as Fig. 2 shows.

FIGURE 2

Succession to Simta sub-district headmanship

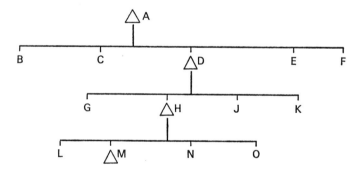

△ = Headman

B, the lawful successor to A, died unmarried; C, who could have succeeded, is said to have been illiterate and so unsuitable; D therefore became headman. G, his first-born son, apparently 'disappeared' in India before his father died, which enabled H to become the next sub-district headman. On his death in 1960 L might have got the title but he is considered something of an incompetent (and a heavy drinker) and much in the shadow of his extremely able and ambitious younger brother, M, the present incumbent. However, in his petition to the revenue authorities (which was not contested) M felt obliged to argue his legitimate right to the title on the grounds that though the second of his father's four sons, he is the first of the eldest wife, while L, though born first, is the son of his father's younger wife.

From time to time, issues of this kind were contested publicly and in such cases contending parties had to be especially ambitious and well-to-do, for the final right of appointment always lay with the administration, and the appeals and petitions necessary to wage a dispute of this kind involved great expense and immense time and trouble. Usually, they had to be referred to a senior member of the government, not uncommonly the prime minister himself.

In sum, political struggles, to the extent that they occurred in Rana times, were confined to intra-village rivalries and occasionally to competition within a larger circle of villages. But village headmen did not contend *with one another*, nor, more importantly, did sub-district headmen, for the administration defined the widest political arena as the major revenue unit. This is not to suggest that the only form of political activity in Belaspur during the century before the revolution revolved around competition for the office of headman. For the factional struggles which have characterized rural political life in so much of South Asia (Nicholas 1968) have not eluded western Nepal. But to the extent that these rivalries were about local issues (including headmanship) they did not alter the essential fact that political activity until 1951 was contained within small-scale contexts.

A point to be noted here is that residents of the bazaar did not receive headmanships, due principally to their minimal involvement in agriculture. Since for many years townsmen were granted a commutation on their own house taxes no collectors were required in the bazaar itself and when the privilege was withdrawn in 1957, they remitted their assessments directly to the revenue office. The few townsmen who owned cultivating land paid taxes to the relevant village headman, but because they were resident outside the revenue units in which their lands were situated, their links to these officials were much more tenuous than those of villagers. Bazaar landowners did not rely on their headmen to settle disputes in which they became involved, but looked to notables within the town itself, or to senior members of the administration with whom they were in constant contact to provide informal mediation. And because government servants were exempt from corvée even the few bazaar households with land (since they generally had members in government employment) escaped this most onerous of obligations to their tax-collectors. So townsmen were not in any significant way the dependants of village or sub-district headmen.

Aftermath of revolution

Between 1846 and 1946 challenges to the regime evolved mainly from within the ranks of the ruling Rana family itself as various factions competed with one another for control of the government. Following the Second World War, and the decision of the British, who had contributed to maintaining the Ranas in power (Joshi and Rose 1966), to withdraw from the sub-continent, opposition became more widespread, and found its organizational base in several parties created by Nepalese exiles in India. With their merger in early 1950 into the Nepali Congress Party, whose stated aims were to bring down the Ranas, alter the system of government they had created and end the country's isolation from the outside world, the stage was set for revolution. Hostilities between the state militia and the 'Liberation Army' (*Raksha Dal*) of the Nepali Congress began later that year. After a series of Congress successes, but before a complete military victory could be achieved, the newly independent Indian government, anxious for a moderate solution, arranged a settlement between the Rana leaders and King Tribhuvan, who supported the revolution which had promised to restore the power of the monarchy. In accordance with the agreement (reluctantly complied with by the Nepali Congress which had not been included in the Delhi negotiations until their final stages) the King, in February 1951, established an interim coalition government composed both of representatives of the previous Rana government and the Congress Party. But since the coalition, as Joshi and Rose note, 'was formed on the basis of a peculiar dialectic logic of combining the incumbent Rana regime with an antithetical Nepali Congress in the hope of producing a democratic political synthesis, conflict was inherent in the scheme of things' (1966:87). The Congress leaders, forced to accept a settlement which fell far short of their aims, took every opportunity to undermine their opponents' position in the coalition cabinet and within a year they had removed the Ranas, at long last, from the government of Nepal.

In Belaspur the revolution passed quickly and quietly. A small detachment of the Congress Liberation Army entered the district but encountered no resistance from the local military garrison which had all but disbanded. A Congress leader assumed control of the district administration and those senior officials of the previous regime who had not already fled in anticipation of Congress's arrival were dismissed and sent home. But with the country's civil service in almost total collapse, replacements for these Rana appointees could only be found from among the local population. For the first time, in other words, residents of Belaspur district had the opportunity of filling senior positions in the district administration.

The political 'instincts' of the district's more ambitious men made them quick to realize that occupants of such posts would have formidable resources at their disposal in terms of patronage, authority and coercive force, not to speak of the financial perks. In addition, they would not only enhance the prestige they already enjoyed in their settlements and neighbourhoods but would be honoured in the district at large. Whereas the prerogatives of headmen during Rana times had been and continued after 1951 to be carefully circumscribed, those of senior members of the administration appeared by comparison limitless, especially in view of the rather weak control exercised in the immediate aftermath of the revolution by the central authorities. These new opportunities thus created or 'liberated' political hopes which had previously been constrained by the structure of tax-collection and the rules of recruitment to headmanship and the district administration.

This is not to suggest that every category of the population could now compete on an equal footing for these offices. First of all, due partly to high caste domination of the national political structure, and partly to the legacy of illiteracy bequeathed them by the Ranas, untouchables fared little better in the early stages of the new regime than they had done in the old. Second, for most of the reasons mentioned earlier, men prominent in the vicinity of the government offices benefited most of all from the new opportunities. In other words, as the political arena within which local leaders opposed each other shifted from the village or sub-district to the district, those closest to the locus of power, i.e. the district capital, found themselves at a distinct advantage in the competition.

In the years immediately following the revolution, senior administrative posts, like less exalted offices during the Rana period, were obtained by establishing personalistic links to centrally-appointed governors from outside the district. Residents of the bazaar who were not only best placed to forge such links, but who had accumulated a wealth of administrative experience during the previous regime, which these governors were reluctant to overlook, succeeded in establishing a strong foothold in the upper echelons of the new administration. One townsman became the highest-ranking official in the district headquarters next to the governor (see below), while others held high posts in the revenue office and the court, which were, at this time, still the three key branches in the local administration. Moreover, despite a rapid turnover of governors in the district (there were three in the three years immediately following the revolution) townsmen were, by and large, successful in retaining their hold on these positions by establishing loyalties not merely to individual patrons but to the Nepali Congress Party itself.

Although villagers also sought and were granted high offices, few managed to retain them for long, due perhaps to their lack of previous experience in government service, or to the practice whereby each new governor replaced many of his predecessor's appointees with his own, or, as many of these erstwhile officials insist, to the machinations of a few jealous and ambitious townsmen occupying key positions in the administration. Whatever the reasons, these villagers, thus dismissed from their offices, along with many others who had aspired to but never received senior administrative appointments, formed a category of potential leaders who were not at all kindly disposed toward the ruling Nepali Congress. Such men and their village followings proved a source of recruits for the opposition parties which, within a year or two of the revolution, began to establish a presence in the district.

The coming of political parties

Following the establishment of the Rana-Nepali Congress government in February 1951, a host of political parties were created to gratify individuals slighted or interests ignored by the coalition.[5] By the middle of 1952 'the political scene in Kathmandu was cluttered with a number of splinter groups', few of which had any base of popular support (Joshi and Rose 1966:136). Only a handful of these, however, reached beyond the confines of the nation's capital. One of the few which did was the Gorkha Parishad, created in 1952 by several members of the Rana family who had been important in the pre-revolutionary establishment. In Belaspur, they sought support among villagers who had, either for personal reasons become dis-illusioned with the Congress regime or were attracted by the platforms, promises and wealth of the party.[6]

A district office was set up in Belaspur Bazaar, and the party's main leadership was provided by a core of men prominent in several villages close by the town, for the most part resident in Bhuka. As already noted, this community contained (and still contains) some of the most notable families in the district, including that of the Simta sub-district headman. Because of their wealth and nearness to the town, many of their members were well educated, by local standards politically sophisticated and, in the opinion of many, entitled to play an important part in the new regime. Certainly, their disappointment at not being allowed to assume a more significant role in the district administration fed their hostility towards Congress. Undoubtedly, too, the handsome salaries offered by the Gorkha Parishad to its district leaders (to say nothing of the generous party finances at their disposal) and the prospect of gaining power in the near future (elections had been promised) encouraged the alignment of these villagers with the opposition party. And, finally, the fact that two highly respected residents of Bhuka had joined the party while in Kathmandu and were actively recruiting members, includ-ing many of their fellow villagers who until that time had no reason to be dissatisfied with the Congress regime, probably contributed further to the heavy representation of Bhukals among the opposition's leadership in the district.

The Gorkha Parishad, then, provided them with the chance to occupy formal office, with its attendant benefits and responsibilities, through which to oppose the town notables who supported Congress and whom they regarded, with slight exaggeration, as having a dominant influence on, if not actual control of, the district adminis-tration in the immediate post-Rana years. Although the resources which the latter could muster were by far the greater, political instability in the country encouraged the opposition groups to attempt to sap the strength of Congress through a continuous series of challenges and provocations. Various forms of harassment, including petitions complaining of maladministration, law suits against officials for corrupt activities, reports accusing government servants of allowing the depletion of forest resources, and occasional civil disobedience, were designed to maintain pressure on an already beleagured Nepali Congress. In the most dramatic confrontation of the post-Rana period, the Gorkha Parishad leaders in the district organized, in May 1953, a demonstration for the declared purpose of removing the Congress governor.[7]

Demonstration

There are few objective 'facts' relating to the events surrounding the demonstration, save that it took place and that it achieved its immediate goal of forcing the governor to flee the district. In the following paragraphs I will relate two fundamentally different versions of the incident given by participants and observers, some of whom were at the time members or supporters of the administration and others of whom were involved as demonstrators. The contradictory accounts they offer are, clearly, related not only to their different alignments in 1953, when these events took place, but to their affiliations in the contemporary political structure (discussed in Chapters 9 and 10). In relating the history of even such recent events, in other words, we are recording the creation of legends, or what Leach in *Political Systems of Highland Burma* calls myths (1954).

The main *dramatis personae* in the events recounted below were:

District governor: a Nepali Congress Party appointee from Kathmandu.
Gorkha Parishad district chairman: a Chetri of Bhuka.
Gorkha Parishad district secretary: a Chetri of Bhuka.
Gorkha Parishad district treasurer: a Chetri of Bhuka.
Jimmawal: The Simta sub-district headman, a Chetri of Bhuka (H in the genealogy in Figure 2 above; he was still alive at the time of these events).
Police Captain: a Thakuri of Bhuka, and a descendant of the former Belaspur kings.
Lieutenant of Militia: a Thakuri from a village near Bhuka.
Assistant, later Acting governor: a Chetri resident of the town.
Harilal: the Acting governor's father. A scribe in the town.
Pandits: Two Brahmins from the village of Duari, bordering Bhuka.

Various policemen, officials, shopkeepers, etc. from both the bazaar and Bhuka.

The main leaders of the demonstration were reputedly the Gorkha Parishad's district executive. The former treasurer is today the head of the district's land revenue office in Belaspur while the ex-secretary is the representative of his ward in the Village panchayat (see Chapter 9). The erstwhile chairman now lives in another part of the country. The former two, with whom I was able to discuss these events, like others involved in the demonstration, stress as its principal aim the removal of a corrupt and unjust official.

Gorkha Parishad secretary (Bhuka): The governor at the time was a thief. He would send his men into the villages to frighten people and take their money under any pretext. He 'looted' the district, took bribes and generally caused the public much misery. I was the general secretary at that time and we came to know about his activities and told him to stop, but he ignored us. So we put up notices telling him to leave this place, and he tore them down. Then we summoned our members to march in a procession to demand that he leave the district. There must have been 12–14,000 people in the procession.

Those who supported Congress, or alternatively opposed adherents of the Gorkha Parishad, do not disagree that the governor at the time was corrupt, but merely maintain that he was no different from his predecessors and so did not warrant treatment of this kind. They consequently condemn the demonstration and those who led it in two main ways. Some, who held then or hold today positions of responsibility in the administration concentrate on the 'legality' of the act. Thus, one Newar bazaariya who was, at the time of the demonstration, a clerk in the district headquarters—he now runs a shop and practices as a scribe—comments:

Clerk (bazaar): If the governor had done wrong he could have been dealt with by legal means. But those Bhukals went beyond the law—they should not have driven him away like that.

The majority of bazaariyas, however, condemn the demonstration as proving (yet again) the determination of Bhukals to exert their influence on district affairs. The explanation given by a former policeman is a more typical reaction:

Policeman A (bazaar): All governors in those days were bad ones (*badmash*) and so was this one. But the real *badmash* were the Bhukals who just wanted to stir up trouble. They believe that because they are wealthy and famous they can dominate everyone else. Their real leader was the Jimmawal (i.e. the Simta sub-district headman).

The import of his remarks becomes clear if it is realized that under the panchayat system introduced in 1961 the bazaar was amalgamated with Bhuka to form a single 'Village' unit[8] for the purpose of electing a council. The hostility between notables in both communities has therefore sharpened and become focussed on their struggles within the new electoral arena of the council. Since Bhuka, by sheer weight of numbers, is able to elect more representatives, townsmen frequently complain of being 'dominated' (*dabaunu*) by their village rivals (see Chapter 9). This ex-policeman, for many years closely involved on the side of bazaar politicians in their struggles against the Bhukals, not only employs a current idiom in assigning a motive for the 1953 demonstration but expresses perhaps more the contemporary than the traditional concern of bazaariyas at the expanding influence of these villagers.

The reference to 'Jimmawal' reflects an unwillingness to concede that the most powerful figure in the villages of Simta revenue unit during Rana times could play a less than commanding part in the affairs of the Gorkha Parishad with which his fellow Bhukals were so clearly identified. It is known of course that the Jimmawal enjoyed the privileges of headmanship at the pleasure of the new Congress authorities and was reluctant to engage openly in party (especially opposition party) politics at this time, but the belief persists among townsmen, probably with some justification, that he controlled the party's activities at the time of the demonstration. This assumption is justified by pointing to the fact that he later stood as a Gorkha Parishad candidate in the parliamentary elections of 1959. Moreover, since the district chairman and treasurer were his close but junior kinsmen and the secretary his son-in-law, the notion that a formal hierarchy of offices in a modern type of organization could diminish his right to influence or even veto their decisions is not seriously entertained. Finally, the active part which his son (the old Jimmawal died in 1960) now plays in district politics serves further to confirm for bazaariyas the influential role which this Bhuka family has played in the area since long before the end of Rana rule.

By contrast with the 'trouble-makers' of Bhuka, most townsmen present their own part in the events as being directed to peacemaking, although most were known as Congress supporters, and later, as election time approached, formed the core of its district organization. One shopkeeper who was for a time the local Congress chairman, comments:

Peace-maker (bazaar): Bazaariyas urged the demonstrators not to cause trouble. We dressed in white, brought a white flag, and shouted 'peace' (*santi*). But these Bhukals took our flag, tore it up and threw it on the ground. They even tried to tear our clothes. We couldn't stop their procession. Even the police and army could do nothing.

Here the role of the police and army in the events becomes important. By 1953 the Liberation Army had been disbanded and responsibility for the security of the region returned to a reorganized militia, recruited almost entirely from within the district, although usually officered by central appointees from outside the area. In the immediate post-Rana years, however, for the same reasons which enabled local residents to assume senior posts in the civil part of the administration, the garrison had mostly local officers. In May 1953, the commander was a lieutenant from a village near the bazaar with whose residents many Bhukals had ties of kinship. Indeed, the officer, a Thakuri, was himself a close affine of one of the Gorkha Parishad's district executives from Bhuka (in charge of its 'publicity' section). The militia consisted of about 80 men with rifles, although only about half that number were apparently available for duty during the crisis.

The police force, which had been established in 1952, had a strength of perhaps 25 men armed with batons (*lathi*) on duty during the demonstration, and was led by a captain who lived then as now in Bhuka village, although on the northern fringes removed from the majority of its notables with whom he shares neither caste (he is a Thakuri) nor political affiliation. Some informants attribute the split to a series of disputes over land between the captain and the Jimmawal, while others date its beginnings to the immediate post-Rana period, when the captain became a fervent Congress supporter on appointment to his post, while most of his co-villagers became affiliated to the opposition. The captain himself refers rather to his descent from the last *rajah* who ruled over a petty kingdom in the area (see Chapter 2) and to the fact that his former 'subjects' (meaning here his fellow villagers) no longer pay him his due respects.

Police captain (Bhuka): How could the governor give everyone jobs in his administration? Could he give those Bhukals jobs if there were no vacancies? So they brought a procession to get rid of the governor, because only in this way could they get important posts in the administration. They brought mostly herd-boys, plough servants, illiterates, and all kinds of such people. They attacked the governor, and his wife and children. They threw stones at the district headquarters building. The procession was unlawful. Even though I am also from Bhuka I did not support them. They shouted at me that I was their own brother. But I could not join them because I had eaten government salt—I was a government employee—and had to serve the government. I had to obey government orders. I was instructed to disperse the procession. I fired over the heads of the crowd—only to frighten them. Then I led a baton charge, but some of the police did not help me. They went to the side of the Bhukals. They didn't obey an officer's command. The lieutenant in charge of the army garrison was ordered by the governor to fire, first into the air, and then at the demonstrators. It was a written order, but he stood by quietly. The Gorkha Parishad had promised him that after the governor was driven away he would get the post. So he did nothing. He must have been imagining himself governor.

There are, in the captain's account, a number of themes. First of all, he subscribes to the not uncommon view, already noted, held especially by townsmen and others who supported Congress, that affiliation to the opposition party can be explained primarily in terms of failure to obtain or hold high office in the post-Rana district administration. Given this reasoning it follows that the purpose of the demonstration was to bring down the regime and replace its appointees with those of the opposition. The behaviour of the lieutenant, already an important member of the administration, is explained by his ambition for even greater power and authority.

Secondly, the captain seeks to discredit the demonstration by referring to the rowdy and unpleasant behaviour of the participants (hurling stones and abuse) most of whom, he charges, were the area's 'riff-raff', i.e. herd-boys and plough servants. In the agricultural economy of the district these tasks are performed by the landless, the untouchables, the poorest and least privileged sections of the society. He also refers scathingly to illiterates, for in latter-day Nepal, as we have seen, literacy is an important source of and adjunct to status. Certainly, no illiterate could hold a responsible post in the administration.

Thirdly, there is an allusion to the unlawfulness of the procession, a point stressed by one administrative clerk (see above) and here noted in part justification of the captain's refusal to recognize the demonstrators' appeal for village solidarity. The captain does not seek to deny the strength of multiplex relationships on which his fellow villagers implicitly based their demands for loyalty, but rather argues the greater importance of loyalty to one's government, especially if one has 'eaten government salt'. He disdains those policemen, many of whom were Bhukals he had appointed, and the militia commander, who refused to honour such obligations. In this he echoes the views of most townspeople.

Policeman B (bazaar): The captain led a baton charge against his own people (*dajyu-bhai*). He had no choice since he was a government employee. You have to fire on your own father if necessary. We have to serve and obey the government. We (bazaariyas) did our duty, but the policemen from Bhuka refused to attack their own men. Instead, they joined the procession and cried out slogans with the Bhukals.

The policemen of Bhuka offer a different version of the events:

Policeman C (Bhuka): The police were ordered to use their batons. We tried our best but how could so few police control so many people? They kept coming. We (Bhukal policemen)—about ten of us—were later dismissed because they said we sided with the procession. We joined the baton charge, but the captain reported that we had not. The army was ordered to fire but they did not. How can one fire on one's own people?

We have here two contradictory accounts of how Bhuka policemen responded to the order for a baton charge. Townsmen and the captain insist that they refused. Those Bhukal police I spoke to claim to have participated. To suggest that they refused to obey an order would be to subvert the ideal that the government must always be obeyed, especially by its employees. The problem, as they see it, is that the captain reported falsely against them. Yet, in the same breath, they justify the army lieutenant's refusal to give his men the order to fire in terms of the gross violation of village norms which such an act would represent.[9]

A leader of the demonstration, however, refuses to see the lieutenant's behaviour as a victory for the demands of kinship and/or village solidarity over those of duty to government, but once again returns to the question of the procession's legality.

Gorkha Parishad treasurer (Bhuka): The army was told to fire but they could not because the procession was not unlawful. The law says you can have a procession. The lieutenant knew this.

The unwillingness or inability of the bulk of the army and the police to disperse the demonstrators, and the refusal of the latter to leave the grounds of the district headquarters apparently led the governor to the conclusion that his life was in danger and that night, accompanied by a few militia men who had remained loyal, left the building by a side entrance and made his way to a village west of the town where he was provided with shelter and given assistance for his journey to the terai.

With the governor out of the way, competition for control of the district administration intensified. A key figure in these struggles was a Chetri townsman who, at the time, was the senior bureaucrat under the governor in the district headquarters, and assumed the latter's responsibilities after he had fled. For the first time (and probably the only time in Belaspur's recent history) a local resident became the chief officer in the district.

Acting governor (bazaar): I was away when I heard the news about the governor being driven out of the district. I returned as soon as I could since I was second-in-command at the district headquarters. When I arrived back I found the lieutenant of the militia was doing the governor's work. I told him that in the absence of the governor I was the officer responsible and asked him to hand over the post. He was still insisting on doing the job when a cable arrived from Kathmandu appointing me acting governor.

I told those Bhuka people that they had acted unlawfully in driving the governor away. 'If you are a man from this district', they told me, 'you should be on our side. But instead of taking our side you tell us we have done the wrong thing.' Then they tried to have me dismissed. They sent a report by wireless telegraph to Kathmandu and said that I was a bad governor. But it did them no good.

They also instigated the lieutenant and some of his men to turn against me, so the militia was divided between those who supported and served me and those who were against me. The ones who were against me also sent a cable to Kathmandu. They said that this acting governor is unfit for his job, that he does such and such, and gives everyone trouble (*dukha*). 'We chose the lieutenant to be our governor', they said, 'and the government should appoint him to this post.'

After seeing these messages, I sent one myself. I told the department that these people who are sending the reports are the same who drove the governor out of his district. They mixed with the Gorkha Parishad instead of obeying the government. Now they criticize his government-appointed successor. They want their own choice for governor. It is clear that they are not on the side of the government. This lieutenant knows nothing of his duty, so he should be recalled and trained in discipline. This is what I told the department in Kathmandu. I asked for 50 militia from another district to help me fulfil my duties. Two days later I received a reply: the lieutenant was recalled to Kathmandu, and militia were to be despatched from Doti to take up duties in Belaspur.

One feature of the struggles which emerges clearly here is the use of appeals to higher authority by all the contending sides. Wireless messages are modern adaptations of a traditional practice. In former times men with serious grievances against district officials would bring their complaints before special roving commissions (*dodaha*) sent periodically from the capital, senior members of the government on their winter hunting expeditions in the terai, or even the prime minister himself in Kathmandu (see Cavenagh 1851).[10]

The former acting governor, like the majority of those in official posts attempting to put down detractors or defend themselves against attack, seeks to equate any opposition to himself as anti-government activity and sentiment, which is not merely reprehensible, but by implication, tantamount to being illegal. His attackers, by contrast, concentrate in their accusations on his propensity (like that of his predecessor) to 'trouble the public'. One of the two Brahmin 'pandits' whose signatures appeared on the first message of complaint about the acting governor comments:

Pandit (Duari village): In our message to the Ministry we said that this acting governor was demanding bribes and frightening the people. We pointed out that he had brought government employees to work in his household, fetching wood and water, and washing his pots and pans, so that all in all he is not fit to be governor. We also mentioned the white speck (*phulo*) in his eye. I had prepared the complaint and took it to my brother's son (actually FBSS) who signed it as well. Then we sent it by wireless. The truth is that the Jimmawal told me what to write—I was his priest at the time. He pretended to be on our side but he was not, really.

The contents of the message are by no means out of the ordinary although several points require a word of clarification. The use of government employees as menials by a superior in his personal household, although officially frowned on, is a not uncommon practice in Nepal (see Chapter 3). It is therefore a charge which can be readily and with justification brought against most senior members of the administration by those seeking to embarrass them. The mention of a *phulo* in the governor's eye appears at first glance incongruous, although this 'charge' was apparently taken as seriously as the others, if not more so, by the authorities in Kathmandu. This is a complex issue which I cannot pursue more fully, but here it is sufficient to note that its importance for those involved relates both to the association which Nepalese make between physical handicap and mental ability and to the fact that one-eyed men are considered inauspicious in much of South Asia (see Freed and Freed 1964). The former acting governor was concerned to emphasize, when relating these events, that his sight in both eyes was perfectly normal. Finally, the accusation that both the decision to send a complaint and its contents were dictated by the Jimmawal requires some appreciation of the relationship between these Brahmins, on the one hand, and notables in both Belaspur Bazaar and Bhuka, on the other.

The two Brahmins from the village of Duari became involved in the struggles we have been examining partly as a result of their pre-eminence as ritual experts. For many years the only two district residents with advanced formal qualifications in Sanskrit (from a college in Benares),[11] these pandits were and still are called on to perform complex and lucrative merit-making rites, requiring their specialized knowledge, for wealthy clients throughout Belaspur, and to serve as household priests to the most prominent families in settlements surrounding their own village, including Bhuka.

Just prior to these events, they were involved in a series of disputes with the head teacher of the *bhasa* school, another Brahmin who had been sent out from Kathmandu by the Rana education authorities when the school was established in 1922. The two local pandits, one of whom had joined the *bhasa* staff, while the other taught Sanskrit in the middle school, hoped to force the dismissal of the *bhasa* head (and presumably assume control of the school) by claiming that he was not properly qualified and that he was in any case too old to discharge his duties (he was over 70 years when these disputes began). For a combination of reasons the old man was aided by several bazaariyas, his principal support coming from Harilal, the father of the man who was to become the acting governor. A wealthy and distinguished resident of the town, having served for many years in the district administration, Harilal was, at the time of these events, a scribe in the town. Some informants report that the latter himself had quarrelled in the past with the pandits and so lost no opportunity to involve them in litigation and offer assistance to whoever their current enemies were. Others note that the mere association of one of these pandits with the Jimmawal—the pandit's father was a village headman under him, while the pandit was his priest—was responsible for turning Harilal against him since he and the Jimmawal are said to have been implacable foes.

The intensity of the rivalry between the two men is probably exaggerated by informants, but that it existed is not surprising when we consider the position of the scribe in this society, especially in regard to disputes which reach the district court. The main arguments of the litigants are contained in a series of petitions and counter-petitions, and because of their peculiar grammatical style and format even literate members of the public must commission specialists to prepare them. Then, in the very nature of their work, scribes amass a great variety of detailed knowledge about their clients' personal circumstances, quarrels, alliances, and so forth. This combined with their accumulated experience of court procedures and other technical legal matters, to say nothing of a familiarity with the predilections of particular judges, confer on these scribes a considerable influence not only on the affairs of their clients, but in the community at large.

At any one time, no more than a handful of these men achieve some degree of fame in the district, a measure of which is the fact that the wealthy and the influential turn to them for advice and assistance. (Informants wishing to be unkind to a particular scribe may suggest that he actively seeks out persons who are quarrelling and encourages one side to take out a court action, or may even, if he can, instigate such a dispute in the first place.) Since each litigant must have a different advisor, it is inevitable that certain scribes find themselves continuously on different sides of a whole range of disputes. Indeed, some come to see themselves, and not their clients, as the true rivals and become, in time, confirmed enemies.

For some years following the end of Rana rule, the two most important scribes working in the town were Harilal and a Bhukal who was a close agnate of the Jimmawal (the latter's FBSS). Although none disputes that the writing talent lay with the Bhuka scribe, it is sometimes suggested that the Jimmawal was his closest confidante, that he spent a great deal of time with the scribe, helping him plan his strategies, and that the Jimmawal took special interest in a case if the opposition was being prepared by Harilal.

Whatever the initial stimulus for the opposition between the pandits and the acting governor's father Harilal, the former became involved in the events surrounding the demonstration on the side of the Bhukals by lending their literary skills and considerable prestige as ritual specialists and teachers to the attack on the acting governor. The pandit's inference that he was drawn, somewhat inadvertently, into the affray by a devious Jimmawal attests, in retrospect, to the serious consequences for the pandits of their acts (see below). It also reflects the split between him and the Jimmawal's family a few years later, when a quarrel led to the severance of their priest-*jajman* tie, and the formation of similar ritual associations with several important households in the town, including that of the acting governor with whom they had once fought so bitterly.

Following the demonstration the government sent a commission of enquiry to Belaspur, which relied heavily for its evidence on submissions by the acting governor and the police captain. The three principal executives of the Gorkha Parishad, as well as its publicity director (all Bhukals) were jailed for one year, some ten other Bhuka villagers were dismissed from their government posts, mainly in the police, and the two Duari pandits lost their teaching jobs.[12] All these men, and a number of others were fined for their part in the disturbances.

Inter-calary roles

The demonstration highlights dramatically the invidious position in which certain members of the administration are placed by virtue of their official responsibilities, on the one hand, and their duties as inhabitants of a village or even district community, on the other. This kind of 'predicament' also existed, of course, for village and sub-district headmen, and I have seen several documents in the 'archives' of district headquarters in which headmen are chastised by the authorities for harbouring villagers suspected of committing offences.

The general problem was first discussed by anthropologists working in colonial Africa, who drew attention to the 'inter-calary' roles of chiefs. As subordinate officers of the white administrative hierarchy, it was explained, they were 'caught in the dilemma of trying to work within that hierarchy under pressure to support its demands and values and at the same time felt pressure in many instances to represent . . . their people . . .' (Gluckman 1968:72). It has recently been suggested that persons filling other than chiefly roles may have experienced similar conflicts (e.g. district commissioners) and, moreover, that the failure of anthropologists to include in their accounts of colonial administration the clerks, messengers, policemen, interpreters, etc. has led to the impression that these problems existed only for the chief (ibid). Certainly the conclusion to be drawn from the actions and statements of those connected with the demonstration discussed above is that the kinds of conflicting demands made on actors in menial positions in the administration (such as policemen) are not fundamentally different from those made on more senior officials (the police captain and the lieutenant of militia) or, indeed, the acting governor himself, who occupied not merely an inter-calary, but to employ Gluckman's more recent term, an 'inter-hierarchical' position.[13] For each, at some stage of the incident, was called on to meet what could be regarded as irreconcilable demands.

The crux of the dilemma, according to some anthropologists who examined the African situation, lay in the opposition between the value systems which informed the two 'sub-structures'. In the instance studied by Fallers, it was a conflict between the universalistic bureaucratic values of the British administration and the particularistic ethic of Soga indigenous society. Because of his inter-calary position the chief was seen by Fallers to embody two views of the world: two systems of beliefs, European and African. Both were institutionalized and accepted as legitimate, yet they contained diverse and conflicting elements, so that there arose situations in which incompatible values and beliefs were widely held by members of the same social system (Fallers 1955).

On one level of analysis the opposition between the ethic of administration and indigenous society is a satisfactory assumption, and I would suggest that it has the widest applicability. Even the Nepalese civil service which, in 1953, certainly did not begin to approximate to Weber's notion of a bureaucratic organization, was still based on norms and values at variance with those of the peasant society it was meant to serve. Despite a large measure of ethnic and cultural uniformity between administrators and members of the public it would be wrong to assume that each sub-structure was guided by the same principles. It is in the nature of an administration, whatever its degree of bureaucratization, to be founded and run on values which at least to some extent conflict with those of the society it administers. I stress this point to turn aside any suggestion that the Nepalese situation is not comparable to the African one because the former was not characterized by an opposition between the two sub-structures.

But while the attribution of basic guiding principles to each is a useful abstraction, it does not constitute an adequate explanation for the behaviour of real actors in real social situations.[14] To present a picture of an African chief 'hemmed in' by two logically inconsistent ethical or normative systems whose contradictory demands at best leave him too paralyzed to act, and at worst exact a 'considerable psychic cost' (Fallers 1955) appears not to take account of the whole range of pressures and constraints guiding any particular decision of someone occupying such an inter-calary position. As Kuper has pointed out, to portray the chief's position as virtually untenable is to ignore or underplay his room for manoeuvre (1970). Indeed, in an earlier chapter I tried to show how even after, indeed, especially after the introduction of a Public Service Commission, local residents could manipulate different and opposing values to ensure for themselves and their kinsmen and neighbours a place in the administration.

By examining in some detail a crisis situation such as the demonstration in its social and political context, we are better able to appreciate the complexity of factors which an individual, confronted with opposing demands, must take into consideration. Neighbourhood and kin ties, party and personal loyalties, financial and political consequences, etc., must all be weighed. Although there is no way of determining precisely how the actors in this 'social drama' came to their different decisions, there is no evidence here of behavioural paralysis. Moreover, the retrospective explanations they offer for their behaviour suggest a number of commonly held principles, at least four of which emerge clearly from their comments. Thus, they attach positive value to: (a) acting 'legally', (b) combating corrupt officials, (c) obeying the government; and (d) demonstrating loyalty to kin/village/district.

First, it will be noted that the principles are sufficiently broad and vague to enable either side in a dispute to proclaim itself and its allies to be their staunchest defenders, and its enemies to be guilty of their unfailing violation. Second, in any given context, the observance of one of these norms may demand or be represented as the desecration of another. Thus, to deal with a corrupt official may require an 'illegal' act; to obey the government may necessitate neglecting village ties; to behave 'legally' may lead to an act of disobedience toward the government, and so on. But it is the anthropologist who perceives or imposes the conflict and not the participants. In explaining their behaviour at the time of the demonstration those who occupied inter-calary roles neither deny the validity of any particular value nor conceptualize it as being in conflict with any other.

If challenged with neglect of one obligation, the actor stresses what for him is, in that context, the greater importance of another. Thus, when the police captain recalls the demand by Bhukals for village unity at the height of the demonstration, he explains his refusal not by denying its importance, but by stressing the over-riding consideration of obedience to government. Similarly, the acting governor does not deny the need to remove a corrupt official (his predecessor) but accounts for his disapproval of Bhuka's procession to accomplish this aim by stating his preference for 'legality'. Thus, in retrospective accounts of their behaviour at the time of the events individuals display no lack of ability to manipulate the universe of norms and values to explain and justify how their decisions were arrived at.

Parliamentary elections

Although the Gorkha Parishad had suffered a temporary setback in the district, within a year, with its leaders out of prison, and the country preparing for elections—promised for 1955 and eventually held in 1959—the party once again regained its earlier momentum, although its activities in this period followed more orthodox lines of building electoral support. Bhuka notables once again assumed control of the district organization, this time with the overt participation of the Jimmawal and the Duari pandits. The Nepali Congress also established an organization in the district, many of whose leaders were townsmen. By this time the acting governor had been transferred, after serving in this capacity for six months, and replaced by a direct appointee of the central government. The former's place as the dominant figure in the bazaar was assumed by a wealthy Newar shopkeeper, who played a key role in the Congress organization.

At election time, the Gorkha Parishad was represented in the constituency which contained Simta sub-district by the Jimmawal. Congress chose for its candidate the man who had commanded the army which 'liberated' Belaspur at the time of the revolution and who was a ritual friend (*mit*) of the Newar merchant mentioned above, and generally much respected in the area. As it turned out, results in the constituency and in Belaspur generally followed the national trend which gave Congress a clear majority.[15] Bhuka, as expected, pro-vided a substantial proportion of the Gorkha Parishad's vote of approximately 1,000, while other villages, along with the bazaar, made a Congress victory certain by providing twice that number.

Five other candidates together received an additional 2,000 votes.[16] The extremely low poll in this constituency (under 20 per cent) obviously reflects a failure on the part of all parties to arouse strong feelings of loyalty among members of the public. The fact that most of those who did vote were residents of a few villages in close proximity to the district capital, i.e. Simta sub-district, attests only partly to their greater 'political awareness'. It signifies, too, a feeling among those outside this perimeter, and one to which they frequently give voice, that the elections were yet another manifestation of an on-going contest between the ambitious men of Bhuka and the bazaar, a rivalry in which they, as outsiders, played and still play little part.

Conclusion

This chapter has examined the growth of political conflict between residents of Belaspur Bazaar and Bhuka, a village on the periphery of the town. Essentially, this is a development which has occurred since the end of the Rana regime. There were, to be sure, enmities and rivalries between individual townsmen and villagers, but these were not conceived in terms of the opposition of groups based on locality. The absence of political competition was, as I have pointed out, a logical correlate of the complementary nature of their economic relations. But it was, at the same time, inhibited by the nature of the political arena, which confined political activity within small-scale social and geographic contexts. The Ranas, moreover, defined and arbitrated the rules of competition for the principal status positions, those of village and sub-district headman.

The period immediately following the revolution of 1950-1 was characterized by the emergence of political parties, upheaval in the country (and especially in the capital), and a weakening of the national administration. In the district, men whose ambitions had previously extended no further than control of a political following in a settlement, village, or at most, sub-district, were quite suddenly presented with unprecedented opportunities. For in this new arena the resources available were, on the one hand, those of national political parties and, on the other, of massive power through control of the highest offices in the district administration.

The competition for these new resources, however, was very largely confined to residents of the district capital and a few surrounding settlements, especially Bhuka. Notables in these two communities found themselves on opposite sides of a deep political divide: the former supporting and holding key positions in both the Congress-controlled administration and its district party organization; the latter aligned with the main opposition party, dominating its district organization, and seeking at every opportunity to challenge and embarrass the administration and the townsmen so closely identified with it.

By 1959, when elections took place, the lines of cleavage were firmly drawn. Within two years, however, with the dissolution of parliament, the abolition of all political parties in the country, and their replacement by a system of 'panchayat democracy', the opposition between townsmen and their village neighbours was directed into new channels.

Notes to Chapter 8

1 If a man rose out of the menial ranks during his government service, for the rest of his life he would be known and addressed by his former title.

2 'The environments in which political contention occurs' (Swartz 1968:271). This is one of several possible definitions suggested by Swartz.

3 Although the use of local tax-collectors was fairly common throughout Nepal, there were significant regional variations (see M. C. Regmi 1963; 1964; 1965).

4 *Mukhiya* is also a clerical grade in the administration.

5 The original Nepali Congress itself splintered into four distinct groups. For a thorough discussion of political events in the capital during the period see Joshi and Rose (1966).

6 Several parties, including the United Democrats and the Communists, later established branches in the district to contest the elections, but their presence was short-lived.

7 It is possible that the Gorkha Parishad attempted to provoke a coordinated series of incidents in various parts of the country. Joshi and Rose write of 'widespread political tension in the hill districts' as a result of the activities of the party and report that in January, 1953 there were clashes between supporters and opponents of the party in Pokhara, a district between Kathmandu and Belaspur, which led to the arrest of its general secretary (1966:139).

8 When referring to the new statutory unit, I capitalize the first letter, viz. Village.

9 There is, of course, a difference of some magnitude between using batons to disperse a crowd and firing on them, which must account in part for this apparent reversal of attitudes.

10 Uberoi (1968) reports a similar system of direct appeal to higher authorities in Afghanistan, stressing how this serves as a check on the arbitrary use of power by district officials.

11 Both attained the degree of *madema*, which is given the same status in Nepal today as a high school matriculation.

12 In some instances (e.g. the pandits) dismissal was accompanied by a ban on holding government appointment again.

13 'Distinct subhierarchies within a total hierarchy meet in one person, who is the lowest member of the superior hierarchy and the highest member of the subordinate hierarchy' (Gluckman 1968:71).

14 Gluckman has attacked the tendency to make comparisons 'between the ideal of one situation and the "worst" features of another'. Thus, the African chief, alleged as administering under the influence of personal ties, is compared with the bureaucratic ideal of our own society—in which personal influence is supposed not to operate (1968:ix–x).

15 In the country as a whole, 74 of the 109 seats in the House of Representatives were won by Congress, which received 38 per cent of the votes cast. The Gorkha Parishad was the second party, with 19 seats and 17 per cent of the votes (Joshi and Rose 1966).

16 One of these was the former secretary of the Gorkha Parishad who joined the United Democrats a few months before the elections.

9

Political Relations
The Village Panchayat

IN December 1960, King Mahendra exercised the prerogatives vested in him by the existing constitution to assume, in conditions of 'grave emergency' all powers attached to parliament and other governmental bodies, and so introduced a period of direct rule through an appointed council of ministers. During the ensuing two year period there was added to this basic political apparatus a framework of statutory panchayats or councils based to some extent on similar institutions in Pakistan, Egypt, India and elsewhere, as well as on previous experiences with more limited schemes of this kind in Nepal itself.

Panchayats

From at least the third decade of this century there have been sporadic attempts by government to establish statutory panchayats in the country. For reasons which need not concern us here, none of the programmes introduced before 1961 was ever fully realized, although the present panchayat system, which embraces the whole country, owes a great deal to them.[1] These statutory bodies should not be confused with the *ad hoc* assemblies of respected members of a community who may be called to settle a dispute or consider any matter involving a disagreement between several individuals or groups. Such gatherings are also referred to as 'panchayats' and, indeed, *pancha* is a term applied to any notable or influential person.

Along with the creation of panchayats the country was reorganized administratively into 14 'Development Zones', each divided into a number of 'Development Districts'. Districts were further sub-divided into 'Towns'—any locality with a minimum population of 10,000—and 'Villages' for the purpose of establishing the basic units in the system. The new panchayat structure was originally intended to mirror this organization with a four tier system of councils. By the time of fieldwork, however, plans had changed and there were only three levels: National, District and Village/Town. I will outline some of the main features of the former two in Chapter 10; the concern here is only with the lowest tier in the system. Since there are no statutory 'Towns' in Belaspur, these are ignored in the discussion.

Because a Village panchayat was meant to represent an area with a population of approximately 2,000 persons, it has usually been necessary to incorporate into a single bloc a number of contiguous traditional settlements (*gau*). Thus, some 280 units of the latter kind in the district of Belaspur[2] have been organized into 57 statutory Villages (also called *gau*), with an average population of 2,400 persons.

Villages are partitioned into nine 'wards' (the English word is used) and in each ward residents 21 years of age and over are entitled to participate in the election of a representative to the panchayat, who need not, however, reside in the ward. In addition to the nine members so chosen, the entire adult population of the Village elects a chairman (*pradhan pancha*) and vice-chairman (*upa-pradhan pancha*).[3]

Despite the introduction of a political organization the recruitment to which is by universal adult suffrage, in contradistinction to the traditional system of headmanship based essentially on ascriptive criteria of incumbency, higher castes in the district, especially Chetris and Thakuris, continue, as in the past, to be over-represented in public office, while those belonging to the lowest ritual strata, especially untouchables, are still grossly under-represented. Table 28 sets the caste affiliation of the 594 members of Village panchayats in Belaspur beside the proportion of each caste in the total voting population of the district.

If the caste affiliations of panchayat chairmen only are noted, the imbalance is even more striking, with Chetris and Thakuris, who together comprise 45·8 per cent of the voting population in the district, providing almost 72 per cent (41) of its 57 Village *pradhan pancha*. Not a single untouchable holds such office.

The Bazaar–Bhuka panchayat

As part of the process of partitioning Belaspur district into a number of more or less equal population blocs, the bazaar was amalgamated with the adjacent village of Bhuka to form a single statutory Village.

TABLE 28

Castes of Village panchayat members in Belaspur district

Caste	No. of panchayat members*	Percentage of total panchayat members	Percentage of voting population
		%	%
Chetri	244	41·7	32·8
Thakuri	158	26·4	13·0
Jaisi	49	8·2	10·5
Brahmin	33	5·4	1·7
Magar	49	8·2	11·8
Other clean castes	31	5·1	3·2
Untouchables	30	5·0	27·0
	594	100·0	100·0

* Thirty-three other places were unfilled at the time these figures were obtained.

More precisely, the Village also contains a third settlement, called Sota, which includes mainly Magars and Muslims as well as some of the overspill population from Bhuka, the houses of which begin where those of Sota end. Save where it is relevant to distinguish this settlement from Bhuka proper, I will include it in the latter.

Six of the Village's nine wards are in Bhuka (including Sota, which constitutes one ward), a consequence of the latter's much larger population (1,421 to the bazaar's 941), but by no means a wholly accurate reflection of their relative numbers. Bhuka wards have not, on the whole, been delineated in the interests of maintaining equal numbers between them. Thus, the smallest contains a population of 167, while the largest has 337 people. Their boundaries have been determined on the basis of natural features such as streams or gullies, or, even more importantly, with a view to maintaining more or less intact, neighbourhoods whose residents share common caste or clan affiliation. Table 29, which gives the population of Bhuka wards, suggests how, with the exception of the Smiths, Cobblers and Chetris, each caste tends to be concentrated in a single ward. In the case of the latter, who form a majority in four and a plurality in one of the six Bhuka wards, a different lineage tends to predominate in each.

Councillors

Councillors (*sadesi*) are elected for a term of six years, but in order

TABLE 29

Population of Bhuka wards

Caste	Ward No.*						Total
	4	5	6	7	8	9	
Chetri	160	99	130	111	222	39	761
Thakuri					61		61
Jaisi					54		54
Brahmin				6			6
Magar						136	136
Gurung						25	25
Smith		80	33			22	135
Cobbler	7	4	36	78			125
Tailor		17		4			21
Muslim						97	97
All	167	200	199	199	337	319	1,421

* Wards 1–3 are in the bazaar. Ward 9 embraces Sota village.

to hold elections more frequently than this (every two years) the government ruled that, in the first instance, only one-third of the elected councillors would serve the full term, one-third would serve four years, and one-third two years. Even so, this did not prevent ward representatives with only two or four year terms from standing for re-election when these had expired, nor indeed, those with six year mandates from resigning after two.

Since 1961, there have been five elections, and two of the eleven members on the present body have served on every panchayat, while two others have had experience of all but one. Examining the composition of the Village council over the years, it becomes evident that there is a relatively restricted nucleus of persons from whom the councillors are regularly drawn. The current membership, elected in 1969, reveals certain characteristics of this category of men.

Firstly, the great majority of councillors are of clean caste. The only two untouchables on the panchayat, a Tailor and a Butcher, represent bazaar wards. Bhuka councillors are presently all of twice-born status, although two untouchables from the village have each spent a two year term on the council.

Second, while panchayat members are all literate, in only one case was literacy acquired in a modern, secular school. Representatives either learned to read and write at home from relatives or neighbours, or attended the *bhasa* school in town for a time. This is largely a function of age, since secular education only began in the post-Rana period. Panchayat members tend to be in their middle years: the average age is 37; only one member is under 30 years, and only one is over 50 years. The new panchayats are recognized as having to deal with matters the understanding of which require good education and a knowledge of the 'modern' world. In present-day Nepal, only young adults possess these qualifications, yet there persists a reluctance to grant people in this age category either the ability or the opportunity to play a role in the panchayats. 'However well schooled', one man remarked, 'can children tell their fathers what to do?' The Village council, then, does not draw its personnel from the reservoir of highly educated young men who, partly for this reason are driven, and for other reasons encouraged, to enter the civil service. The small numbers who manage to attain high rank in government employment are, as I have noted, increasingly likely nowadays to persevere in an administrative career. Only those who leave the service without having achieved any advance, therefore, may seek council membership. Seven of the eleven present council-lors have spent some time (3–14 years) in the district administration, although none occupied a senior post. The result is that neither the younger, better educated nor, measured by administrative rank, more distinguished residents of the Village, are likely to enter the panchayat.

Third, panchayat personnel tend, economically, to be associated with the 'middle range' of the population. All representatives belong to households of sufficient wealth to allow them a measure of free time to engage in panchayat activities. This applies to the two untouchable members from the bazaar as well. In this connection, seven of the 11 representatives do not rely exclusively on agriculture for a livelihood, although all, save the Tailor (whose holding is small) produce enough grain from their own lands to feed their members. Two Bhukals (a Chetri and a Jaisi) and two townsmen (a Newar and a Butcher) run shops in the bazaar; the Tailor practices his craft; while two Chetris from Bhuka own dwellings in the town from which they derive rent.

Notables and the Village panchayat

Panchayat members do not belong to the wealthiest category of the population. The households which comprise such a category may be identified by the fact that they have considerable holdings of land—many outside the district (see Chapter 6); that the majority of these lands are cultivated by tenants; that such households can afford to maintain plough-servants (*hali*) to work their remaining fields in the hills;[4] and that they regularly sell substantial quantities of grain, mainly paddy. In addition, most of these households have considerable cash incomes from a combination of sources such as government service, shopkeeping, contracting and document-writing.

The score of households in this category, sixteen of them in Bhuka, four in the bazaar, are not only the wealthiest, but (partly by virtue of this wealth) the most influential and important in the Village. Before 1951, many of these families provided not only local, but sub-district leadership, while in the immediate post-Rana period they were active in political party affairs at the district level (see previous chapter). With rare exceptions, men of such prominence have not sat and do not sit on the Village council.

Their reluctance can be attributed to several kinds of factors. A number of these notables had succeeded in entering administrative employment during the Congress regime or soon after its downfall (almost without exception in senior posts) and for reasons already noted, would not be tempted away from their lucrative and increasingly secure careers into the panchayat. Thus, half of the heads of the 20 wealthiest and most prominent households in the Village, including the acting governor and the Gorkha Parishad treasurer at the time of the 1953 demonstration, have been in bureaucratic service continuously since before the panchayat was inaugurated. By law, they can not hold positions in both.

The attitude to the panchayat of certain prominent men, at least in the very early years of the system, is also understandable when the atmosphere surrounding its introduction is appreciated. Considering the fate of previous experiments of this kind, few thought its chances of becoming established on a country-wide basis, let alone of enjoying long life, were anything but exceedingly thin. Moreover, those who had been closely involved in political party organization had seen a number of their national leaders jailed or exiled following the abolition of political parties. The dismissal of parliament by the monarch was justified largely on the grounds that the nation's party politicians had brought the country almost to the point of ruin, that they had misused their powers, 'set aside the interests of the country and the people, and wielded authority in a manner designed to fulfil the party interests only. . . .'[5] This strong anti-party theme, reiterated constantly in public messages, certainly contributed to the wariness with which former party activists regarded the Village council.

The resolve of notables to remain aloof from close involvement in the council was related also to its rather insignificant rewards. Certainly, measured against the considerable power and resources accruing from high rank in the civil service, or wielded by former party leaders in the district, the Village panchayat in the early years offered minimal prestige and few other perks. On the contrary, it demanded considerable time and effort from the representatives, without commensurate rewards. Even now a chairman's administrative responsibilities, in particular, are extremely heavy, and few prominent men are willing to devote their energies to dealing with the detailed chores of this office. Chairmen not infrequently resign their posts because they find it takes up too much of their time. Participation in panchayat activities carries occasional risks, as well. Thus, a reputation can be severely damaged by an electoral defeat, and a notable must weigh carefully his chances of victory in a public contest which has a wide element of unpredictability due to a secret ballot and an equal vote for all adults of whatever status. Members of Village panchayats, especially chairmen, are also in an exposed and so extremely vulnerable position. They are harassed by opponents who subject them to a continuous barrage of complaints, accusations and petitions, many of which are taken beyond the Village to government offices or the district panchayat. Partly as a consequence of this constant sniping, their every move is scrutinized by officials who sometimes interpret their disputes and political manoeuvrings as a lack of commitment to the panchayat ideal of selfless devotion to national development.[6]

Finally, also of significance is the fact that the traditional structure of tax-collection coexisted for some five years alongside the councils—which meant that headmen continued to enjoy their benefits and influence until as late as 1966–7, when their duties were finally assumed by the panchayats.

The transfer of these functions is only the latest in a series of government moves which, without manifestly aiming to do so, have produced a situation where a formidable degree of power now resides in the Village panchayat. Since its inception this body, in addition to taking over tax-collecting duties from headmen, has assumed responsibility for the allocation of ever-increasing development funds, the issuing of a variety of permits and testimonials to residents which they require to travel or work abroad, trade locally, etc., and the administration of government programmes such as land reform. Although fundamental decisions about these matters are taken at national and district government levels, and the Village panchayat is charged mainly with their implementation, there is considerable leeway available to councils enabling them to take decisions of policy which affect the manner in which the benefits and burdens of these programmes are distributed. Moreover, the Village Panchayat Act has defined a fairly wide area within which these bodies may exercise additional prerogatives (see below).

Now, too, the entire weight of government propaganda extols the virtues of the panchayat system, and continually calls on the populace to support its aims and programmes. Public holidays, occasional 'cultural' performances, and frequent visits paid the district by outside dignitaries become occasions to remind the people of the kingdom's aspirations under the new system and the dire consequences for the nation's progress if support is not forth-coming. Moreover, there is implicit in this constant re-iteration of panchayat ideals the notion that for individuals and groups to engage in political struggles wholly outside the framework of the councils is tantamount to rejection or even subversion of the regime.

This 'mystification' of the panchayats coupled with their assump-tion of increased functions and powers have wrought significant changes in the attitudes of many notables to the panchayat system generally and to the Village council in particular. Men who in the past considered this body to be unviable or trivial now seek to control it and exploit the resources it commands, not the least of which, as will become evident in the course of the discussion, is access to the next tier in the system, the district panchayat.

There are three principal, but not mutually exclusive, ways in which prominent men attempt to exercise their influence on the Village council. One is by seeking election to it, generally to the office of chairman, and thereby to dominate council business, although, as I have shown, there are drawbacks in such a course. Thus, in the neighbouring Village of Duari one faction leader became chairman of the panchayat, so strengthening his position in local political struggles.

A second strategy is to become indirectly involved, by being present at council meetings and participating in its discussions, without actually seeking election to it. In a Village panchayat in east Nepal whose workings I observed, most decisions are in fact taken by an informal body which includes not only council representatives, but a number of influential notables who attend meetings regularly and tend to dominate the proceedings. The existence of such a plenary body can be explained by the fact that one of the two main faction leaders in the Village had managed to take control of the council (he was its chairman and 'packed' it with councillors who would not challenge his authority) so that the wider group was essentially a creation of the rival faction to maintain 'surveillance' of the council (L. Caplan 1970).

Influence over the Bazaar-Bhuka panchayat is sought in yet a different manner. Although notables also drop in uninvited to meetings and exercise the privilege of any resident to voice an opinion, none attends regularly and no meeting is likely to find more than one or two in attendance. Rather, they seek to exert their influence in panchayat matters either by sponsoring candidates for council who in the context of daily life are largely dependent on their support and goodwill, or, by establishing such links with existing councillors.

Competition for control of the council mirrors, as we might expect, the opposition between villagers and townsmen. If anything, it has intensified as a result of the amalgamation of the two communities into a single statutory Village. The leading personalities of the previous period, because of age, death, or for other reasons indicated above, are no longer in the forefront of the struggle. The Chetri who served for a time as acting governor is now a permanent senior civil servant (at present, a district judge) who spends only an occasional leave at home and so plays little part in local affairs. His father, Harilal, an extremely prominent townsman in his day, by 1961 had become too old to take more than a passing interest in the council; he died in 1968.

The leadership of the bazaar coalition[7] has passed to a wealthy Newar shopkeeper whom I shall refer to henceforth simply as the Merchant. His great-grandfather had been born in Kathmandu Valley, come to Belaspur with a Rana governor, and stayed on to marry and settle in the town. The Merchant inherited a small general shop and some land from his father and, somewhat exceptionally for a bazaariya, never sought administrative service. Instead, he concentrated on expanding his patrimony and today he is certainly one of the wealthiest men in the district, with landholdings both in Lakandra and the hills, and the largest retail business (cloth shop) in the bazaar (see p. 111).

In Bhuka, leadership continues to reside in the family of the sub-district headman. As I have noted, the Jimmawal was extremely influential in the Gorkha Parishad organization, at first informally and later more openly, and represented the party in the parliamentary elections of 1959. On his death a year later, he was succeeded by his son who, until 1966-7, when the traditional system of tax-collection was finally abolished in the district, served as sub-district headman. Even before this date, however, he had begun to take an active interest in the panchayat, so that the struggle for its control has become, in essence, a contest between the coalitions led by the Jimmawal and the Merchant.

In one sense, the outcome of such a contest is inevitable—the domination of the council by Bhukals, which proceeds from the unequal distribution of population and wards between the bazaar and the village. In the following paragraphs I indicate certain manifestations of this control.

Bhuka domination of the council

To begin, it is apparent in the fact that all five chairmen of the Village council since 1961 have been Bhukals. It is evident, moreover, when several of the more significant matters dealt with by the panchayat over the years are examined in the light of the comparative effects on the two principal sectors of the Village.

One concerns the allocation of development funds. In the past, statutory panchayats were concerned to a large extent with dispute settlement: the programme introduced in some parts of the country (but not in Belaspur) in 1953, for example, made provision for a special court in each Village. The primary emphasis in the present system, however, is on the initiation and implementation of 'self-help' development schemes. As early as four months after the abolition of parliament in December, 1960, when plans for the new panchayat system were still in their early stages, the king noted in his New Year's message that 'various works of common welfare and national development have been set afoot . . . through the basic organization of rural town and district councils' (Mahendra 1961:42).

The stress on self-help schemes is apparent in regular panchayat meetings and in the bi-annual Village assemblies (*sabha*) at which all adults are invited to discuss and approve panchayat budgets. At one Village assembly I attended, of the 18 items on the agenda, one dealt with a tax on commerce, another with a proposed rise in the salary of the panchayat secretary,[8] two were expressions of support for recent government pronouncements, and a fifth was a resolution approving the proposed budget. The remaining thirteen items referred to development projects either planned or under way.

Village panchayats are encouraged to propose development projects and to match, in voluntary labour (*sramdan*) the cash contributions of the government, which distributes these development funds through the district panchayat, and provides, where necessary, technical advice and assistance. In the six years to the spring of 1969,[9] just under rs 250,000 were distributed among the district's 57 Villages, with the largest share, approximately rs 100,000, devoted to bridge construction. The remaining funds supported work on irrigation channels, springs (*dhara*), schools, panchayat meeting houses, and other miscellaneous schemes.

Bazaar-Bhuka Village has received more than its fair share of these grants, a total of rs 13,800 over the six-year period, against an average of rs 4,300 per panchayat in the district. Residents of the town, however, complain that the projects supported by this money have benefited mainly Bhuka villagers, and themselves little if at all. Thus, a substantial part of the development money received (37 per cent) has been allocated to the construction of irrigation channels and springs which, they point out, benefit Bhukals almost exclusively.

In fairness, however, it must be noted that those schemes which government officials most avidly encourage and support, and for which they are best able to provide technical assistance, are precisely those which benefit the rural, agricultural sector of society. But landowning bazaariyas, whose fields are dispersed among many different Villages, do not benefit specifically from improvements in Bhuka.

Further, townsmen argue, while some of the money has helped to build a new primary school in New Bazaar, this serves primarily the children of villagers and not their own, who mainly attend the school in Old Bazaar.

According to bazaariyas, even the limited advantages of a 'social centre' constructed in New Bazaar have accrued primarily to Bhukals. Completed in 1968, the building, which absorbed half of all grants to the Village, was first utilized as a government guest house and, more recently, converted into temporary quarters for the district jail. Thus, while neither townsmen nor villagers have enjoyed these facilities, the former point out that, unlike most development projects, this one was entrusted to a Bhuka man (an agnate of the Jimmawal) who acted as contractor and, in the process, they insist, spun a handsome profit, while utilizing the voluntary labour of all Villagers, including that of bazaar inhabitants.

Townsmen also get less than what they regard as their fair share of credit allocations under the land reform programme. All households are required to contribute to a special savings (*bacat*) fund, a proportion of which may be loaned out to individuals for agricultural improvements. Since the terms of credit, 10 per cent and a not too stringent policy of collateral security, are extremely favourable in local eyes, the savings fund is an attractive, if limited, source of credit. In the two years during which the scheme has been in operation, loans totalling about rs 3,000 have been granted to 16 Bhuka villagers (average about rs 190) and rs 1,000 to nine bazaariyas (average rs 110). Townsmen tend to attribute the discrepancy to the fact that the special panchayat sub-committee which considers applications, contains four villagers and only one resident of the town.

Here again, it is difficult to assess the degree to which this inequitable distribution of the credit fund is due to a deliberate policy on the part of Bhukals of favouring fellow villagers or to the fact that loans are required to be made for specified agricultural purposes only, a stipulation which tends, inevitably, to discriminate against town dwellers.[10] In any case, bazaariyas make relatively few applications and so probably obtain a smaller proportion of these loans than their numbers would appear to entitle them to.

The panchayat's taxation policy is another frequent object of attack by townspeople who contribute the major share of this revenue. When Village councils were granted the right in 1963 to impose taxes, it was assumed that their major source of income would derive from a ten per cent surcharge on central government land taxes. The intensity of opposition to such a tax on a national scale, however, forced the government to withdraw this prerogative a year later. This left councils with virtually no alternative but to utilize their remaining powers to impose taxes on 'trades and professions', to bolster their otherwise meagre income from fees for preparing documents, gun and radio licences, commissions on taxes collected on behalf of others, etc.

In the local context, 'trades and professions' is interpreted to mean those engaged in retail commerce or practising, either whole- or part-time, non-agricultural—and so mainly untouchable— occupations. The tax burden, therefore, falls most heavily on bazaar residents of all castes. It is carried to a lesser extent by some 25 Bhuka untouchables, mainly iron Smiths and a few Tailors, who still practice their traditional crafts, and the eight shopkeepers resident in the village, two of whom, it should be recalled, represent Bhuka wards on the council.

But if certain panchayat decisions inadvertently favour villagers at the expense of townspeople because they are constrained by and in a sense the outcome of official government policy, others appear to achieve a similar effect by more conscious or deliberate design. Perhaps the most far-reaching in its repercussions was the council's decision to create New Bazaar.

Until recently, as I noted in Chapter 7, Bhukals, like villagers throughout the district, played a negligible part in the commercial life of the town. The former made a tentative entry into this sphere only around 1959, when the then Jimmawal and one of his wealthy agnates, a prominent scribe, purchased land from a bazaariya in what were the northern limits of the town and built several dwellings on the site. The scribe, who had already established a reputation as a successful document-writer in the district capital, had previously practised on the public green or wherever else was temporarily convenient. He now set up an 'office' on his premises, while the Jimmawal rented out the buildings he owned to various government offices and, on occasion, to a fellow villager anxious to try his hand at shopkeeping.

By 1964, the prospects for commercial expansion of the town had become evident and a new land reform programme was encouraging many wealthy peasants to think of exploiting these new opportunities. One avenue to further growth of their enterprise in the town lay in purchasing the property of existing residents, a strategy which, for obvious reasons, was meeting with little success. The alternative was to encourage economic expansion by extending the area of the bazaar, a policy which required neither the acquiescence nor the uprooting of the resident community. The panchayat thus decided, against the strongest opposition of townsmen and their representatives in the council, to organize the sale, for commercial development, of public land north of the existing ribbon of settlement. To ensure that bazaariyas would not derive any benefit from the expansion, the panchayat ruled that anyone who already owned a dwelling in the town could not apply for a plot of land in New Bazaar.

Bhukals themselves submitted one-third of all applications (32 out of 96) and indicated—in response to a panchayat questionnaire—a readiness to invest rs 70,000 in stock alone, or an average of rs 2,100 per applicant, over and above the cost of the site and construction of the building. Since the number of requests for plots exceeded the land available, a 'draw' was arranged, and Bhukals won 17 of the 48 plots, the largest number for any single settlement.

The main effect of the panchayat's decision, therefore, was to shatter in a single, dramatic move, the virtual monopoly of commerce which townsmen had enjoyed since the creation of Belaspur Bazaar some 200 years earlier.

In sum, then, the introduction of a panchayat system created in the main to promote development has placed villagers in a distinctly advantageous position *vis à vis* townsmen as regards the distribution of resources channelled into the Village. A majority of Bhuka representatives on the panchayat ensures that whenever the interests of villagers conflict with those of townsmen the issue will be resolved in favour of the former. The advantages of education, administrative experience and proximity to government offices which enabled bazaariyas to play so prominent a political role in the immediate post-Rana period are of no account in the contemporary arena of the Village panchayat.

The constant frustration of bazaar aspirations results in regular and vociferous complaints by townsmen to government officials and public threats to withdraw from the union and form a separate council. At the first Village assembly following the elections of 1969 townspeople brought a petition urging secession which led the chairman, a villager, to disband the meeting on a technicality, and so avoid bringing the issue to a vote.

If a bazaar leader can, at best, only seek to mitigate the extent of the imbalance in the allocation of resources, what is the purpose of his continued interest in the council? In a word, because it is only through the Village panchayat that he can hope to pursue political ambitions beyond it. The first step in this process is to become a delegate to the district assembly (*sabha sod*)—there is one from each Village—and thus earn the right to vote in elections for the district council and, indeed, to seek a place on this higher panchayat body. To become a delegate he must gain the votes of the majority of Village councillors. To achieve this goal in the face of a greater number of representatives from the village, he must exploit certain structural divisions within it.

Divisions in Bhuka

The majority of Bhuka's inhabitants (53·5 per cent) is Chetri. Of the 133 households belonging to this caste, 100 are associated with the Thapa 'clan' (*thar*), a patrilineally-defined, non-exogamous unit. This is, in turn, divided into three principal exogamous lineages (also *thar*), each of which tends to be identified with and numerically dominant in one or more wards. Thus, the Bagati lineage (with 19 households) forms the majority in one ward; the Ragmi lineage (39 households) is similarly preponderant in two wards; while the Sadal group (34 households) to which the Jimmawal belongs, is a majority in one and a plurality in another ward. A fourth Thapa lineage in Bhuka, the Sinjel, is small (eight households) and insignificant.

The households belonging to the three major Thapa lineages are not only numerically, but economically and politically preponderant in their respective wards. It is not that panchayat representatives must necessarily be drawn from among these groups (see below), but no one could hope to represent a ward without the full backing of its dominant lineage.

In the context of Village panchayat politics, domestic units which share a common descent group affiliation tend, on the whole, to exhibit a certain solidarity in the face of other, similar groups. This is to some extent a function of inheritance in the male line which emphasizes the bonds among agnates created and sustained by the sharing of rights in a common patrimony. Not infrequently, for example, even after the partition of a domestic group, certain of its lands will remain undivided and the benefits distributed among several households of close agnates. Then, the norm of virilocal residence after marriage ensures that male patrikin with common interests continue to inhabit the same locality. The bonds of agnation are therefore reinforced by ties of neighbourhood, by the exchange of labour services and other cooperative ventures, by worship of common deities, and so on. Generally, the community of households sharing common lineage affiliation is further buttressed by the fact that one member of the group (or occasionally several) emerge(s) to represent its unity. These men are in no sense traditional lineage leaders, but are, rather, respected for the resources and favours they dispense directly, or, are able to call on from others.

However, although the dominant lineages of the Thapas may be represented as solidary groups which compete in the context of the Village panchayat, it must be stressed, as P. Caplan remarks of a similar situation in Duari, that these lineages 'are not opposed politically on the basis of segmentary principles' (1972:71). Moreover, the groups in question are by no means equals in the sense of commanding similar resources of wealth or manpower. The most important of the three is the Sadal lineage which, in the past, provided the headmen of the Simta sub-district and whose members have dominated the village for generations. Nine of the sixteen wealthiest Bhuka domestic units (see pp. 179–80) belong to this group, and today the Jimmawal, with the assured backing of the Sadals is still acknowledged as the village's most powerful figure. The Bagatis, by contrast, are fewer in numbers and of considerably more modest economic status: there are no Bagatis among Bhuka's wealthiest households. Nevertheless, they control the votes in one ward and in recent years have tended to ally themselves with the Sadals. This is attributable mainly to the fact that the most prominent Bagati household head served for many years as a kind of estate manager (*khotari*)[11] for the Jimmawal, and has received numerous forms of assistance from the latter, including support in his successful bid to become the panchayat's vice-chairman in 1967, a post he held for two years (see below).

The principal cleavage in Bhuka is between the partners in this alliance and the Ragmis. The origins of this opposition are not wholly clear, although it is probably traceable to the time when Bhukals were prominent in the Gorkha Parishad party (see Chapter 8). Both the chairman and the treasurer of the district organization at the time of the demonstration were Ragmis and although much of the responsibility for its planning and execution can be laid at the feet of important Sadal families (including the Jimmawal's), they managed to escape official displeasure and retribution since they acted only 'behind-the-scenes' and were not formally linked with the events. The Ragmis, whose two most important notables were jailed and fined—one is now in the civil service and the other no longer resides in the district—still resent the Sadals for what they regard as the latters' craftiness (*jal*). Although their wealth is not comparable to that of the Sadals, their numbers enable them to control two wards, and so to form an important dissident bloc within Bhuka itself. It is the existence of such a bloc which provides the opportunity for the bazaar leader to organize a viable opposition to the Jimmawal.

Village panchayat elections: 1967

The current delegate to the district assembly was chosen in 1967, shortly after elections for the Village panchayat had been completed. In fact, elections took place only for chairman and vice-chairman. Ward representatives were chosen by informal consultations among prominent household heads of the main Thapa lineages, the principal coalition leaders and the aspiring councillors. The panchayat was composed as follows:

Chairman. The successful candidate was a Ragmi, resident in ward 7, whose campaign was encouraged and aided by the Merchant. His opponent was the sister's son of the Jimmawal, who backed his candidacy. In 1965–6 this man had been the chairman of the Village council; however, his suspension in mid-term by the district council on suspicion of mishandling funds (see p. 228) was made much of by his rivals and was probably an important factor in his defeat.

Vice-chairman. The person elected to this office was a Bagati from ward 8, whose campaign had been directed by the Jimmawal. A shopkeeper in New Bazaar, he is beholden to the Jimmawal for manifold favours (see above). The Bagati had little trouble defeating his opponent, a bazaar inhabitant of Thakuri caste and a supporter of the Merchant who had, among other things, helped to obtain a job for him in government service several years before.

Ward representatives:

Ward 1 (bazaar). Although the ward is composed almost entirely of Cobblers, their representative was a respected Butcher shopkeeper resident among them. He regards the Merchant as his patron and supports the latter unquestioningly.

Ward 2 (bazaar). The ward has an overwhelming majority of Newars, and was represented by the mother's brother's son of the Merchant, of whom he is a devoted follower.

Ward 3 (bazaar). The Merchant, with the full approval of the residents, most of whom are Tailors, chose this ward as his 'constituency' since, to be eligible for a place on the district assembly, he had first to win a seat on the Village council. The Tailor who had been the ward representative on the previous council, stood aside in favour of the Merchant (see ward 8 below).

Ward 4 (Bhuka). This is a Ragmi ward and returned a member of the
lineage who had represented it on a previous council. His candidacy
was promoted by the Merchant.

Ward 5 (Bhuka). The Sadals have a plurality in this ward, which also
contains a large population of untouchables, mainly iron Smiths
(Kami). The Jimmawal proposed one of the latter for ward representative; he is linked by *jajmani* ties to many important Sadal households,
including that of the sub-district headman.

Ward 6 (Bhuka). The majority in this ward are Sadals, and the representative was a classificatory younger brother (FFBSS) of the Jimmawal.
He is completely loyal to his agnate/patron who helped him secure a
lucrative contract from the district headquarters. This man also served
on a previous council.

Ward 7 (Bhuka). The bulk of the population is Ragmi, although the
representative was from the large minority of Cobblers in the ward.

Ward 8 (Bhuka). The majority here are Bagatis, and the Jimmawal chose
this ward as his constituency. The Jaisi who had previously represented
the ward, like the Tailor in ward 3, stood aside (see above).

Ward 9 (Bhuka). Most of the inhabitants are members of non-twice-born
castes. The representative was from the largest single group, the
Magars.

By skilfully exploiting the cleavage within the Thapa clan in
Bhuka the Merchant was able to gain a majority in the Village
council to support his candidacy for district assembly delegate.
First, by ensuring that bazaar votes were added to those of Ragmi
inhabitants of wards 4 and 7 he succeeded in steering the Ragmi
candidate for Village council chairman to victory, thereby earning his
gratitude and, later, his support in the contest for delegate to the
district assembly. Through the chairman's influence, moreover, he
was able to count on the vote of the Ragmi representative from ward
4. Finally, he drew the Magar member for ward 9, otherwise
unaligned, to his side. These, in addition to the three bazaar councillors, earned him six votes against the Jimmawal's five. The latter
secured the votes of the Bagati vice-chairman, the Smith and Sadal
representatives from wards 5 and 6, his own, and that of the Cobbler
representing ward 7. Although from a Ragmi dominated ward, the
Cobbler had been a plough-servant for the Jimmawal's household
for 13 years and, in the end, sided with the latter.

It is significant that in the only version I heard (that of the
Ragmi chairman) which presented a somewhat different alignment,
it was claimed that the Cobbler had in fact supported the Merchant,

and that the chairman himself had given his vote to the Jimmawal. This may, of course, have been the case (voting was by secret ballot and there is no way of knowing precisely how each individual cast his ballot) but it is equally if not more likely a version designed to avoid the embarrassment of admitting to having voted for a bazaariya and against a fellow villager.

Village panchayat elections: 1969

Generally, the struggle for control of the Village council would abate following the designation of a district assembly delegate. This is because he holds office for six years[12] whereas Village panchayat elections are held every two years to choose a new chairman and vice-chairman and one-third of the ward representatives (see p. 178). Thus, in the normal course of events coalition leaders would not take more than a passing interest in 'interim' elections. However, the most recent voting in May, 1969, generated as much concern as the previous one as a result of a new government ruling that chairmen and vice-chairmen of Village panchayats would henceforth hold office for four years, instead of two. This meant that the executive and most of the ward representatives on the council after the elections would still be in office when the time came to choose the next district assembly delegate in approximately three-and-a-half years.

In the 1969 elections there were, again, no contests in any of the wards,[13] but a number of changes in representation occurred which could alter the previous alignment of forces. The Magar who had been the ward representative of Ward 9 had lost interest in the panchayat and would not stand again. The issue of who would replace him was decided when the Jimmawal's sister's son (the elder brother of the ex-chairman) moved there from Ward 5 and announced that he proposed to stand. This man was a former parliamentary candidate (see note 16 p. 174) and no-one was apparently ready to oppose him publicly. The new member, although independent-minded, is regarded as an ally of the Jimmawal.

One other substantive alteration occurred when the Cobbler representative of Ward 7 was asked to resign by supporters of the Merchant, and was replaced by a Ragmi whose loyalties were more predictable. The remaining changes involved merely the substitution of new personnel for old: thus, the previous Ragmi representative for Ward 4 resigned and was succeeded by a close agnate; the Smith from Ward 5 also resigned when the Bagati vice-chairman suffered defeat on seeking re-election (see below) and was 'given' Ward 5 by the Jimmawal. Finally, the two ward representatives who had stood aside in the elections of 1967 to make way for the principal coalition leaders, and had then returned to their seats in bye-elections held after the voting for district assembly delegate,[14] continued to represent these wards (3 and 8). Both were loyal followers of their respective leaders.

The vice-chairmanship was contested by the incumbent Bagati and a Ragmi who was another recent settler in Ward 9. The latter received the backing of the Merchant, and with the votes of bazaar residents, the two Ragmi wards, and a large proportion of his new neighbours in Ward 9, managed to achieve a narrow victory. The incumbent Bagati did his own cause no good by antagonizing a number of his regular supporters on the eve of the ballot. A gratuitous insult issued to a prominent Sadal (the scribe mentioned earlier) encouraged enough of them to abstain and probably contributed to the Bagati's defeat, much to the Jimmawal's chagrin. Such an incident serves to underline how internecine quarrels, jealousies and rivalries within the two main camps may have a crucial bearing on the outcome of any particular confrontation, including an election. Following his defeat, the Bagati was returned unopposed as representative of Ward 5, whose incumbent member, the Smith, was asked to resign.

The elections for chairman not only highlighted the cleavage within Bhuka, but stressed again the fundamental opposition between village and bazaar. The first to announce his candidacy was the man who had been the council's chairman in 1965–6, but had been suspended in mid-term by the district council, and subsequently suffered a defeat in the 1967 poll. In the election of 1969, he had the full backing of his mother's brother, the Jimmawal. The incumbent Ragmi chairman also stood for re-election, hoping, as in the past, to receive the Merchant's support. The latter, however, sensing that there might be a fairly equal split in the Bhuka vote, put his weight behind a bazaar candidate, the Newar representative of Ward 2, his mother's brother's son. This drew the wrath of the Ragmi, who accused the Merchant of betrayal.

On the first ballot, the latter received just under 200 votes, mainly from the two Ragmi wards (4 and 7). The other Bhuka candidate obtained 340 votes, from the Sadal and Bagati wards (5, 6 and 8) and Ward 9 (where his older brother had become the representative).

The Newar received over 300 votes from the three wards in the town. Since no candidate had procured a majority, a second ballot was held to choose between the two leading contestants, and the result was an overwhelming victory (543–292) for the Jimmawal's candidate. Clearly, the Newar picked up none of the Ragmi's votes, a situation which can be explained partly by the latter's annoyance that the Merchant had introduced a third contestant, thereby diminishing—in the event, demolishing—his chances of victory. But it must also be seen as the refusal of Bhukals under any circumstances to support a bazaar candidate for chairman. 'No Bhukal', I was told time and time again, 'would ever urge his supporters to vote for a bazaariya'.

Table 30 indicates the power balance within the panchayat after the elections of 1967 and 1969.

TABLE 30

Alignment of Village panchayat members, 1967 and 1969

	1967		1969	
	Merchant	Jimmawal	Merchant	Jimmawal
Chairman	*			*
Vice-chairman		*	*	
Representatives:				
Ward 1	*		*	
Ward 2	*		*	
Ward 3	*		*	
Ward 4	*		?	
Ward 5		*		*
Ward 6		*		*
Ward 7		*	?	
Ward 8		*		*
Ward 9	*			*

The elections of 1969, therefore, resulted in a slight shift in the balance of power within the Village panchayat. In the previous council which took office in 1967, according to a wide consensus of informants, the Merchant could count on the allegiance of representatives from the bazaar wards (1, 2 and 3), one Ragmi ward (4) and, at least at the time of the crucial delegate vote, Ward 9, as well as that of the chairman himself. After the elections of 1969, he can still rely on the three bazaar representatives and (now) the new vice-chairman. But he has 'lost' the chairmanship to the Jimmawal, the new representative of Ward 9 is solidly in the latter's camp, and he is considerably less certain of how the two Ragmi ward members will behave when the time comes to choose the next district assembly delegate.

Conflict outside the panchayat

The focusing of bazaar-Bhuka conflict in the Village panchayat does not obscure the extent of confrontation occurring in other organizations as well. Indeed, it appears at times that virtually every formal association established in the district capital, whatever its manifest purpose, becomes yet another medium through which the opposition of town and village is channelled. In the remainder of this chapter I consider recent events involving two such associations.

The youth club

In 1967 a handful of college students resident both in the bazaar and Bhuka decided to form a Youth Club,[15] ostensibly to promote the 'physical and mental development' of young people locally. Since the idea was first mooted by the younger brother of the Merchant, at the time about to enter university in Kathmandu, he became its first president, by acclamation, but thereafter, no meetings nor other activities were held again until 1969. In April of that year several of the key members who had recently returned home from their studies in Kathmandu, decided to revitalize the club and choose a new executive. Over 80 members were recruited, many of them employees of the administration from both within and outside the district. Each paid a small enrolment fee.

The incumbent president stood for re-election, and several of the more active club members from Bhuka, anxious that he should not go unopposed, but unwilling themselves to risk the humiliation of what they feared would be certain defeat, persuaded a middle-aged civil servant from Bhuka to stand against the Newar. The latter was returned by a 58–25 majority. The secretaryship was contested by another inhabitant of the town, employed in the district administration, and the Jimmawal's second son, a high school teacher with an Intermediate degree[16] from Kathmandu, who won by a vote of 46–35. The club members then proceeded to choose a nine-man committee (from a list of twelve nominees). The results were interpreted as a draw, with each 'party' (as they are referred to) electing four members, and the loyalties of the ninth, a villager from outside the immediate area who is employed in the district administration, undecided.

The Bhuka side comprised two Sadal high school teachers, one of them the Jimmawal's eldest son, an affine from a nearby village, and another villager whose reasons for siding with the Bhukals I was unable to discover. The bazaar side of the committee was composed of the Merchant's son and his wife's younger brother, both of whom hold senior posts in the district administration, and another senior civil servant from outside the district, who is a close friend of the latter. Its fourth supporter is the son of the Merchant's Brahmin priest from Duari.

The excitement generated by the elections for the Youth Club executive was out of all proportion to the manifest rewards attached to the offices being contested. Balloting took place during two consecutive evenings and throughout this period candidates and their 'agents' (the English word was used) campaigned vigorously. The voting itself was conducted with much attention to detail, under the supervision of a chief returning officer (a senior member of the administration from outside the district), who prepared mimeographed voting forms, conducted a secret ballot, and even entertained complaints about underhanded electoral practices. Still, almost immediately the contest was over the club lapsed once again into complete inactivity and a few months later, before returning to Kathmandu to resume his studies, the president resigned.

It is no coincidence that the intense burst of Youth Club energy occurred only a month before the Village council elections (described above); in other words, during one of those periodic 'encounters' when the principal coalitions test their relative strengths (Bailey 1969). The visit of the speaker of the National panchayat to the district a few days after the Youth Club elections became the occasion for another public confrontation. The executive had decided to hold a reception for this dignitary. Arrangements for the event, however, were taken in hand by the president and several committee men from the bazaar, apparently neglecting deliberately to consult members from Bhuka, including the club's secretary (a son of the Jimmawal). The latter arrived purposefully and demonstratively towards the end of the preliminary speeches, and proceeded to inform the gathering that he could not have known when the meeting began, since his assistance in the planning had not been sought, and went on to remonstrate with the bazaar executives much to the discomfort of the guest of honour.

The high school

In the same month several of the leading actors in these events were involved in yet another incident. This began as a demand by two high school teachers, one of them a Sadal who is a member of the Youth Club executive, for a rise in salary. They approached the secretary of the High School Management Committee, an appointee of the chief district officer in whose department he fills a senior post. As it happens, the secretary is a Newar, a bazaar inhabitant, the younger brother of the Merchant's wife, and also a member of the Youth Club executive committee. Without calling a meeting of the School's Management committee, the secretary refused the teachers' request claiming that the school had no funds available. The teachers, angered by his behaviour, and backed by their two colleagues, both sons of the Jimmawal, and the head teacher (a Brahmin from outside the district) decided to hold a token strike in support of their claim. They were promptly arrested by the police on the instructions of the senior official in charge at the district headquarters. The governor was away at the time. This official is also a member of the Youth Club committee and, as noted, a close friend of the School Management Committee's secretary.

For the better part of two days the district capital was in a high state of excitement, with delegations of young Bhukals attempting to negotiate the release of the teachers, and a number of bazaar youths, including the president of the Youth Club, urging the dismissal of the strikers. In the end, the president of the district panchayat—and ex-officio chairman of the School Management Committee—intervened to secure the release of the staff, who promised in return not to engage in further strike action (which is illegal in Nepal). The pay claim was also granted.

Since Bhuka provides three of its five teachers,[17] villagers regard the high school as somehow their preserve, and view a bazaariya in the secretary's job on the Management Committee as part of a scheme by the Merchant and his followers to dominate every aspect of life in the district capital. Bhukals argue that this office should be made elective and feel certain that if it were, someone more amenable to their interests would get the post, since at least half the committee is composed of Bhukals. They interpret the strike settlement as a humiliation for the secretary, a condemnation of his 'dictatorial ways', and a vindication of their own actions.

The bazaar people, for their part, purport to see only unsavoury motives behind the strike: some talk of subversion and revolution, but most sum it up as an attempt to promote villagers' interests at the expense of the nation's progress.

The idioms of conflict are varied, but the competition both within the Youth Club and the School Management Committee may be seen as an extension of the opposition between townsmen and villagers beyond the age category from which the panchayat draws its members and the coalitions their leadership.

Conclusion

During the past decade the hostility which had developed between bazaariyas and Bhuka villagers in the years following the revolution has been channelled into a number of recently established formal associations, principally the panchayat. The imbalance in population and the allocation of wards results in Bhuka's domination of the Village council in the sense that villagers derive a disproportionate amount of the benefits increasingly available under the national development programme. Nevertheless, the bazaar coalition has been successful in winning more than its share of support from representatives on the council by exploiting a structural division between Thapa lineages in Bhuka. This has not resulted in—nor was it intended to achieve—an alteration in the flow of resources away from the village into the town. But it means that a bazaar leader can secure a decisive vote in the contest to represent the Village on the district assembly. The significance of this achievement will become apparent in the ensuing chapter.

A word might be said here about the position of bazaar untouchables. Despite their high numbers and comparatively strong economic position within the town, their part in its present political life is hardly more significant than it was in the past. While they now exercise a voice in the Village panchayat, it is, in effect, that of the bazaar leaders of clean caste, whom they seem prepared to follow unquestioningly. There is, in short, no political consciousness among them.

Notes to Chapter 9

1 For some details of these earlier programmes, see Joshi and Rose (1966:397–8); L. Caplan (1970:163–4).

2 This number was obtained from the district panchayat secretariat. It must be understood, however, that any settlement may itself be divided into a number of named hamlets or neighbourhoods.

3 Until 1966, members of the public had no direct voice in the elections of the chairman and vice-chairman, who were chosen by the nine ward representatives from among their own numbers.

4 Such wealthy people make arrangements with men of poor households, usually untouchables, to work their fields on a long-term basis. The latter are given interest-free loans and become plough-servants until the loans are repaid. In addition, each ploughman receives an agreed annual quantity of grain from his 'master' (*riti*).

5 Royal Proclamation, December 15, 1960.

6 There is a substantial literature on the relation between community development and the ideal of village harmony (see Thorner 1953; Berreman 1963).

7 See Mayer (1972) and Boissevain (1971; 1972) for a discussion of the relative merits of various terms to suggest collectivities which are not quite so formal as groups nor yet as unstructured as categories. I use 'coalition' in its dictionary sense—'a temporary alliance of distinct parties for a limited purpose'— because, as Mayer points out, it does not necessarily imply egocentricity, as does 'faction'. The alliances I am referring to are generally led by but do not necessarily rely for their survival on particular individuals.

8 The secretary is a paid employee of the Village panchayat, occasionally appointed by the administration, but more usually by the panchayat itself, and then sent for periodic training to conferences and meetings organized by the ministry in charge of panchayat affairs. Since its inception, the secretary of the Bazaar-Bhuka Village council has been a neighbour and affine of the Jimmawal (and father's brother's son of a former chairman).

9 Nepalese calendar and fiscal years are concurrent; they begin and end in the spring.

10 In 1968 this section of the Lands Act was amended to enable loans to be made for marriage and funeral expenses, but at the time of fieldwork this had not yet become widely known in Belaspur.

11 A *khotari* visits and may even reside for a time on the landowner's more distant properties, generally those outside the district, which are cultivated by tenants, to ensure that the owner's interests are safeguarded. Such a responsibility calls for a person in whom the owner has complete trust, so that generally a less prosperous kinsman, affine or neighbour whom he has known over many years is given this task. The reward may be a portion of the produce, or other more diffuse benefits.

12 As with the Village council, terms of office of district assembly delegates were staggered after the first elections held according to proper procedures in 1963, and the Merchant 'drew' a four year term, which forced another contest in 1967.

13 This is fairly common practice over much of Nepal. Indeed, contests for Village panchayat executives are a relatively new phenomenon. In 1969, there was still no balloting for chairman in one-third of Belaspur Villages.

14 A man who becomes his Village council's delegate to the district assembly retains his seat on the council unless he also wins election to the district

panchayat, in which case he vacates his place on the former body. This is what happened to the Merchant. The Jimmawal, after his defeat in the ballot for district assembly delegate, withdrew from the Village council (see Chapter 10).

15 This is to be distinguished from the Youth Organization (*Yubak sangatan*), one of a number of 'class' organizations set up by the government alongside the panchayat system to represent the interests of various categories of the population.

16 The 'Intermediate' degree is generally awarded at the completion of a two year course, the 'Bachelor' after four.

17 In fact, shortly after this incident, two more Bhukals were added to the staff, one of whom was later to become head teacher.

10

Political Relations
The District Panchayat

IN the previous chapter I explained the concern of coalition leaders with the outcome of Village panchayat elections largely in terms of their rivalry to represent the Village on the district assembly. For it is this assembly, composed of delegates from all the Village councils in the district, which elects from its own ranks the powerful eleven-man district council (including the president (*sabhapathi*) and vice-president (*upa-sabhapathi*)). This body, in turn, has a crucial part in the choice of Belaspur's representative on the national panchayat, undoubtedly the summit of a local man's ambition. In this chapter, I follow the bazaar-Bhuka conflict out of the Village, to examine its manifestations in district political affairs. Several factors are isolated which have a bearing on the outcome of rivalries at the district level. One is the nature of informal ties between locally-resident senior bureaucrats and their colleagues from outside the district; another, the links between top administrative officials and panchayat executives. Moreover, candidates for high electoral office in the district must adapt themselves to an arena characterized by a quite different basis of association between aspiring leader and follower than that of the Village. Put crudely, in the latter, relationships founded mainly on kinship, neighbourhood and other traditional, ascribed positions constitute the candidate's basic resources. At the district level, by contrast, far greater dependence must be placed on a wide range of achieved linkages which have little place in the small-scale context of the Village, including those created by 'bribery'.

The district panchayat
The legislation establishing district panchayats assigns a wide range of powers and duties to these bodies, which include the execution of all district-level development projects initiated by the government as well as the formulation of others; disbursal of the grants made by the

government among Village panchayats; inspection and supervision of the work of these lower councils, and assumption of their functions where these have not been fulfilled; construction and repair of major tracks, bridges, etc.; provision for primary and secondary education; imposition of a variety of taxes, fees, etc. Such a concatenation of privileges and responsibilities confers on the district panchayat immense power and prestige, and no political leader with aspirations beyond the Village can hope nowadays to fulfil his ambitions without first entering this body.

Its president, elected every two years, is a person held in high honour and respect throughout the district. Unlike the other members of the council, he is engaged in panchayat business on a full-time basis. He commands a small administrative staff of his own, recruited locally,[1] and draws the salary of a relatively senior civil servant. As district council president he sits on a number of committees dealing with a variety of matters from recruitment of government servants to the management of the high school (see Chapter 9). He addresses innumerable public gatherings, whether or not they officially relate to panchayat matters and, less formally, his advice on a host of issues and his mediation in disputes large and small are constantly sought. In the range of its concerns and the breadth of its powers, the office of district council president is comparable to the most important positions of leadership available to locally resident notables in the past.

As a category, members of the district panchayat resemble in many ways those who serve on Village councils. Thus, they belong mainly to twice-born castes: of the 18 men (two Brahmins, eight Thakuris, seven Chetris, and one Newar) who have served at one time or another on the Belaspur district panchayat, only one—the Newar—does not wear the sacred thread. They are mainly in their late thirties or early forties and so too old to have benefited from the middle and high schools in the district, although all are of course fully literate. The crucial difference between them and their Village panchayat counterparts is that the former tend to be much wealthier and more influential.

The first district council was actually set up in 1961, apparently in an atmosphere of undue haste and general confusion. Village panchayats had only just been formed when the establishment of a district assembly and council was called for. District officials were unable adequately to prepare themselves or members of the public for these elections and the result was an extremely *ad hoc* body, mainly appointive, which served for an interim period. During this time, it had no development funds at its disposal and only minimal functions and powers. Virtually nothing is remembered of this council; few could recall who its president was—a wealthy resident of a village at some distance from the bazaar, whose interest in the district panchayat lapsed when new elections were held. What is certain is that the notables of the bazaar and Bhuka had nothing to do with it. Most people refer to the succeeding panchayat as the 'first'.

Assembly delegates, in 1963, chose as their president, by acclamation, the Merchant who had, on that occasion, obtained his delegate's seat on the assembly without opposition in the Village council: at that time the Jimmawal had not yet become involved in panchayat affairs. Delegates elected as their vice-president a Bhuka resident who is something of an entrepreneur. The son of a wealthy peasant farmer, he had become, by his own efforts, one of Bhuka's richest inhabitants, mainly through investment in a variety of 'unorthodox' ventures. He was one of the few men in the district who managed not only to acquire and plant but to derive some benefit from improved paddy seeds available in parts of the terai to small numbers of men willing to cooperate in agricultural experiments under government supervision. He had also, a few years previously, bid successfully for the contract to feed the militia and, by all accounts, had done well out of it financially. He is still known locally as the Contractor (*tekadar*). Finally, he was one of the first villagers to buy property and erect buildings in the town, and had made substantial earnings from renting accomodation to government offices.

The Contractor reached the district assembly by registering his official residence in another Village where a ritual brother was the dominant political figure on the council and arranged for him to be elected without opposition as delegate for his adopted Village.[2] There are no agreed evaluations of such a tactic since it is so rare, the result, perhaps, of a surfeit of politically ambitious men in Bhuka. But informants who did comment expressed disapproval, and one likened the person who adopts such a course to a *ghar jouin*, the uxorilocally settled son-in-law, a figure of ridicule in most parts of Nepal where virilocal norms obtain.

By choosing this circuitous route to the assembly, the Contractor avoided having to challenge the Merchant's control of the Bazaar-Bhuka council. In so doing he displayed a shrewd appreciation of his own position within Bhuka. For although a Sadal Thapa, he was not at all popular with the remainder of the Sadals, their allies, and the Jimmawal and some say that he went to live in Sota (Ward 9) because of his inability to get along with them. They regarded him as something of an upstart and very much of an opportunist. He had offended many of his fellow villagers in the immediate post-Rana period by appearing to follow the Gorkha Parishad until Congress achieved its electoral victory, whereupon he switched his loyalties to the party of government. Moreover, as a member of a Sadal branch genealogically at some remove from the Jimmawal, he certainly had no traditional claim to leadership, and his comparative youth (he was in his late twenties at the time) entitled him to no special respect from his fellow villagers. All in all, he lacked a following in the village and could expect no backing if he had contemplated an attempt to challenge the Merchant for a seat on the assembly.

At the next district pachayat elections, in late 1965, the Contractor challenged the Merchant for the presidency, and defeated him. The Merchant, however, retained a place on the district council, and in 1967 made a successful bid for Belaspur's seat on the national panchayat. His opponents were the Contractor, at the time the district panchayat president, and the Jimmawal. The latter, after his defeat in the elections for assembly delegate, resigned his seat on the Bazaar-Bhuka Village council and, like the Contractor, transferred his official registration to another Village, where a former headman in the Jimmawal's sub-district had become the 'kingpin' in the panchayat. He thereby both became a delegate to the district assembly and ran successfully for a place on the district council, which entitled him to participate in elections for the national body (see below).

In late 1967, elections for district panchayat president were again held; the main contestants were the Contractor (the incumbent president), the Jimmawal, and a third candidate, a Thakuri ex-Indian army Serviceman, whose candidacy was promoted by the Merchant—as Belaspur's member of the national panchayat no longer eligible himself—anxious that a man more sympathetic to his own interests hold this important office, and that his Bhuka foes be prevented from winning it. The Serviceman was elected and, at the time of fieldwork, was still the district council president.

To summarize, here is a brief chronology of these panchayat elections:

1961 —*Ad hoc* district council formed, apparently without proper elections.
        President—a villager no longer involved in panchayat affairs.
1961 —District council elections.
        President (unopposed)—the Merchant (Belaspur Bazaar).
        Vice-president—the Contractor (Bhuka).
1965 —District council elections.
        President—the Contractor (defeated the Merchant).
1967(a)—National Panchayat elections.
        Representative—the Merchant (defeated the Contractor and the Jimmawal to become Belaspur's representative on the N.P.)
1967(b)—District council elections.
        President—the Serviceman, resident of a village at some remove from the town. (Supported by the Merchant, he defeated the Jimmawal and the Contractor.)

Thus the struggle for the presidency and, through this office, control of the district panchayat, may be viewed as yet a further expression of, and contribution to, the hostility between the bazaar and Bhuka, although the contest is waged outside the Village arena. Before examining in greater detail the alignment of forces within the district assembly, it is important, at this juncture, to consider the part played by bureaucrats in these political affairs.

Bureaucrats and politicians

We might look first at those members of the district administration holding senior rank who are resident in the bazaar and Bhuka. From events surrounding the Youth Club and High School recounted in the previous chapter, it is evident that bureaucrats are involved directly in coalition rivalries outside the panchayats. They are, however, excluded by law from serving on elected councils; but this does not prevent them from recruiting votes and generally seeking to influence the outcome of elections in favour of the alliances with which they are associated.

Moreover, in serving these interests, they attempt to utilize, whenever possible, the close ties they have with senior administrators from outside the district. In the following paragraphs I examine the manner in which informal relationships develop between high-ranking civil servants resident within the district and their colleagues from outside.

Bureaucrats: locals and outsiders
During Rana times, as pointed out in Chapter 3, there was little likelihood of any local resident rising above a position of low-level clerk in the district administration. This meant that many of what have been termed junior and all senior posts were filled by men from outside the district. During the last decade of the regime's existence there were just over 200 posts in the district administration, and approximately 12 per cent of these were of a rank which could not be appointed locally. Whatever bonds developed among the men in this latter category, therefore, served only to reinforce the divisions between themselves as high-ranking outsiders, and locally resident, low-ranking government servants.

The division between outsider and local resident is no longer coincident with that between higher and lower bureaucratic rank. Belaspuris making a career in the civil service can and do reach positions of importance in the district administration. Although most outsiders are in senior posts, not all such posts are held by those whose homes are outside Belaspur. On the contrary, the majority are filled by district residents. Of 48 senior administrative and 19 technical posts, Belaspuris hold 31 of the former and seven of the latter, i.e., 38 of the 67 top jobs in the district administration. Nineteen of them are held by residents of the town (eleven) and Bhuka (eight).

Informal ties of friendship evolve between these local inhabitants and outsiders sharing roughly equal rank in the bureaucracy. A variety of mainly recreational contexts exist which enable and encourage such out-of-office relationships. Receptions at the district headquarters to which most senior (administrative) personnel are invited, are held from time to time to honour a visiting dignitary, welcome a new or bid farewell to a departing governor, or celebrate a national holiday. Periodically, dance and drama shows are held and senior officials invariably organize and usually participate in these performances. They are the main participants, too, in celebrations surrounding Holi, a Hindu festival only nominally observed in the villages of Belaspur. Most evenings, after office hours, and before dark, a number of senior officials meet in front of the district headquarters to play badminton, and tournaments are held from time to time. Saturdays, when offices are closed, are occasions for organizing picnics, drinking, playing cards, visiting temples, or merely calling on friends. The wives of government servants who visit one another occasionally also provide a means whereby contacts among their husbands can grow, although fewer than one-third of high-ranking outsiders have their wives with them in Belaspur. Weddings and other festivities in the homes of local residents offer other opportunities for indigenous bureaucrats to invite non-resident officials to be their guests.

The development of close bonds among senior officials is encouraged, too, by their common possession of certain attributes. Such men tend to be young: in the Belaspur district administration their average age is 30·7 years. The great majority come from wealthy families with adequate lands. Approximately two-thirds of outsiders and half of local residents of senior rank belong to households whose fields produce well in excess of their grain requirements. Of greatest importance, however, is the fact that these bureaucrats enjoy, by comparison with other members of the administration as well as the general public, superior educational qualifications obtained in the secular school system established in the country after 1951, although the men from outside the district have a higher average (11 years) of schooling than their Belaspuri colleagues (with 8·3 years). Many of the latter, however, have either studied or worked outside the district, and not a few have spent time in Kathmandu. As a result of their studies and their travels, a number of local inhabitants share with outsider colleagues knowledge both of a universe beyond the confines of the district, and of national and international affairs inaccessible to those without their experiences.

These special advantages, to say nothing of the prestige and authority they derive from their high offices, contribute to a feeling among them of constituting an extremely privileged sector of society. In that the Youth Club provides a formal organization for this relatively well-educated elite, it serves as a vehicle to clarify and stress their shared interests and values. This emerged starkly during the contest for Youth Club president when one middle-aged senior civil servant, a man educated only in the local *bhasa* school, began to read aloud the voting instructions in the slow, halting, sing-song manner of the barely literate peasant, to be met by a howl of derision from the young men gathered for the balloting.

Indeed, Youth Club members' admiration for 'qualifications' probably counted as much in the electoral victories of the Merchant's brother (as president) and the Jimmawal's son (as secretary), both of whom are university trained, as their abilities to recruit followings.

Six of the Youth Club's nine committee members are also high school graduates or better.

Finally, it is of interest to note that the bonds created by these young men through their identification with such a 'culture of privilege' cuts across the variety of castes to which they belong.[3] (The only untouchable in this category is in a technical post and spends most of his time outside the district capital on assignment. He does not participate in any of the activities described above.)

There are two main types of constraint on the cultivation of informal ties with out-of-district colleagues. One relates to the problems posed by distance of residence from the bazaar. The majority of senior bureaucrats who live in the district commute daily to their offices from home. If their houses are at some distance from the town they cannot remain for long in the bazaar after office hours because of the time taken in commuting, nor can they return easily to the bazaar on holidays. Some do live away from home during the week either because they are obliged to live in government-provided accommodation or because their homes are too distant to enable them to commute daily, in which case they find rented rooms in the district capital or stay with relatives in nearby villages. Generally, they too return to their villages at week-ends and for holidays. Even bureaucrats who reside in relative proximity to, but outside the town, leave the bazaar before or shortly after sunset and spend most Saturdays and holidays on their farms. The implications of residence are therefore clear: those who live in villages even as close as Bhuka tend to spend considerably less free time in the bazaar than senior officials who actually live there permanently. In consequence, it is townsmen who are best placed to develop the kinds of relationships with outside colleagues which enable them to wield strong influence with the latter.

Another type of constraint on the formation of close links between Belaspuri and outside bureaucrats has to do with gradations of rank within the category I have referred to as 'senior'. For our purposes, three such gradations may be identified: (a) that which contains the highest officials in the three key branches of the district administration—the governor,[4] chief district officer, and district judge. Since the introduction of a Public Service Commission, men in these sensitive positions are invariably non-residents so the question of local bureaucrats establishing bonds of friendship with outsiders at this level does not really arise, since such bonds assume equality of status; (b) those bureaucrats ranking just below these top officials, who are either their deputies or in charge of other (less strategic) branches of the district administration; (c) the lowest category of senior official, composed of men whose rank is essentially a reflection of the technical skills demanded in the job, and not a measure of the administrative responsibilities attached to it. Thus, for example, the land reform office in Belaspur employs a large contingent of senior staff mainly because their duties demand relatively advanced literary and numerical skills. Categories (b) and (c) contain both outsiders and inhabitants of the district.

It is within grade (b) that friendship ties between residents and non-residents are likely to have the greatest impact on local political struggles. The manner of the district headquarters' intervention in the teachers' strike, for example, becomes clearer when it is realized that the Newar secretary of the High School Management Committee (against whose refusal to consider their claim the teachers were protesting) is not only a bazaar resident but one of a close circle of bureaucrats who drink, play cards and picnic together regularly and which circle also includes the next-ranking official to the governor, a Brahmin from outside the district. It was the latter who, with the governor temporarily out of the district, instructed the police to arrest the teachers. The dearth of Bhukals in category (b) and their absence from this friendship circle in particular, puts the village coalition at a disadvantage in the competition between the two sides to utilize the potential benefits of administrative authority and influence.

Lateral ties of friendship among high ranking bureaucrats, however, do not exhaust the extent of linkages between resident and non-resident members of the administration. Vertical bonds of an informal nature also develop within an office. Those between the head and his immediate subordinates who regularly advise him, to whom he delegates part of his responsibility, and on whose abilities and discretion his own professional reputation may largely rest, are of special interest here. For where these subordinates happen to be local inhabitants they are in a position to derive certain advantages from such a connection. Thus, I noted in Chapter 3 the implications of these kinds of informal links for the recruitment of local personnel to menial grades. The possibility of occasional intervention by a governor or chief district officer on the side of one protagonist in a local dispute at the urging of a close subordinate (who is directly or indirectly connected with the dispute) cannot be discounted. Through the Newar High School secretary's links to the governor's Brahmin assistant and his own direct tie to the chief district officer (in whose office he holds senior rank), the bazaar coalition, in which the secretary plays an important part (he is the Merchant's wife's brother) clearly has access through several crucial channels to the centres of power in the district administration. These links are shown in Figure 3.

FIGURE 3

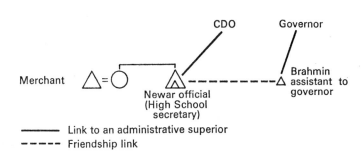

The involvement in local political contests by the district's top officials results also from the lack of clear definition of authority both within the administration and between it and the elected panchayats. Within the district bureaucracy, as noted in Chapter 3, the governor exercises 'general supervision' over various government departments in the district (a responsibility he now shares with the CDO). Whereas in the past the virtual absence of effective communication with Kathmandu gave him all but absolute power in the district, nowadays improvements in the links between the capital and outlying regions enable central departments to exercise closer control over their district branches (Malhotra 1958).

This results, from time to time, in disputes over jurisdiction between a top official and the heads of branches in the district.[5] Where such quarrels do occur adherents of the principal coalitions may seek to become involved on one or the other side. Their support is not unwelcome since the protagonists may require attestations from prominent local people as to the correctness of their behaviour.

Thus, when the deputy head of the district council secretariat and for a time acting-CDO (an outsider and a close friend of his Newar colleague) arrested an employee of the health centre on suspicion of selling government-issued medicines illegally, several high school teachers who are aligned with the Bhuka coalition demonstrated in support of the latter and threatened to report the acting-CDO to Kathmandu. The latter's concern to keep the incident from reaching the ministry responsible for health must certainly have played some part in his decision to release the accused that same day without preferring charges. In another, more serious instance, the district police chief challenged the governor's right to discipline a member of his force. Relations between the two men grew so estranged that a commission of enquiry had to be despatched from Kathmandu to settle the matter. Here again, each of the coalitions competing for power in the district sided with one of the disputants, and provided witnesses during the enquiry.

Bureaucrats and panchayat leaders

Since 1960 the relation between top district officials and the panchayats has been a complex one, indeed much more complex than the formal division of responsibilities between the administration and these elected councils would lead us to suspect. When the system of panchayats was first mooted it was envisaged that these bodies would gradually assume the administrative functions which were then the responsibility of district governors, and that the president of the district panchayat would become the principal executive officer. Despite the allocation of some of the governor's traditional duties to these elected bodies, however, the central government, as Joshi and Rose note 'intends to move slowly and cautiously in devolving powers upon the district panchayats' (1966:401). In fact, Kathmandu through its district authorities, maintains a tight control on the activities of the panchayats and reserves the right to dissolve a district council or to remove any of its members. In April 1969, for example, without prior notice or any but the most cursory explanation, it suspended all incumbent district panchayat presidents and vice-presidents, although their terms were not due to expire for several months, and called for temporary replacements until new elections could be held.

A similar balance of power exists at a higher level as well. Although the national panchayat has considerable advisory and legislative

functions, the monarch reserves 'broad and essentially unchallenge-
able veto powers which cannot, in the final analysis, be overridden
by the National Panchayat' (Joshi and Rose 1966:404). Moreover,
cabinet ministers, who are chosen by the crown, 'can be dismissed
or retained by the King without reference to the support (they) may
enjoy in the National Panchayat' (ibid: 405).

Despite what amounts to an overwhelming concentration of
power in the administration, the district's top officials are generally
very sensitive about their relations with panchayat principals. This
is because, as I have indicated, the latter can, if unduly provoked, go
above the heads of local officials and, at the very least, cause them
some embarrassment, or, by persistently refusing co-operation, bring
the panchayat to a virtual standstill. Because the professional esteem
of top government servants is based no longer only on maintaining
land revenues and law and order, but also on their success in further-
ing the panchayat system, to the survival of which the monarchy is
so strongly committed, they are reluctant to 'show their strength'
where such behaviour might antagonize council leaders. This does
not mean that they remain aloof from panchayat affairs, however.
Local politicians whose ambitions and activities threaten, in the
view of district officials, to paralyze or in any way thwart the work of
district councils (and so endanger their reputations) are opposed
while those who are adjudged to portend no such disruption are
encouraged and, where possible, abetted. These bureaucrats, can
not, indeed, dare not avoid becoming involved to some extent in
political contests waged for control of the district council.

On the whole, over the past decade, the weight of interventions by
top district officials in local political affairs has been biased in favour
of the bazaar coalition at the expense of the Bhukals. This is due, in
part, as I have pointed out, to the virtual monopoly by townsmen and
their close friends and associates of key senior posts (i.e., category
(b) posts) in the district headquarters and the district panchayat
secretariat, the two main decision-making departments of the
administration. It has been encouraged, moreover, by a series of
disputes involving the Contractor and two successive governors.

The earliest occurred shortly after the Contractor was elected
vice-president of the district panchayat and concerned the Women's
Organization (*mahila sangatan*) one of the 'class organizations'
established in conjunction with the panchayat system.[6] These
organizations are supposed to be structured in much the same way

as panchayats, with village, district and zonal/national committees. Because of a virtual absence of literate women in the villages of Belaspur, however, there is only one committee in the district, and this is made up almost entirely of women resident in the town.

Its first president was a young Chetri woman, Laxmi Debi, who almost single-handed had organized the committee at the request of the Contractor, who, for a time before he entered the district council had been employed in the secretariat and responsible for setting up class organizations in the district. There matters stood until the arrival in Belaspur of a new governor, whose wife was a member of the central committee of the Women's Organization. When the time came to elect a zonal representative to the central body (which, in turn, chooses representatives to the national panchayat), Laxmi Debi announced her intention to stand against the favoured candidate, a terai woman, who, for reasons to do with central committee politics, was the candidate whom the governor's wife strongly supported. The latter was extremely annoyed with Laxmi Debi and campaigned vigorously against her and on her rival's behalf. After the vote, held in the terai, which went against Laxmi Debi, the governor's wife sought her resignation from the district committee, and when this was refused, challenged the committee's legitimacy on the grounds that it was in the hands of persons who were opposed to the idea of panchayats. With the blessing of her husband, the governor, she established another committee and chose as president of the new organization a Thakuri woman from the town who had no ambitions beyond the district and was ready, according to informants, to reward this official patronage with docile co-operation. Moreover, the Thakuri woman's family has a long association with the Merchant's coalition, although the latter is not said to have been directly involved in the dispute. Laxmi Debi refused to acknowledge the rival committee and a series of petitions from both sides claiming recognition were sent to the relevant ministry in Kathmandu.

The Contractor, by this time vice-president of the district panchayat, had been drawn into the dispute by virtue of having initially sponsored Laxmi Debi and later giving her his full support in the zonal elections. The claims of the governor's wife that the first committee was controlled by opponents of the panchayat system was a serious accusation probably aimed as much at him as at the members of the committee he helped to set up.

The issue remained unsettled until the eve of a visit to the district by a member of the royal family, when both committees embarked on preparations to greet the distinguished guest. At that point the governor arrested both the Contractor and Laxmi Debi, accusing them of being 'anti-national elements'. News of the arrest reached the royal visitor who apparently ordered their release and an enquiry into the affair. The governor was shortly thereafter replaced and some claim it was as a result of the arbitrary use of his special emergency powers. In the end, Laxmi Debi resigned her office and took up an administrative post outside the district. The two committees were amalgamated under the presidency of the Thakuri woman, who has occupied the office ever since.

Relations between the Contractor and the governor's successor began peacefully enough but soured soon after the former's election as president of the district panchayat in 1965. The initial clash took place following a bad harvest when grain was sent into the district by the central government to relieve the crisis and stabilize prices. A difference of opinion developed between the district council president and the governor over the extent of the shortage and the methods of distribution. The Contractor appealed to Kathmandu over the head of the official and, although the governor's policy was finally vindicated, the incident created a climate of intense and lasting mistrust between the two men. They quarrelled over a number of subsequent issues, and soon came to regard one another as implacable foes. Where panchayat matters were concerned the proposals of one would almost invariably meet with the disapproval of the other.[7] The inauguration and implementation of development projects in the district, sluggish at the best of times, slowed to an imperceptible crawl, putting at risk the reputations and ambitions of both men.

With the approach of new elections in 1967, the governor, by this time eager to see the defeat of the Contractor, openly, if discreetly, gave his support to the Serviceman challenger (see above). He praised the latter for his positive attitude to panchayat-led development, and compared this to the incumbent president's interest only in self-aggrandizement. The entry of the Jimmawal into the contest at this stage gave him no particular comfort, for although the two men were on amicable terms, the governor made no secret of the fact that he regarded the former sub-district headman as a man of the past, of the Rana period, unsuited to responsible leadership in the modern panchayat era.

The governor might very well have been further encouraged to resist the candidacy of both Bhukals, i.e., the Jimmawal and the Contractor by the fact that the Merchant, who was promoting their chief rival, the Serviceman, had by now become a member of the national panchayat. Such a person moves in important political circles in the nation's capital; he may serve on or even chair one of a number of key committees and, in time, could become a minister. As a result, he is constantly courted by administrative and high government officials in the nation's capital, and therefore can exert a not inconsiderable influence on a governor's behalf, or, indeed, to his detriment. Within the district, moreover, he is, without doubt, the most important notable, with all the privileges and powers that such notability entails. The head of the district administration must therefore be extremely cautious in his relations with that district's representative on the national panchayat, even if the political structures in which they operate are formally exclusive.

The extent to which assembly delegates, who choose the district council, are influenced by the preferences of top officials is impossible to say. The election of the Serviceman as president in 1967, however, was certainly contributed to and welcomed by the governor, and helped to re-establish cordial relations between himself and the district council.

District panchayat elections

The man who aspires to become a delegate to the district assembly looks for support to members of the Village panchayat with whom he probably shares a variety of multiplex links of the kind normally associated with 'face-to-face' communities. A candidate for membership of the district council, however, has to create followers out of assembly delegates most of whom are only vaguely familiar to him; with many of whom, in other words, his links are simplex in character. How, we might ask, does he build a following?

To gain the votes of a sufficient number of delegates to the district assembly does not require an open campaign, with speeches and elaborate platforms. This is not to say that in informal discussions in tea shops and other meeting places during the campaign the contestants are not extolled or denigrated and, following the election, their successes and failures not explained in 'ideological' terms. Since the introduction of the panchayat system the public statements of candidates must be phrased in the language of national development and a prospective district councillor or contender for the presidency must be seen and heard to subscribe to this philosophy. Men seeking election to the panchayat criticize incumbents for their failure to develop the district and stress their own suitability for the task. Those already in office point to their record in this programme, and accuse rivals of threatening to thwart national goals by caring only for their selfish interests. Older candidates, especially those who were politically active during the Rana or Congress regimes sometimes find it difficult to employ the idioms appropriate to a development-oriented system of elected councils. At home in the language of a previous period or a different arena they are promptly labelled by their enemies as backward-looking men of a bygone era and, moreover, are stigmatized by their association with these now discredited regimes (the Jimmawal is a case in point).

A delegate, then, may be influenced by a candidate's ability to manipulate the appropriate symbols. Alternatively, delegate voters publicly recognize and subscribe to the formal political ideology which stresses the duty of a citizen to vote for the candidate who is most likely to further the national goals, for that is the essence of a 'partyless panchayat democracy'. Indeed, I have been regaled with stories from the Mahabharata offered to justify such a policy of favouring the common as opposed to the parochial good.

But a delegate's support is likely to be sought and given on more pragmatic grounds as well. For an entrenched set of values also exists which arises from and vindicates quite different grounds for conferring allegiance. A person is greatly constrained to assist his 'own man' (*apne manche*) and to follow the dictum that 'a distant (benign) god is not as good as a nearby (malevolent) spirit'.[8] In the following paragraphs some of the main bases of alignment in panchayat politics at the district level are identified through an examination of the district presidential elections of 1967.

Since the terms of office of a number of delegates had expired and voting to select their replacements had not been held in time for the district panchayat elections, the assembly consisted of only 42 voting delegates out of the full complement of 57 members. Candidates for president thus had a fairly compact set of voters to reach. In the pursuance of votes, they attempted to establish links to delegates directly or through intermediaries, or activate those already in existence, and thus to mobilize what has been described as an 'action set' (Mayer 1966).

The recruitment of support does not begin when assembly delegates gather in the district capital for the balloting, but prior to Village panchayat elections. At that time prospective presidential candidates and their chief backers and lieutenants tour as many areas as they can in an effort to influence the composition of Village councils, and especially the choice of chairman, so that in as many cases as possible a sympathetic delegate will be sent to the assembly (see below). Mayer (1963:87) notes the use of similar tactics at election time in the Dewas district of Madhya Pradesh.

I discussed the possible alignment of the 42 delegate voters with five informants who were personally acquainted with the candidates and collectively, though not individually, with all of the delegates. They were asked their opinions of which delegates voted for which candidates and on what basis. There was a striking degree of consensus among informants as to how each member of the assembly had voted, although considerably less agreement, as I note below, as to the reason for many votes going the way they did.

On the first ballot delegates had a panel of six names before them. One candidate received only one vote (his own) while two others received two votes each. A fourth candidate, the Jimmawal, received eight votes, including his own, and informants were unanimous in identifying the nature of the links between this candidate and his supporters. Three main kinds of ties were stipulated: close kinship (one delegate was the Jimmawal's son's wife's father, another his sister's son, and a third his mother's sister's son); ritual service (one delegate belonged to the household of the Jimmawal's priest); and headmanship. Three delegates who are believed to have given their votes to the Jimmawal were former village tax-collectors who, it is claimed, still respected and honoured a sub-district headman, although only one of the three had actually been in the Jimmawal's revenue unit and so directly subordinate to him.

The remaining two candidates, the Contractor and the Serviceman received 16 and 13 votes respectively, and so went forward to the second ballot held on the following day. The result was a draw with 20 votes each; one delegate who had voted on the first day did not show up, while another, anxious to demonstrate his attachment to both candidates, destroyed his ballot publicly. In the end, the issue had to be decided by lot, and the Serviceman won.

Each candidate relied on one major intermediary who earned a significant number of votes for him. The Serviceman's principal intermediary was the Merchant. The latter utilized ties to economic clients, former Congress friends, business associates and even his Brahmin 'teacher' (*guru*) to amass a substantial bloc of votes for his protégé. The Jimmawal, after his humiliating defeat on the first ballot, was determined to see the Merchant, who had already out-flanked him in the Village and national panchayat elections, humbled, and threw his support behind his younger agnate and fellow Bhukal, the Contractor. He apparently succeeded in convincing all his voters to back the latter on the second ballot, although, of course, several were also related, even if more distantly, to the latter.

Not less than a third of each candidate's vote, and in the case of the Serviceman, probably as many as half, was recruited through the two major intermediaries.

Apart from his reliance on the Merchant, the Serviceman was also dependent on several other intermediaries. Thus, two of the candidates who were eliminated on the first ballot switched their few but important votes to the Serviceman, while a third supporter, the latter's vice-presidential 'running mate', also backed by the Merchant, had a father's brother among the delegates who was persuaded to support the Serviceman as well.

Intermediaries are not invariably other members of the district assembly. Occasionally, a prominent village notable who is not directly involved in panchayat affairs may bring pressure on the assembly delegate from his Village to vote for a particular contestant. More frequently, however, candidates establish links with Village council chairmen who then act as their intermediaries since, on the whole, assembly delegates are appointees or followers of the chair-men.[9] The leader of the strongest faction in the Village I studied in east Nepal was content to exercise control of the panchayat and allow a considerably less influential figure in the Village to represent it on the district assembly. The chairmanship of a Village panchayat usually constitutes the height of ambition of a peasant notable. It is only when he seeks power beyond the Village arena that it becomes important to gain a place on the assembly, and to do this he may consider it essential to win control of the lower level council, at the same time eschewing its chairmanship. For although there is no rule which prevents a chairman from representing his council on the district assembly, regulations stipulate that on becoming a member of the district council a delegate must forfeit his seat on the Village body, so that only a man who has no desire to enter the district council can be both a chairman and a delegate. But there are no attractions to being an ordinary assembly delegate and few chairmen in fact consider it worth the time. Of the 57 current assembly members, only four are also the chairmen of their Village councils.

Apart from his reliance on the Jimmawal, the Contractor established most of his links with voters directly. As I have noted, he entered the district panchayat in its early years and over time built up a number of political friendships with others inside the assembly and especially the council. At the time of these elections, the district assembly contained three men who had served together with the Contractor on the two previous panchayats (i.e., for four years) and another six who had been councillors with him for two years. Thus he was able to count on support from members of what was referred to as his 'group' (using the English term): those who, as a consequence of their acquaintance and co-operation on former district councils, had become political allies.

But his relatively long and central involvement in district panchayat affairs had resulted in the Contractor having a number of political enemies as well, men whom he had offended, failed to support or, for a variety of reasons, on whose opposing side he had found himself in most council matters. Such men, of course, gave their votes almost as a matter of course to his opponent, whatever the latter's other claims on them might have been, although in this case their decision was reinforced as well by association with the 'group' of the Merchant, who had also served for a long period on the district council.

The Serviceman, who had only recently returned to Belaspur after a number of years in the Indian army, had little basis of personal support among the delegates, but by the same token, had no long-standing enemies among them either. The majority of his votes, as I have stated, were recruited by various intermediaries. He did establish a few direct links through his identification with the ex-serviceman's association—one of the delegates was its former president—and by kinship. Informants also suggested the possibility of obligations being created by residence in neighbouring Villages, although this was presented as speculation and without the degree of certainty with which other links were explained. The Serviceman resides in and represents a Village in the north-western part of the district, some two days' walk from the bazaar, and he is said to have drawn some support from delegates representing other Villages on the same ridge (*darda*).

But the Contractor who lives in and has most of his closest relationships in the area of Bhuka was not credited with having established any links founded specifically on locality.

Like neighbourhood, caste affiliation is another basis on which the Serviceman, but not the Contractor, is alleged, by most informants, again speculatively, to have relied for votes. The alignment of delegates, however, suggests that caste could not have been more than a peripheral factor in securing loyalties. Of the sixteen delegates whom informants are agreed voted for the Serviceman, six were members of the same (Thakuri) caste, while five were Chetris and five belonged to other groups. A similar pattern emerges for the Contractor's supporters: of his fifteen voters about whom there is consensus, only six were Chetris like himself, while four were Thakuris and four belonged to other groups.

The attribution of particular strategies to one candidate which also could be, but are not attributed to his rival is understandable when we remember that the alliances of the Contractor are more commonly known than those of the Serviceman, who as I have noted, is a very recent arrival on the political scene. Informants are thus encouraged to speculate about the possibilities of caste or neighbourhood as bases of loyalty when they cannot find other linkages which 'explain' voting patterns more categorically.

There is, in other words, a notional continuum along which bonds may be placed, ranging from those, like close kinship or clientage, which are thought to represent virtually a bounden duty to vote for a candidate to those, like caste or neighbourhood which, at best, imply only a tenuous and easily avoided obligation to do so. Stated otherwise, the extent of a delegate's commitment is an aspect of the relationship between himself and the candidate or candidate's intermediary. The more intense and multi-purpose the bond, the more likely is the voter to recognize and/or accept an obligation to support the candidate. Where the relationship tends to be non-diffuse or simplex, the obligation is correspondingly thin.

In general, a candidate's efforts are directed at this end of the spectrum, where he seeks to convert tenuous and fragile ties into multi-purpose ones. Thus, a link established in the days of political parties, and since grown cold, is revitalized and bolstered when the candidate or his intermediary promises assistance in obtaining a government post for the delegate's son. Similarly, a bond based only on common opposition to a rival is further cemented by the creation and maintenance of ritual kinship. The initiator of such a tie visits the household of his potential ally during the Hindu festival of Tiwar and, in exchange for a gift, receives a ceremonial mark on the forehead (*tika*) from a female member of the household. (In this way, the Contractor had become the ritual brother, wife's brother, and sister's son of several assembly delegates.)

It is with such a paradigm of the aspiring politician's differential relationships to his potential voters that we may approach the problem presented by yet another, frequently employed explanation for a delegate's adherence to a particular candidate: namely, 'bribery'.

Bribery

Activities labelled 'bribery'[10] have existed in Nepal since at least the unification of the country under the Gorkha conquerors. For with the establishment of an administrative structure in the districts which was dominated by outsiders, two essential ingredients for such behaviour were introduced: new administration-controlled benefits mainly in the form of government jobs, and the transformation of links between ruler and ruled from those which were primarily diffuse to those which were tenuous and potentially exploitative. To explore the implications of such a change I will return briefly to the discussion begun in Chapter 3 on the ways in which local inhabitants procured jobs in the district administration during Rana times.

It will be recalled that governors had the final right of appointment to all posts filled locally. Three main avenues were open to Belaspur residents to obtain such posts. The first was to use an existing personal link to someone already in an administrative job, usually a kinsman, fellow villager, patron or client. The second, called *chakari*, was to ingratiate oneself over a period of time with the governor by bringing small gifts of food, or performing unsolicited services. The third involved offering a cash payment (*ghus*).[11]

It is impossible to say how frequently each of these three channels to an administrative post was actually utilized. A job aspirant's choices would certainly have been influenced and constrained by (a) the extent to which local residents already employed in the administration were included in his personal network, and so might be expected to assist him in getting a post; (b) the time available to the job-seeker to embark on a programme of *chakari*, which required persistence over, in some cases, many months; (c) the amount of cash available to him, since this was in very short supply prior to 1951; (d) the predilections of those able to grant jobs. Some senior officials are said never to have accepted cash payments while others were notorious for their rapaciousness.

But if we cannot give precise figures for the proportion of supplicants using each of the principal avenues to a place in government service, we can suggest a fundamental sociological difference between, on the one hand, reaching the sources of these appointments by utilizing personal links and, on the other, doing so by offering favours in the form of cash or kind. In the former instance, local inhabitants exploit the multiplex nature of their day-to-day social relationships, some of which, if they are fortunate, happen to penetrate the administration. In the process of obtaining jobs, they merely create new obligations or discharge existing ones as part of an ongoing system of social ties. Alternatively, local inhabitants with government posts recognize obligations to assist others within their own spheres of multiple links to obtain these valued jobs.

By contrast, favours (bribes) are offered when supplicants are unable to activate personal ties in the administration which could lead them to the source of appointments. Here, relations are, as I have said, tenuous, and the bribe must be seen as an attempt to create a degree of certainty and predictability where none exists. Stated otherwise, bribery occurs at points in the social structure where relationships are anomalous.

Such a conclusion might apply as readily to the ways in which loyalties are sought and given in contemporary elections within the district assembly as to the manner of job-seeking and conferment in Rana times. In each context, moreover, cash bribery (*ghus*—the same term is used in both) is strongly condemned. Elsewhere I have considered why, of the two modes of bribery, it is that involving cash and not kind which is regarded as morally reprehensible (L. Caplan 1971). Here, we might note that whereas the giving of favours in kind are more or less public events, cash favours are invariably secretive and private, a fact which contributes to and emerges from the differential moral evaluations applied to each. The universal expression of disapprobation for cash bribery, and its clandestine nature, moreover, help to explain the frequency of *allegations* of such behaviour, which may bear no direct relation to its actual occurrence. These allegations constitute, like charges of witchcraft, an eminently suitable means of explaining certain personal misfortunes, justifying one's own actions, or condemning those of others.

Accusations of bribery

Charges of bribery—I am referring now only to cash offerings[12]— operate at two levels: general and specific. The former are made publicly and refer to broad categories of people. Thus, senior government servants nowadays characterize all officials of the pre-1951 era as bribery-prone. The district governor remarked to me on one occasion that when the Ranas sent their representatives to take charge of a district 'they were given only one instruction—"earn as much as you can"'. Even nowadays, bribery is often attributed to administrators by unsuccessful applicants for government jobs: 'to get a post you have to bribe officials' is a remark frequently heard. In like manner, those who have suffered setbacks in the court may bemoan an absence of impartial justice, and suggest that cases are decided not on their merits but on the strength of the bribes received by members of the judiciary.

In electoral politics similar views obtain. Each political party of the post-Rana period is accused by those who supported its rivals of having bought its votes, while people without previous affiliations might accuse all parties of such practices. In the course of a tea-shop discussion about the parliamentary elections of 1959, one man, making the appropriate gesture of rubbing his thumb against the first two fingers of the same hand, remarked how those elections had been 'entirely a matter of green rhinos' (Nepalese 100 rupee notes). In the contemporary panchayat context, a comment heard time and again is that 'only money wins elections', or that 'people only give their votes for bribes, and care nothing for ability'. The persons making such statements thus offer a general comment on the moral climate of a period, past or present, or explain personal failures by expressing a non-specific grievance against institutions from which they derived or appear to be deriving no benefits.

The second kind of allegation differs from the first in that it names specific individuals, but privately in that those accused are not confronted directly with the charge. The same person, of course, can make both a general and a specific accusation. But whereas each affords a convenient explanation for personal misfortune, the latter usually arises from and reveals a hostile relationship between accuser and accused.[13] Where no such relationship exists an allegation is more likely to be non-specific. Thus, although many unsuccessful applicants for government posts attribute their failures to the occurrence of bribery, I have heard no specific charges directed against their successful opponents or particular officials, and I suggest this is due to the absence of political or personal antagonism between the parties concerned.

In this regard, it is worthwhile noting that whereas an act of bribery involves at least two participants, the briber and the bribed, specific allegations of such activity are often made against only one individual or party. A few examples will illustrate the point. In the course of a discussion among several supporters of the bazaar coalition the subject of Bhuka's domination of the Village panchayat arose and one man remarked that the Jimmawal was rich and powerful only because his agnatic forebears had bribed the land revenue department to obtain the sub-district headmanship. On another occasion when I was questioning a number of Bhukals about the events of 1953 (discussed in Chapter 8) one observed quite gratuitously that the acting governor's father (Harilal) had grown wealthy by taking bribes while an employee of the court. It will also be recalled that one of the reasons given by the Bhuka supporters of the Gorkha Parishad for the demonstration against the Congress governor was his proneness to demand bribes from persons in the district. In these instances a particular enemy is cited as having engaged in bribery, and any others who were presumably involved with him in this activity—the person(s) to whom the Jimmawal's ancestors offered or from whom Harilal received bribes—because they have no part in the hostile relationship, are not specifically named in the accusation.

When allegations include both briber and bribed it is because the two are regarded as enemies by the accuser. This is what generally happens in the context of panchayat elections. In their recounting of the 1967 Village panchayat ballot for district assembly delegate supporters of the Jimmawal's coalition explain their defeat in terms of the Merchant's bribery of the Ragmi chairman and the Magar representative of Ward 9. By their assumed alignment with the bazaar coalition these men become enemies and so liable to specific allegations of bribery.

However, as I have already intimated, allegations (and, in all probability, practices) of this kind are more likely to be found outside the Village context than within.[14] This is because political loyalties in Villages are likely to be founded on the kinds of diffuse links created by kinship, neighbourhood and close economic and ritual interdependence which we associate with small-scale communities. The Bazaar-Bhuka panchayat is probably atypical in that it amalgamates two communities between which, for reasons already cited, few such links exist. At the district panchayat level and beyond, political alliances certainly must be forged on a much wider variety of bases, only some of which grow out of these 'primary' relationships.

Where the ties between a candidate and his potential supporters are tenuous, conditions for the occurrence of bribery exist and allegations of such behaviour are, accordingly, encouraged. This is explicitly recognized by those who follow and comment on political events. It is commonly stated, in one form or another, that for a man seeking election who has few close ties to his electors 'there is only one way—*peysa* (cash)'.

The structure of national panchayat elections tends, if anything, to invite such practices, and certainly encourages the conviction that to achieve a place on this body requires the expenditure of considerable sums of money in the form of bribes. Aside from a minority of representatives chosen directly by the crown or sent by university graduates and class organizations, members of the national panchayat are elected by zonal assemblies—there are fourteen in the country—each of which is composed of all the district councillors in the zone. Thus, with five districts, the zonal assembly of which Belaspur is a part, consists of 55 members, who as a body elect one representative from each district to sit on the national panchayat. Candidates are, therefore, required, in effect, to create immediate followings among zonal delegates since the assembly meets in one of the district capitals for only three or four days at election time. They are likely not to have any personal knowledge of all but a handful of district councillors from other areas, since the zonal assembly does not ordinarily meet and has, as far as I was able to learn, no other functions.

In sum, then, bribery is believed to play a crucial part in panchayat elections especially above the Village level, and will be assumed by one side to have occurred where no 'moral' link is otherwise known to exist between an opposing candidate and his supporter.

We may now examine more closely the extent to which voting patterns in the 1967 elections for district panchayat president were explained by bribery. The five informants (who were not chosen systematically) were asked separately how each of the enfranchised assembly delegates cast his vote, and on what basis. Informants were able, on average, to suggest how some 33 of the 40 delegates had voted on the second, decisive ballot, and there was, as I have noted, a wide consensus about the alignments of 31 delegates,[15] but a clear difference of opinion about the loyalties of the remaining nine. Less agreement obtained about the precise reasons for particular delegates assigning their votes to particular candidates, and especially regarding the role of bribery in creating political adherents. There follows a brief summary of each informant's place in the context of coalition rivalries and his assessment.

Informant A. A member of one of the two Joggi households in the bazaar, he enjoys close ties both with the Contractor, whose mother is the Joggi's father's sister[16] and the Merchant who is his neighbour, creditor and patron. This informant, therefore, although an astute observer of local politics and a veritable fund of information about these matters, refrains from active involvement on either side. He made not a single allegation of bribery.

Informant B. The Jimmawal's son and a teacher in the high school. He is, of course, strongly committed to the Bhuka coalition, although marginally less so to the candidacy of the Contractor who defeated his father on the first ballot. This informant attributed 10 of the 30 votes he claimed to have knowledge of to bribery: eight of these were alleged to have been offered by the Serviceman/Merchant alliance, and the remaining two by the Contractor, a reflection perhaps, of the rather cool relations between the latter and the Jimmawal.

Informant C. The Jaisi representative of ward 8 on the Village panchayat, and a completely loyal follower of the Jimmawal (see above). He offered an opinion on the voting preferences of 34 delegates, and alleged that five of these had exchanged their votes for cash offered by the Serviceman/Merchant side. The Bhuka candidate, he categorically stated, had not used bribery.

Informant D. A close affine of the Merchant, resident in the town, and though not a key member of this coalition, a strong supporter of its leader. He claimed knowledge of 29 delegate voters and accused six of accepting bribes from the Contractor. No such practice was attributed to the Merchant (or Serviceman).

Informant E. Chairman of the Village panchayat in 1965–6 and elected again in 1969, he is the Jimmawal's sister's son and, as already noted, dependent on the latter for whatever political successes he has achieved. Thirteen of the 31 votes he purported to know about were attributed to bribes, and five of these, he claimed, were offered by the Contractor. These two men have been involved in a series of disputes which apparently began in a domestic context, when they were neighbours in Bhuka's ward 5, and soon spread to other contexts. These led to the Contractor contriving, during his first term as district panchayat president, to have his fellow Bhukal suspended from the chairmanship of the Village panchayat. The remainder of the allegations were against the Serviceman/Merchant alliance with whose cause, for reasons already made clear, he has even less sympathy.

The fact that one informant attributed to bribery two in every five votes with which he claimed acquaintance, while another made not a single allegation of this kind reflects, to a degree, a differential knowledge among informants of the personal and political linkages between candidates and delegates. As stated, where ties are known to be diffuse, informants refrain from any suggestion that bribery is involved, while where the precise nature of ties are not known or thought to be tenuous, there may be a tendency to assume bribery as the only means of establishing voting obligations. On several occasions informants rationalized delegates' votes in terms of common caste or neighbourhood shared with the candidates, then added that such a link, in itself insufficient, was probably secured by a cash payment. But lack of precise knowledge cannot fully explain the range of bribery accusations, since every informant refrained from offering an explanation on the voting behaviour of a substantial proportion—on average, one quarter—of the assembly delegates, claiming no knowledge of their affiliations. The pattern of bribery allegations clearly reflects both the personal alignments of the informants and the hostile relations between them and the accused, either candidates or delegates, or both.

Conclusion

This chapter has examined the competition between bazaariyas and Bhukals for control of the principal offices in the district panchayat. It has eschewed detailed description of their manoeuvrings and sought, rather, to highlight certain significant features of the political process at this level. First of all, the importance of links between the rival coalitions and top officials in the district administration were noted. There are, on the one hand, those between such officials and locally resident senior bureaucrats, who may be attached to one or other coalition. Politically useful links arise either from their formal subordinate/superordinate attachments within the same office, or from the informal friendships of local residents with outsider colleagues who are so placed. On the other hand, there are those relationships (friendly or hostile) between top officials and district council leaders or prospective leaders which emerge inevitably as a consequence of their common, but by no means identical, interests in the success of the panchayat system.

Secondly, I have attempted to distinguish the ways in which political alignments are formed within the district council and to indicate how these differ from the bases of loyalties within a Village council. In the latter, they arise mainly from existing multiplex relationships which imply expectations to receive and obligations to provide support. In contests beyond the Village, ties to prospective voters are, on the whole, tenuous and unpredictable, and aspiring leaders must devise ways of transforming these fragile relationships into more categorical, multi-purpose ones.

In this connection, it becomes clear from the discussion that outside the face-to-face community successful leaders are those best able to go beyond the traditional methods of political recruitment on ascriptive grounds and build followings on quite novel bases, even if these include bribery. Men like the Jimmawal, who would continue to apply the idioms and strategies of an earlier political order to the contemporary context outside the Village (even if they are still meaningful *within* this context) find themselves losing ground.

Finally, it is to be noted that although political contests outside the Village have, since 1951, remained the virtual monopoly of townsmen and Bhukals, the nature and scope of the confrontation has undergone a significant change since the introduction of panchayats. For whereas bazaariyas and their village neighbours dominated entirely the political party organizations in the district between 1951–59, the panchayat system demands an extension of the arena to include the representatives of Villages beyond these narrow confines. In their ability to deny or confer allegiance, men from distant parts of the district now possess the wherewithal to affect the fortunes of aspiring leaders and the latter are increasingly compelled to take account of their aspirations and ambitions.

Notes to Chapter 10

1 These people are recruited in the same way as, and work alongside, employees of the district council secretariat, but their salaries are paid out of general council revenues.

2 This is a perfectly legal device, providing that the person concerned registers his name only in his adopted Village.

3 On those occasions when they eat together publicly—as at a formal reception given by the governor—a Brahmin prepares the meal, which normally includes *pullao*, a mixture of rice and either vegetables or meat fried in oil, but never boiled rice. Since chairs are placed side by side, to avoid eating in the same row, officials stand with their plates of food and face away from those next to them until the meal is over, when all wash their hands and return to their chairs.

4 To avoid confusion, I use the term governor to refer to the highest official in the district headquarters, although nowadays he has a different title (see Chapter 3).

5 In their economic study of Kosi zone in eastern Nepal, Ojha and Weiss (1972) suggest that the relative independence of district administrative offices contributes to the difficulties of regional planning.

6 Class organizations for farmers, youth and ex-servicemen have also been established in Belaspur district but these are, with the exception of the latter, virtually moribund.

7 At that time the post of chief district officer had not yet been introduced, and the governor had an effective veto over panchayat affairs in the district.

8 *Tardako deota bhanda najiko bhut ramro cha.*

9 Mayer notes how in Dewas district the Village panchayat may be represented on the next highest body (the Central Committee) by its chairman, his ally, or even his rival, chosen in return for supporting his opponent for the Village chairmanship (1963:90).

10 By 'bribery' I mean the offer of favours with a view to influencing the recipient's judgement or conduct (see Stirling 1968; Nye 1967; Bayley 1961).

11 From the verb *ghusnu*, to pierce, thrust into (Turner 1931).

12 *Chakari*, for obvious reasons, cannot be employed as a device to obtain votes.

13 Mair makes the point that witchcraft accusations may have more to do with quarrels and factional divisions than with any intrinsic 'tension' in specific social relationships (1969:216).

14 '. . . many voters in India would consider the purchase of a vote a perfectly legitimate transaction. If one does something for nothing, one does it for oneself, one's family, one's castemen, or fellow villagers. A stranger—and for most electors the candidate is outside this narrow circle of obligation—could reasonably be expected to pay for the favour of a vote' (Bailey 1963a:32).

15 By consensus I mean that at least four of the five informants agreed on how a particular delegate voted.

16 This is the only instance of marriage ties between clean caste residents of the town and Bhuka.

11

Conclusion

THIS book has examined the manner in which events taking place far beyond the confines of a small town in the remote hills of western Nepal have impinged on the traditional social institutions and relationships of townsmen and affected their links with neighbouring villagers. In considering the local manifestations of national and international currents, it has adopted what Cohen refers to as a 'micro-historical' perspective (1969:26). In tracing institutions and relationships and their interconnections through time, it has also been concerned to examine some processes of social change.

Unlike the situation in many parts of the third world under colonial rule, where exogenous influences were introduced gradually and filtered down slowly to remote tribal and peasant communities, Nepal's exposure to the external world, its ideas and its technology, was sudden and dramatic. The revolution of 1951 ended more than a century of stagnation under a Rana autocracy, and within a few years the country had set off, with massive assistance from every corner of the globe, on the familiar path of economic growth. Shortly thereafter, and certainly by the time I arrived to do fieldwork in 1969, some, at least, of the implications of these developments had become apparent, even in a relatively isolated region of the country like Belaspur. To demonstrate the nature and direction of the changes which have occurred in the past two decades in and around the district capital the narrative has systematically compared the contemporary social pattern to that which persisted during the years of Rana rule.

Throughout the latter period, indeed, probably since the creation of Belaspur Bazaar as an administrative centre in the late eighteenth century, the principal economic mainstay of the town's clean caste inhabitants was government service. Although administrative posts were conferred without benefit of formal appointment procedures, townsmen were more successful in finding and retaining such employment than other residents of the district. This was because of their historical association with the administration—most were settlers and the descendants of settlers who came to the area as government servants—and thus their cumulative administrative experience, their proximity to educational facilities in the town, and their daily contact with the officials in their midst. Even so, townsmen were enlisted, like all inhabitants of the district, only in menial and lower clerical posts—the only ones recruited locally—which, along with all administrative ranks in the country, were subject to annual review and their incumbents, therefore, to not infrequent dismissal and replacement.

The insecurity of government service was cushioned by the involvement of clean caste townsmen in petty commerce during their spells of unemployment or when they could no longer hope to obtain administrative posts. But shopkeeping thereby came to be regarded as a peripheral occupation to be abandoned readily in favour of administrative work, so that the scale of these enterprises remained extremely limited. At the same time, the attitudes of townsmen to retail trade were at least partly conditioned by the commercial insignificance of the bazaar. Its growth in this respect was inhibited by a variety of factors such as systems of gift-giving and requisitioning which ensured that officials from outside the district were supplied directly by villagers, without the intervention of bazaar middlemen; a virtual absence of demand for consumer goods in the district; and a practice whereby households obtained their limited externally-produced needs by selling stocks of clarified butter directly in the plains.

Bazaar untouchables, for their part, hardly engaged at all in commerce and, to the extent that they were employed in government service, filled mainly caste-tied posts in the militia. Three of the four groups, Butchers being the single exception, practised their traditional occupations for which there was ample demand because of a relatively small population of these castes in the district. Tailors were tied to hereditary clients both in the town and neighbouring villages, and supplemented their incomes by spending winters sewing clothes in the plains and, less regularly, went north to work in the summer months. Cobblers had few ongoing ties to clients: the shoes they made were bartered with other townsmen and villagers for goods (including grain) and services. They, too, spent occasional winters in the plains and summers in the north. The gold/silver Smiths relied entirely on providing their services within the district, and like the majority of Cobblers, had no hereditary clients, but exchanged their own for other services and products. Untouchable households who, for one reason or another, could not practice their caste specializations, or who derived an insufficient living from them, provided, like the Butchers, a pool of agricultural labour for surrounding villagers.

But townsmen of whatever caste were either landless or only very marginal landowners, and relied for the bulk of their regular supplies on wealthy peasants with grain to spare. For the latter, such sales were a welcome means to earn cash locally, since they took little interest in government service and none at all in commerce. The relations of townsmen and villagers in Rana times, then, were based essentially on an interdependence of economic roles.

Furthermore, there were no political contexts in which these two categories of the population interacted. This correlated with the complementary nature of their economic links, but it was reinforced, as well, by the confinement of political struggles to small-scale social and spatial contexts. The Ranas and their favourites from outside the district monopolized senior government posts in the district and so denied local inhabitants any significant part in the comprehensive power and authority of the administration. The principal offices available to local people (village and sub-district headmanships) were, in any case, largely ascriptive and, ultimately, arbitrated by the Ranas. Moreover, residents of the district capital, because of their minimal involvement in agricultural pursuits, neither received such headmanships themselves, nor were in any significant way dependent on villagers who did.

Relations between townsmen and villagers are today no longer organic, but characterized rather by intense competition. This transformation has been attributed to a host of innovations—in education, transport and communications, land reforms, self-help development schemes, etc.—introduced during the past two decades by the successors of the Ranas. For the people of a remote area like Belaspur, the immediate and primary expression of these reforms has been a dramatic expansion and reorganization of the district administration. Essentially, this has brought two kinds of benefit locally. The first relates to the substantial increase in the availability, security and conditions of government service and, more especially, to the fact that Belaspuris now have access to senior bureaucratic ranks. The second concerns the unprecedented injection of cash into the district, to pay the salaries of government employees and finance the overall costs of development. This has led to increasing monetization in the district generally, and thus stimulated the growth of commerce in the bazaar.

The attractions of these enlarged opportunities coupled with government land reforms which discourage further investment in subsistence farming have inclined some peasants to extend their range of activities outside the traditional agricultural sphere. Today, villagers own a substantial proportion of the buildings and a majority of shops in the town, and have begun to enter the upper reaches of administrative service. Those who have enjoyed the most success in these ventures are wealthy members of the highest castes. On the one hand, only they are seriously affected by ceilings on land holdings, restrictions on lending and new tenancy arrangements introduced under the land reform programme. On the other hand, they alone can afford the education needed to gain access to senior bureaucratic levels, and the capital required for investment in bazaar enterprises. Moreover, it is primarily that category of wealthy villager resident close by the town which has been best able to exploit these opportunities. The case of Bhuka village was cited as an example of the considerable advantages conferred on a peasant community by its proximity to the district capital.

Thus, in the past two decades villagers, especially those in the immediate environs of the town, have begun to encroach on what had previously been regarded as the occupational preserves of townspeople. Nevertheless, the latter have continued to maintain their strong position in the local administration, and contribute a disproportionate number of its senior ranks. Their interests in shopkeeping have expanded as well, and several have built up substantial businesses. But the intense competition they now encounter from villagers has heightened awareness of the risks inherent in an exclusive reliance on these sources of livelihood. Residents of the bazaar have, therefore, been encouraged to invest their earnings from government service and their profits from shopkeeping in land, and thus to diversify their own economy.

This rivalry has led to strong feelings of hostility between townsmen and neighbouring villagers. Despite an increasingly similar (but not yet identical) set of economic interests, they perceive themselves virtually as different species, with separate occupations, cultures and identities. One feature, emphasized particularly by villagers, is their own caste 'purity', maintained by endogamous marriage practices, in contrast to the hybridization of townsmen, occasioned by their marriages across (clean) caste lines.

The interconnectedness of households in the town fosters and encourages their unity in the face of the political rivalry which has also arisen between themselves and nearby villagers during the past twenty years. With the overthrow of the Ranas, inhabitants of the district were recruited by the Nepali Congress authorities to fill senior positions in the local administration, thus providing unprecedented positions of power and prestige. Residents of the district capital quickly established a strong foothold in the upper echelons of the new administration, while villagers, at least in the immediate aftermath of the revolution, were somewhat less well represented. For this and other reasons, there was a further polarization between bazaariyas, who became identified with the ruling Congress government, and villagers, in particular the inhabitants of Bhuka, who aligned themselves with and formed the leadership of the main opposition party in the district.

The cleavage between the two communities became even more pronounced when panchayats replaced the parliamentary system abolished in 1960, and it continues to underlie leadership struggles at every panchayat level.

Thus, at the very time they were beginning to compete for the economic benefits emerging locally as a result of programmes formulated in the kingdom's capital, other national and international events led to changes which gave this competition a sharper focus by channelling it into new political contexts.

Post-Rana currents have affected certain institutions and relationships among townspeople as well. I noted how, despite the formalization of administrative procedures, 'nepotistic' practices have replaced the traditional *chakari*—the offer of prestations in kind, over time— as being of primary significance in determining how posts are awarded locally. Broadly speaking, prospective government servants no longer need rely on creating links to outsider officials, but utilize primary, multiplex ties to locally-resident bureaucrats, who since 1951, have occupied senior positions. Townspeople clearly benefit from these developments. By virtue of their high educational qualifications they fulfil the new criteria for recruitment to jobs above menial rank. Then, those already in such employment assist their kinsmen and neighbours in the bazaar to obtain posts as these become available.

But for an individual to pursue a long-range career in the senior ranks of administrative service, which implies regular transfer out of the district, he is compelled to leave his household estate, or his share in such an estate, which with growing interests in land and commerce is a considerable equity, in the charge of a senior relative. There is evidence, tentative though it may be, that there is much more concern nowadays among the clean castes in the bazaar to delay the partition of households than there was in Rana times, when government service was insecure and held out no prospects for advancement.

These new career possibilities have not benefited bazaar untouchables, although a few Butchers have obtained (non-caste-specific) menial jobs in government service. This is due partly to their low educational achievements and partly to the fact that they must compete for jobs without the benefit of 'reserved' places, as exist, for example, in India. But I have also suggested that, on the whole, untouchables practising their traditional occupations in the district capital are able to exploit a comparatively secure occupational niche. Since 1951, especially, increasing monetization in the district, occasioned, as already noted, by the expansion of administrative activities, has enhanced their economic prospects, although each group has been differently affected by this development. The Tailors, whose services are in ever-increasing demand both within and outside the bazaar, have sought to withdraw from their relationships with hereditary clients in favour of more impersonal exchanges in a free market. The Smiths and Cobblers, for their part, now find that barter and other exchange relationships in which they traditionally participated are being rapidly replaced by cash transactions. Moreover, a significant minority of untouchable households now cultivate their own land. The overall effect has been to make these groups less dependent on clean castes than in the past. But despite their growing economic independence, they play only a passive role in local political affairs, although they remain closely aligned with other residents of the district capital. (This is in stark contrast to the untouchables of Duari who, with increasing economic self-reliance, have begun to play a more active part in village politics.)

This discussion has highlighted certain aspects of the problem of how resources which find their way into remote areas as a result of national development programmes are distributed amongst the local population. Anthropologists have pointed out that traditional peasant elites are best placed to exploit the new opportunities at the expense of the less affluent members of rural society (Rao 1963). The evidence from western Nepal suggests that when these benefits emerge in specific physical loci such as an administrative or market centre, spatial considerations perhaps even more than economic ones may determine which categories of the populace will be best poised to take advantage of their appearance. Thus, it is villagers resident in the immediate hinterland of Belaspur Bazaar who, along with townsmen, provide the overwhelming majority of district administration personnel recruited locally; together, they own virtually every private building in the bazaar, and dominate its commerce. Furthermore, they have all but monopolized contests for and positions of leadership since the end of Rana rule, first in the local party organizations and latterly in panchayats at the district level and beyond.

Thus, the notion of an 'urban field' or 'umland' (see p. 7) can be useful not only to plot the spread and nature of links between a town and its hinterland, but also to identify the manner in which new resources channelled through the town are distributed in the region at large.

The book has touched briefly on other themes, as well. One relates to the question of endogamy as a defining characteristic of a caste system. I noted that despite the close unity wrought by marriages between members of different clean castes in the district capital, townsmen regard themselves as belonging to separate ritual groups, hierarchically ranked and culturally distinct. It was argued that such marriage practices do not fundamentally affect the conceptualization of ritual difference where there are unambiguous principles of status conferment which are validated by shared values and symbols.

Inasmuch as inter-caste marriages, as distinct from those which extend or re-define the boundaries of endogamous groups, are increasingly found in urban areas (Kannan 1963), it is to be hoped that other such studies will consider further the implications of these 'deviations' from the traditional caste model.

The problem of 'inter-calary' roles was also discussed in the context of a detailed case study of a demonstration against the district governor organized by the main opposition party, led by residents of Bhuka village, to embarrass and challenge the ruling Congress party and its bazaar supporters. One fact to emerge clearly from a consideration of this event is that the kinds of dual pressures—from bureaucratic superiors, on the one hand, and kinsmen/neighbours, on the other—experienced by someone occupying an 'inter-hierarchical' position (governor, or chief) are not fundamentally different from those faced by locally resident occupants of the most menial administrative posts. Moreover, the discussion emphasized the difficulty of inferring behavioural paralysis solely from the opposition of conflicting demands or, especially, value systems to which persons may subscribe by virtue of their inter-calary roles. It underlined, rather, the wide room for manoeuvre which incumbents of such positions may, in fact, enjoy.

Anthropologists have long noted the ability of individuals to handle conflicting role sets and their concomitant values by stressing different aspects of one or the other in any given context. Indeed, Bailey offers the term 'bridge actions' to describe 'situations in which the actor may play upon the roles which he has in different systems of social relationships . . .' (1960:251). To suggest that roles which are 'inter-calary' somehow present special problems for the actor may after all be an unwarranted assumption.

Another theme which arose in the course of the narrative concerns the sociological significance of bribery. Attention was drawn to two main points. First of all, there is a need clearly to distinguish the occurrence of such behaviour from allegations of its occurrence. Accusations of bribery resemble those of witchcraft in many small-scale societies, for on the one side they provide a convenient explanation for personal failure or misfortune and, on the other, reveal relationships of hostility between accuser and accused. Secondly, I emphasized that bribery, to the extent that it takes place, occurs not haphazardly, but at points in the social structure where relationships are anomalous and thus tenuous.

It should not be necessary to stress that bribery does not arise from any natural affinity of the Nepalese for these practices. It is to some extent encouraged by a system of indirect elections above the Village level which compels an aspiring leader to build a compact political following from among a numerically limited, identifiable category of electors (a district or zonal assembly). Clearly, under a different, e.g. constituency system of voting, where large numbers of electors are involved, direct bribery is not a viable strategy (Bailey 1963a:33).

But there is a fairly substantial corpus of writing which suggests that acts termed 'bribery' occur with regularity in many developing countries, both past and present, not only in elections but in other contexts as well (see Scott 1972; L. Caplan 1971). The prevalence of bribery has been explained in a number of ways: by the lack of a national value consensus (McMullan 1961; Braibanti 1962), the vast gap between literate official and illiterate peasant (Nye 1967), or the dissociation of wealth and political power (Greenstone 1965–6). For the sociologist, the explanation might more fruitfully be sought in the process whereby face-to-face communities are absorbed into more complex societies. In the widest sense, this study has dealt with such a process.

The crucial point must surely be that as a nation begins its programme of economic development a situation is created which demands the expansion of the scale of politico-economic contexts within which individuals and groups interact. People in the most remote areas, as these chapters have made plain, are being overtaken by an economic system no longer local, but district-wide, national and even international in scope. The new political structures, such as district and national panchayats in Nepal, subsume the age-long arenas of village or sub-district. Those who compete in these new contexts are required to build and maintain relationships on grounds to a large extent outside their previous experience. How can they establish bonds with others who do not share kinship or neighbourhood, rights in land or other traditional economic enterprise? How do they forge alliances where no community of interests exists?

But the problem is not one of society merely outgrowing its traditional smallness of scale, but at the same time having, in this transitional period, few of the associational bases found in industrial countries. Cohen has recently pointed to the inadequacy of characterizing urban society as 'impersonal' and of the relationships found within it as 'overwhelmingly simplex' (1969:197–8). As societies grow technologically more advanced and urbanized, there emerge a seemingly inexhaustible range of associational frameworks through which people, and especially those with political aspirations, can develop intense and manifold ties. Thus, Lupton and Wilson (1959) have shown how Britain's 'top decision makers' are not only related to one another through kinship, but by their common educational background, club membership, leisure pursuits, and the like. Similarly, Beteille identifies the common cultural basis of certain sections of the new elites in post-independence India (1967). Such associational structures allow for the creation of relationships no less personalized or morally binding than those in small-scale communities, and equally give rise to intense loyalties, thereby effectively undermining the 'need' for bribery.

Appendix A

Government and quasi-government branches and agencies in Belaspur Bazaar

ALTHOUGH the governor and the chief district officer between them supervise and coordinate all administrative offices in the district, each office is responsible at the same time to its own central department or ministry in Kathmandu, where policy formulation and ultimate control reside. In April, 1969, the Nepalese cabinet consisted of seven ministers with portfolios divided as follows:

1. Finance, General Administration, Palace Affairs
2. Defence, Forests
3. Foreign Affairs, Health, Information and Broadcasting
4. Works, Communications, Transport, Water and Power
5. Industry and Commerce
6. Education, Law and Justice
7. Home, Panchayat, Land Reform, Food and Agriculture

The number of government offices in a district capital depends on a variety of factors such as the size and population of the district and its particular needs, the financial and manpower resources of any particular ministry or department, national development priorities, and so on. From the little information available about other administrative centres in the country, it would appear that the numbers of branches and agencies in Belaspur represent an average for the kingdom's 75 districts.

It is not my intention here to describe and analyse the Nepalese administrative structure or even a district segment of this structure. The brief outline of district offices and their activities which follows is intended only to provide some details to supplement the work on Nepal's public administration by experts such as Malhotra (1958), Goodall (1966), Shrestha (1965, 1969) and others.

The chart below presents basic data about the establishment of each branch, its budget, number of personnel, etc. This is followed by a brief description of their principal activities. I must stress that the 'ethnographic present' is 1969, and that changes have already taken place in the administration since that time.

Office	Year est. in town	No. of per- sonnel	Rank of senior official*	Budget in rupees†	Central Department or Ministry
District					
Headquarters	*c.* 1790	23	G.2	58,000 (R)	Home, Panchayat
Militia	*c.* 1790	9	N-G.3	12,000 (R)	Defence
Post Office	*c.* 1800?	42	N-G.3	71,800 (R)	Communications
Jail	*c.* 1800?	7	N-G.3	23,500 (R)	Home, Panchayat
District Court	1887	23	G.3	33,300 (R)	Law, Justice
Land Revenue	1926	15	N-G.2	22,400 (R)	Finance
Telegraph	1950	3	N-G.1	8,600 (R)	Communications
Police	1952	61	G.3	90,000 (R)	Home, Panchayat
Health Centre	1954	12	G.3	23,100 (R & D)	Health
High School	1961	8	N-G.1	16,900‡	—
Education	1962	7	N-G.1	11,700 (R)	Education
District Council					
Secretariat	1962	26	G.2	44,700 (D)§	Home, Panchayat
Class Organizations	1962	2	N-G.1	5,900 (D)	Home, Panchayat
Bank	1966	7	G.3	22,800	(Head Office)
Land Reform	1967	26	G.3	74,800 (D)	Land Reform
Malaria Eradication	1967	63	N-G.1	125,500 (D)	Health

* In the case of officials (such as the high school's head teacher) who are not members of the regular administrative establishment, ranks are approximations based on salary. G (Gazetted); N-G (Non-Gazetted); 1 (1st class); 2 (2nd class); 3 (3rd class).

† Figures given here represent total expenditures. R indicates financing under the Regular Budget, D under Development Budget.

‡ One-third is derived from a government grant; the remainder from fees and public subscription.

§ In addition, a special budget of rs 69,000 for development projects.

District headquarters

The district headquarters has a wide variety of functions in view of its role as a coordinating agency. The most important of these is responsibility for internal security. The governor thus controls the police and an undisclosed number of 'plain-clothes' agents, and enjoys powers of arrest and imprisonment under the state security laws. He also investigates charges of corruption against officials of the administration, and sends his findings either to the zonal commissioner or direct to Kathmandu for further action.

More routine matters in the charge of district headquarters include overseeing implementation of the land reform programme in the district, surveillance of retail prices in the bazaar and their control, imposition of duty on imports of manufactured goods into the district, awarding of certain contracts (such as the monopoly to distil spirits), licensing of private firearms, and issuing identity documents to persons intending to travel or work outside Nepal. The governor's office also distributes aid to persons suffering personal misfortunes as a consequence of fires, landslides, etc.

Belaspur, along with two other hill districts and two terai districts belong to a zone with its capital at Balnagar. Belaspur's chief official is also technically in charge of the zone's other hill districts, which compels him to spend a considerable amount of time visiting the district capitals, as well as Balnagar, where he reports periodically to the zonal commissioner.

Militia

Throughout the Rana period and for some years following its demise, the military garrison constituted the largest single government 'department' in Belaspur. In 1968, when most of its personnel were moved to Lakandra, there were over 100 men, under the command of a lieutenant. Until 1952, when a separate police force was set up, the garrison's functions included normal police duties, but since that time its role has been more circumscribed. In terms of everyday duties, the garrison performs largely ceremonial functions, guarding the fort and occasionally parading on national holidays. Whereas the militia was traditionally an integral part of the district headquarters—Rana governors even held high military rank, even though they had no other contact with military affairs—it has for some years now been responsible directly to Army H.Q. in the Ministry of Defence. The governor could, however, call in the militia to help deal with any situation which could not be contained by the police.

Post Office

For about 150 years Nepal's postal service was the principal means by which Kathmandu maintained contact with the outlying regions. Despite the use of wireless telegraph by the administration during the past two decades, the postal system has continued to expand along with the rate of literacy in the country. In its most recent fiscal year the Belaspur post office handled approximately 110,000 letters, representing an increase of 12·5 per cent over the previous year.

Mail is carried into and out of the district on foot in a series of relays along a network of 'lines' leading in various directions to other postal centres.

Jail

Persons held in the jail may be sent there by the district court, or by the governor under his special powers of arrest and detention. At the time of fieldwork there were 18 prisoners, including several women. The prison regime is extremely relaxed, with provision for spouses to visit for extended periods. Inmates are provided with rations and prepare meals themselves.

District Court

The district court is the lowest formal judicial body in the country's legal system, although in fact it deals with many cases arising from the efforts at mediation and arbitration of various informal and quasi-legal agents (e.g. headmen) at village level. Decisions of the district court may be referred to an appeal court in Doti, and thence to the Supreme court in Kathmandu.

Although increasingly government legal officers are being attached to district courts as the range of offences classified as crimes against the state increases, the overwhelming majority of cases heard in the Belaspur court are still privately prosecuted. Occasionally, private 'pleaders' represent clients (see p. 117) but generally the judge has before him the written arguments of both sides as well as any supporting documents, and questions the litigants directly, in addition to any witnesses he chooses to call. His judgements tend, on the whole, to apportion blame between the disputants, often in equal measure, and refrain from finding one party totally at fault and the other completely innocent. The result is usually a compromise solution which will favour neither side unduly. It is not uncommon, therefore, for fines to be imposed on both sides in a dispute. Imprisonment is seldom resorted to: in a recent year during which some 500 cases were heard, jail sentences totalled only three years and 15 days, while litigants were fined approximately rs 10,000. District courts in Nepal, therefore, unlike those in India influenced by British legal custom, do not differ radically in their approach from the traditional methods of dispute settlement found in the rural areas (see Cohn 1959).

A perusal of the court diary over a six-month period in 1969 reveals that the largest single category of cases—close to half—concerned the dissolution of marriages. Over a third (35·5 per cent) involved divorce proceedings, many instituted by women who only recently have earned the right to do so. An additional 12·1 per cent of court cases arose from married women leaving their husbands for other men. Such a situation entitles (indeed compels) the cuckold to sever the existing marriage tie and claim compensation from the woman's new 'husband', or, in certain circumstances, from her natal family (see L. Caplan 1970:84 ff).

By contrast with the high proportion of marriage disputes, a surprisingly low ratio (15·7 per cent) of cases which came before the court pertained to land and debts. This is probably because disagreements over such matters are now resolved in the course of registering land and credit dealings with the land reform office. It is likely, however, that much of the litigation classified as being concerned with the clarification of kinship ties ('*samanda*')—7·6 per cent of cases before the court—deals, in fact, with disagreements about claims to inheritance of land and other property.

Since caste is no longer recognized in law, conflicts over ritual status now appear before the court as slander ('*bejatti*'): 12·9 per cent of cases were of this kind. Finally, disputes classified as assault (4·8 per cent), theft (2·0 per cent), and rape (2·4 per cent) were heard by the court, as were a number of miscellaneous disputes which together made up 7·0 per cent of all cases.

Land Revenue

The principal function of this office is to collect land taxes. Traditionally, this was done through special headmen (see Chapter 8) but nowadays responsibility for collection lies with the Village council, which receives a commission of five per cent. All transfers of land by sale or mortgage must be registered with the revenue authorities. In addition, officials may, after investigating claims, decide to grant a commutation of taxes on fields carried away by landslides, a not infrequent occurrence during the monsoons. They are, moreover, still called upon to help settle disputes over boundaries or involving inheritance claims, but this mediation no longer, as in Rana times, carries the weight of law, and the central department from time to time reminds district officials to refrain from involving themselves in such matters. One other important function of the land revenue office has been abolished during the past few years: traditionally, the revenue branch acted as 'banker' for all government offices in the district, holding and disbursing money as required (during the Rana era, no branch could keep more than rs 500 in its premises, the surplus having to be deposited in the revenue office). In 1966, with a fiscal reorganization of the administrative service, each branch took complete control of its own financial affairs.

Radio Telegraph

First established in 1950, at the very end of the Rana period, the country's radio telegraph network was expanded with foreign technical assistance in the 1960s. Belaspur's new post, built in 1965, is linked to Kathmandu through its area control at Balnagar in the terai, as well as directly to other centres in the far western hills. Contact with these stations is made at fixed times during the day or week, when messages are sent and received (or rather shouted back and forth). Operators are trained for several months in area centres before being posted to wireless stations.

Police

With the establishment of this force in 1952, police assumed responsibility for the maintenance of order in the district, previously the main preoccupation of the militia. An 'armed branch' provides guards for the district headquarters, land revenue office, bank, and jail. In addition to police headquarters in the bazaar, there are two small posts in other parts of the district.

Health Centre

Prior to 1954, the town and surrounding countryside had to rely for medical help entirely on ayurvedic physicians either attached to the military garrison or practising privately in the bazaar. The establishment of the health centre, therefore, introduced the population to 'western' medicine. For most of 1969 the person in charge was a fully qualified physician, but he was only the second medical doctor posted to Belaspur's health centre since its inception (the previous one served for only a few months). For much of the time the centre has been run by a health assistant, who is trained over a period of two years in para-medical techniques. The main problem is not the quality of its personnel but the fact that the centre is constantly short of medicines and drugs. In an annual budget of some rs 23,000, less than rs 3,000 is spent on medical supplies. This may explain the recent decision by the Village council which encompasses the town to open a public ayurvedic clinic.

In 1968, a programme, assisted by development funds, to vaccinate the population against smallpox was introduced. Although under the aegis of the health centre, a team of vaccinators has been specially recruited and trained for the task.

High School

Although not officially a state institution, Belaspur's high school (grades 6–10) follows a set curriculum leading to the country-wide School Leaving Certificate examination, a pre-requisite for university entrance. Teaching includes Nepali, Sanskrit, English, geography, law and history of Nepal, mathematics and science. Of the 153 students, all but six are fee-paying. The head teacher is answerable to a Management Committee, the most important members of which are the District council president and the chief district officer, who is nominally responsible for education above primary level.

Education

Although there was for a time an education section within the district headquarters and later the district council secretariat, the establishment of a special office in the district to deal with primary schools signalled the intention of the government to undertake a major programme of educational expansion. The office recruits candidates for teacher training courses, maintains liaison with school management committees in the villages, and seeks to promote common standards and curriculum.

District Council Secretariat

Several years following the overthrow of the Ranas (*c.* 1956) a village development service was established within the district headquarters to engage in agricultural, educational and public health programmes. In

Belaspur its activities were sporadic and made little impact (in 1969 few people could recall its existence). With the creation of a panchayat system, dedicated to the introduction of 'self-help' development schemes, this organization was dissolved and the new secretariat undertook supervision of the development programme in the district. Although meant primarily to execute and to provide advice and technical assistance for projects decided upon by Village and District councils, the Secretariat, by virtue of its monopoly of expertise and control of the necessary funds, plays a major part in the actual decision-making process (see Chapter 10).

In the context of Nepal's development programme, the Secretariat also includes among its responsibilities the operation of schools beyond primary level, the collating of census records gathered by Village councils, the running of a library service in the district capital, the organization of Village and District council elections, as well as the nominal supervision of all government agencies in the district capital other than those concerned with defence, internal security, and land reform.

Class Organizations

Along with the establishment of a panchayat system, the government created a number of 'class organizations' to represent the interests of youth, women, farmers, ex-servicemen, students, children and labourers. Only the first four of these organizations have been established in Belaspur, and this office functions to channel communications from the national executives of the class organizations to their officers in the district, supervise periodic elections and maintain records of personnel, fee collections, etc.

Bank

This is a branch of a government-owned commercial bank. Aside from handling monetary transfers for most government offices in the district capital, its main concern is provision of credit for agricultural and commercial enterprises. Of the rs 132,500 loaned in its last fiscal year, 72 per cent went to farmers, and 26 per cent to merchants. The bank has also begun encouraging people to open savings or current accounts, but it has achieved a modicum of success only among administrators and merchants.

Land Reform

The land reforms suggested in the Lands Act of 1964 (see p. 133) and subsequent legislation were introduced at first in the terai and only reached the far western hills in early 1967. This office has as its primary task the collection and maintenance of up-to-date records of land-holdings, tenancy agreements and credit dealings of every resident in the district as well as the implementation of the compulsory savings scheme. In the absence of a proper cadastral survey, the determination of land areas is primarily based on statements given by individual owners of the amount of seed sewn in each field and the translation of this figure into an estimate of its size. In consequence, much of the work of land reform officials involves the settlement of conflicting claims.

Malaria Eradication

There has been a systematic programme to eradicate malaria in Nepal since at least 1961, although no organization was established in Belaspur until several years later. The bazaar is the headquarters of an area office—areas are not synonymous with districts—comprising four segments, one of which is also centred in the district capital. Every house in low-lying regions where the disease occurs is periodically sprayed, and offices contain basic facilities for detection by blood sampling of infected persons.

Appendix B

Grain production and consumption

FOLLOWING the practice adopted in my earlier study of east Nepal I have given land measurements in terms of productivity. All production figures have been translated into units of edible grain. In doing so, I have followed the calculations of local cultivators: they assume that paddy with the husks removed yields half its measure in rice, while maize off the cob, millet and wheat yield more or less full measure of edible food. A unit is the amount of edible grain (rice, wheat, maize or millet) a person over 14 years of age eats in a year. Bazaariyas, like villagers, eat two meals a day, but consume about one-third less than the latter, i.e., one and one-third *mana* (pounds) daily (see P. Caplan 1972:29). A child 10–14 years consumes half this amount, one aged 3–9 years, one-quarter. Children under three years old may be disregarded. Thus a household containing two adults and two children, 11 and 5 years old, would require 2¾ units of grain to meet their normal annual food requirements. A unit therefore equals approximately 480 *mana* or 60 *pathi* or 3 *muri*.

Appendix C

The profits of shopkeeping

MERCHANTS in Belaspur Bazaar do not keep books other than credit lists, and therefore have no precise idea of the profitability of their businesses. The estimates given in Table 21 of net profits of tea shops are based on approximate costs of raw materials (tea, milk, sugar and firewood) set against the merchants' statements about daily sales. Where tea shops also carry items of general merchandise, profits on these are estimated in the same way as for cloth and general shops.

Here the key figure is annual investment in stock. Since sources of supply are so distant, and journeys can only take place during the comparatively brief cool, dry season, shopkeepers are unable to make more than two trips a year to purchase goods, and many make only one. These merchants, as well as those who do not make the journey themselves, but are supplied by Jorbaji itinerant traders, must attempt to lay in stocks for the entire period (April–November) during which the bazaar is effectively cut off from its commodity sources in the plains (although the monsoons end in late September, no journeys are undertaken until after the paddy harvest). Because of limited financial resources all but a handful of the largest merchants accumulate barely adequate supplies for the coming months, and not a few shops are forced to close for lack of merchandise a month or two before the trading cycle is complete. It is therefore possible to reckon on what Mines calls a 'capital turnover'—the length of time required for sales to equal the value of working capital (1972:48)—every twelve months. In other words, I assume that in any year a shop will sell its entire stock. The figures given in the table, then, are based, in accordance with the statements of informants, on a net profit of 25 per cent of gross sales, i.e., the total annual investment in merchandise marked up by 50 per cent.

References

ABRAHAMS, R. G. 1961. Kahama township, western province, Tanganyika. In A. Southall (ed), *Social change in modern Africa*, London: O.U.P. for the International African Institute.

ALBROW, M. 1970. *Bureaucracy*, London: Pall Mall.

ATAL, Y. 1968. *The changing frontiers of caste*, Delhi: National.

BAILEY, F. G. 1957. *Caste and the economic frontier*, Manchester: U.P.

— 1960. *Tribe, caste, and nation*, Manchester: U.P.

— 1963. 'Closed social stratification in India', *European journal of sociology*, IV, 107–24.

— 1963a. *Politics and social change*, Berkeley and Los Angeles: University of California Press.

— 1969. *Stratagems and spoils*, Oxford: Blackwell.

BARTH, F. 1962. The system of social stratification in Swat, North Pakistan. In E. R. Leach (ed), *Aspects of Caste in south India, Ceylon, and North-west Pakistan*, Cambridge Papers in Social Anthropology, 2, Cambridge; U.P.

BAYLEY, D. H. 1961. The effects of corruption in a developing nation. In A. Amitai (ed), *A sociological reader in complex organizations*, New York: Holt, Rinehart and Winston.

BERREMAN, G. D. 1960. 'Caste in India and the United States', *American journal of sociology*, 66, 120–7.

— 1963. 'Caste and community development', *Human organization*, 22, 90–4.

— 1967. Stratification, pluralism and interaction: a comparative analysis of caste. In A. de Reuck and J. Knight (eds), *Caste and race: comparative approaches*, London: Churchill.

BETEILLE, A. 1967. Elites, status groups, and caste in modern India. In P. Mason (ed), *India and Ceylon: unity and diversity*, London: O.U.P.

BOISSEVAIN, J. 1971. 'Second thoughts on quasi-groups, categories and coalitions', *Man* (N.S.), 6, 468–72.

— 1972. 'Quasi-groups, categories and coalitions', *Man* (N.S.), 7, 644–5.

BOSE, A. 1964. 'A note on the definition of "town" in the Indian census: 1901–61', *The Indian economic and social history review*, 1, 84–94.

BRAIBANTI, R. 1962. 'Reflections on bureaucratic corruption', *Public administration*, 40, 357–72.

CAPLAN, L. 1970. *Land and social change in east Nepal: a study of Hindu-tribal relations*, London: Routledge and Kegan Paul; Berkeley: University of California Press.

— 1970a. 'Education policy in Nepal', *Venture*, 22, 8–11.

— 1971. 'Cash and kind: two media of "bribery" in Nepal', *Man* (N.S.), 6, 266–78.

— 1972. 'The multiplication of social ties: the strategy of credit transactions in east Nepal', *Economic development and cultural change*, 20, 691–702.

— 1974. Inter-caste marriages in a Nepalese town. In C. von Furer-Haimendorf (ed), *Contributions to the anthropology of Nepal*, London: Aris and Phillips.

CAPLAN, P. 1972. *Priests and cobblers: a study of social change in a Hindu village in western Nepal*, San Francisco: Chandler.

— 1973. 'Ascetics in western Nepal', *Eastern anthropologist*, 26, 173–81.

CAVENAGH, O. 1851. *Rough notes on the State of Nepal, its government, army and resources*. Calcutta: W. Palmer.

COHEN, A. 1969. *Custom and politics in urban Africa*, Berkeley and Los Angeles: University of California Press.

COHEN, R. and J. MIDDLETON, 1970. *From tribe to nation in Africa: studies in incorporation processes*, Scranton: Chandler.

COHN, B. S. 1959. 'Some notes on law and change in North India', *Economic development and cultural change*, 8, 79–93.

COHN, B. S. and M. MARRIOTT, 1958. 'Networks and centres in the integration of Indian civilization', *Journal of social research*, I, 1–9.

DUMONT, L. 1964. 'Marriage in India: the present state of the question. Postscript to part one', *Contributions to Indian sociology*, 7, 77–98.

ELDER, J. W. 1970. Rajpur: change in the jajmani system of an Uttar Pradesh village. In K. Ishwaran (ed), *Change and continuity in India's villages*, New York: Columbia University Press.

EPSTEIN, A. L. 1967. 'Urbanization and social change in Africa', *Current Anthropology*, 8, 275–95.

FALLERS, L. 1955. 'The predicament of the modern African chief: an instance from Uganda', *American anthropologist*, 57, 290–305.

FIRTH, R. 1967. Themes in economic anthropology: a general comment. In R. Firth (ed), *Themes in economic anthropology*, ASA Mono. 6, London: Tavistock.

FOX, R. G. 1969. *From Zamindar to ballot box: community change in a north Indian market town*, Ithaca: Cornell University Press.

FREED, S. A. and R. S. FREED, 1964. 'Spirit possession as illness in a north Indian village', *Ethnology*, 3, 152–71.

FURER-HAIMENDORF, C. VON 1956. 'Elements of Newar social structure', *Journal of the Royal Anthropological Institute*, 82, 15–38.

— 1957. 'The inter-relations of castes and ethnic groups in Nepal', *Bulletin of the School of Oriental and African Studies*, XX, 243–53.

— 1962. 'Caste in the multi-ethnic society of Nepal', *Contributions to Indian sociology*, 6, 12–32.

— 1964. Comment on Dumont, L. 'Marriage in India', *Contributions to Indian sociology*, 7, 99–102.

— 1971. 'Status and interaction among the high Hindu castes of Nepal' *Eastern anthropologist*, 24, 7–24.

GABORIEAU, M. 1972. 'Muslims in the Hindu kingdom of Nepal', *Contributions to Indian Sociology* (N.S.), VI, 84–105.

GILLION, K. L. 1968. *Ahmedabad: a study in Indian urban history*. Berkeley: University of California Press.

GINSBERG, M. 1958. 'Social change', *British journal of sociology*, 9, 205–29.

GLUCKMAN, M. 1968. Inter-hierarchical roles: professional and party ethics in tribal areas in south and central Africa. In M. J. Swartz (ed), *Local level politics*, Chicago: Aldine.

— 1968a. Foreword to N. R. Sheth *The social framework of an Indian factory*, Manchester: University Press.

GOODALL, M. 1966. Administrative change in Nepal. In R. Braibanti (ed), *Asian bureaucratic systems emergent from the British imperial tradition*, Durham: Duke University Press.

GREENSTONE, J. D. 1965–6. 'Corruption and self-interest in Kampala and Nairobi: a comment on local politics in east Africa', *Comparative studies in society and history*, 8, 199–210.

HARPER, E. B. 1959. 'Two systems of economic exchange in India'. *American anthropologist*, 61, 760–78.

HAZLEHURST, L. W. 1968. 'The middle range city in India', *Asian survey*, 8, 539–52.

HEADY, F. 1966. *Bureaucracies in developing countries: internal roles and external assistance*. Comparative administrative group; American society for Public Administration (Occasional papers).

HITCHCOCK, J. T. 1966. *The Magars of Banyan Hill*, New York: Holt, Rinehart and Winston.

JANAKI, V. A. and Z. A. SAYED 1962. *The geography of Padra town*, Baroda: M. Sayajiro University Geographical Series No. 1.

JOSHI, B. L. and L. E. ROSE 1966. *Democratic innovations in Nepal*, Berkeley and Los Angeles: University of California Press.

KANNAN, C. T. 1963. *Intercaste and inter-community marriages in India*, Bombay: Allied.

KARVE, I. and J. S. RANADIVE 1965. *The social dynamics of a growing town and its surrounding area*, Poona: Deccan College, Building Centenary and Silver Jubilee Series, No. 29.

KOLENDA, P. M. 1968. Region, caste, and family structure: a comparative study of the Indian 'joint' family. In M. Singer and B. S. Cohn (eds) *Structure and change in Indian society*, Chicago: Aldine.

KUMAR, S. 1967. *Rana polity in Nepal: origin and growth*, Bombay: Asia Publishing House.

KUPER, A. 1970. 'Gluckman's village headman', *American anthropologist*, 72, 355–58.

KUPER, L. and M. G. SMITH (eds) *Pluralism in Africa*, Berkeley: University of California Press.

LANDON, P. 1928. *Nepal* (2 vols.) London: Constable.

LA PALOMBARA, J. 1963. *Bureaucracy and political development*, Princeton: University Press.

LEACH, E. R. 1954. *Political systems of highland Burma*, London: Bell and Sons.
— 1962. Introduction: What should we mean by caste? In E. R. Leach (ed), *Aspects of caste in south India, Ceylon and North-west Pakistan*, Cambridge papers in social anthropology, No. 2, Cambridge: University Press.
— 1967. *Caste, class and slavery: the taxonomic problem*. In A. de Reuck and J. Knight (eds). *Caste and race: comparative approaches*, London: Churchill.

LITTLE, K. 1959. Introduction to Special number on Urbanism in West Africa, *The sociological review*, 7, 5–12.

LUPTON, T. and S. WILSON 1959. 'Background and connections of top decision-makers', *Manchester School of economic and social studies*, 27, 33–51.

254 *Administration and Politics in a Nepalese Town*

LYNCH, O. 1969. *The politics of untouchability*, New York: Columbia University Press.

MCDOUGAL, C. 1968. *Village and household economy in far western Nepal*, Kirtipur, Nepal: Tribhuvan University.

MCMULLAN, M. 1961. 'A theory of corruption', *Sociological review* (N.S.), 9, 181–201.

MACFARLANE, A. D. J. 1972. *Population and economy in central Nepal: a study of the Gurungs*. Unpublished Ph.D. thesis, University of London.

MAIR, L. 1969. *Witchcraft*, London: Weidenfeld and Nicolson (World University Library).

MAHENDRA, H.M. KING 1961. New Year's Day Message, April 13, 1961. In *On to a New Era: some historic addresses by H.M. King Mahendra*, Kathmandu: Department of Publicity and Broadcasting.

MALHOTRA, R. C. 1958. 'Public administration in Nepal', *Indian journal of public administration*, 4, 451–64.

MANDELBAUM, D. 1970. *Society in India*, Berkeley: University of California Press.

MAYER, A. C. 1963. 'Some political implications of community development in India', *European journal of sociology*, 4, 86–106.

— 1966. The significance of quasi-groups in the study of complex societies. In M. Banton (ed), *The social anthropology of complex societies* (ASA Monograph 4), London: Tavistock.

— 1972. 'Quasi-group or coalition?' *Man* (N.S.), 7, 317.

MIDDLETON, J. 1966. *The effects of economic development on traditional political systems in Africa south of the Sahara*, The Hague: Mouton.

MIHALY, E. B. 1965. *Foreign aid and politics in Nepal: a case study*, New York: O.U.P.

MINES, M. 1972. *Muslim merchants: the economic behaviour of an Indian Muslim community*, New Delhi: K. R. Seshagiri Rao, for the Shri Ram Centre for Industrial Relations and Human Resources.

NICHOLAS, R. 1968. Structures of politics in the villages of southern Asia. In M. Singer and B. S. Cohn (eds) *Structure and change in Indian society*, Chicago: Aldine.

NYE, J. S. 1967. 'Corruption and political development: a cost-benefit analysis', *American political science review*, 61, 417–27.

OJHA, D. P. and D. WEISS 1972. *Regional analysis of Kosi Zone/eastern Nepal*. Berlin and Kathmandu: German Development Institute and (Nepal) Centre for Economic Development and Administration.

PARKIN, D. J. 1972. *Palms, wine and witnesses: public spirit and private gain in an African farming community*, San Francisco: Chandler.

PIGNÈDE, B. 1966. *Les Gurungs: une population himalayenne du Nepal*, Paris, La Haye: Mouton.

POCOCK, D. F. 1957. 'Difference in east Africa: a study of caste and religion in modern Indian society', *Southwestern journal of anthropology*, 13, 289–300.

— 1962. 'Notes on jajmani relationships', *Contributions to Indian sociology*, VI, 78–95.

— 1972. *Kanbi and Patidar: a study of the Patidar community of Gujarat*, Oxford: Clarendon.

RAO, M. S. A. 1963. Rural development programmes—a sociological analysis. In M. S. Gore (ed) *Problems of rural change*, Delhi: University of Delhi School of Social Work.

— 1968. 'Occupational diversification and joint household organization', *Contributions to Indian sociology* (N.S.), II, 98–111.

REGMI, D. R. 1961. *Modern Nepal*, Calcutta: K. L. Mukhopadhyay.

REGMI, M. C. 1963. *Land tenure and taxation in Nepal*. Vol. 1: *The State as landlord: raikar tenure*, Berkeley: University of California Institute of International Studies.

— 1964. *Land tenure and taxation in Nepal*. Vol. II: *The land grant system: Birta tenure*, Berkeley: University of California Institute of International Studies.

— 1965. *Land tenure and taxation in Nepal*. Vol. III: *The Jagir, Rakam and Kipat tenure systems*, Berkeley: University of California Institute of International Studies.

RIGGS, F. W. 1964. *Administration in developing countries: the theory of prismatic society*, Boston: Houghton and Mifflin.

ROSSER, C. 1966. Social mobility in the Newar caste system. In C. von Furer-Haimendorf (ed), *Caste and kin in Nepal, India and Ceylon*, Bombay: Asia Publishing House.

Sample census of agriculture 1962. Kathmandu: Government of Nepal.

SCOTT, J. C. 1972. *Comparative political corruption*, Englewood Cliffs: Prentice-Hall.

SHRESTHA, M. K. 1965. *A handbook of public administration in Nepal*, Kathmandu: Ministry of Panchayat Affairs.

— 1969. *Trends in public administration in Nepal*, Kathmandu: Ministry of Information and Broadcasting.

SINGH, K. N. 1959. 'Functions and functional classification of towns in Uttar Pradesh', *National geographical journal of India*, 5, 121–48.

SINGH, R. L. 1955. *Banaras: a study in urban geography*, Banaras: Nand Kishore.

SINGH, R. L. and S. M. SINGH 1960. 'Mungra-Badshahpur: a rurban settlement in the Ganga-Ghagara Doab west', *National geographical journal of India*, 6, 200–6.

SINHA, D. P. 1968. *Culture change in an intertribal market*, London: Asia Publishing House.

SJOBERG, G. 1960. *The preindustrial city: past and present*, New York: Free Press.

— 1969. The rise and fall of cities: a theoretical perspective. In G. Breese (ed) *The city in newly developing countries: readings in urbanism and urbanization*, Englewood: Prentice-Hall.

STIRLING, P. 1968. Impartiality and personal morality. In J. G. Peristiany (ed), *Contributions to Mediterranean sociology*, Paris, The Hague: Mouton.

SWARTZ, M. J. 1968. *Local level politics*, Chicago: Aldine.

TAUB, R. P. 1969. *Bureaucrats under stress: administrators and administration in an Indian state*, Berkeley: University of California Press.

THORNER, D. 1953. 'The village panchayat as a vehicle of change', *Economic development and cultural change*, 2, 209–15.

TUCCI, G. 1962. *Nepal: the discovery of the Malla*, London: Allen and Unwin.

T'UNG-TSU CH'U 1962. *Local government in China under the Ch'ing*, Harvard East Asian Studies, No. 9. Cambridge: Harvard University Press.

TURNER, R. L. 1931. *Nepali Dictionary*, London: Routledge and Kegan Paul.

UBEROI, J. P. SINGH 1968. 'District administration in the northern highlands of Afghanistan', *Sociological Bulletin*, 17, 65–90.

VINCENT, J. 1971. *African elite: the big men of a small town*, New York: Columbia University Press.

WARD, B. E. 1960. 'Cash or credit? An examination of some implications of peasant commercial production with special reference to the multiplicity of traders and middlemen', *Economic development and cultural change*, 8, 148–63.

WATSON, W. 1958. *Tribal cohesion in a money economy*, Manchester: University Press.

YALMAN, N. 1962. The flexibility of caste principles in a Kandyan community. In E. R. Leach (ed) *Aspects of caste in south India, Ceylon and North-west Pakistan*, Cambridge Papers in social anthropology, No. 2, Cambridge: University Press.

Indexes

Author Index

Abrahams, R. G., 2, 10n.
Albrow, M., 52-3
Atal, Y., 145

Bailey, F. G., 9, 80, 197, 230n., 238
Barth, F., 145
Bayley, D. H., 230n.
Berreman, G. D., 145-6, 200n.
Beteille, A., 240
Boissevain, J., 200n.
Bose, A., 1
Braibanti, R., 239

Caplan, L., 6, 102, 122n., 132, 142, 147n., 183, 199n., 223, 238, 244
Caplan, P., 18, 30n., 44, 48, 51, 62, 78n., 132, 133, 148n., 190, 250
Cavenagh, O., 31, 32, 165
Cohen, A., 231, 239
Cohen, R., 9
Cohn, B. S., 10n., 244

Dumont, L., 142

Elder, J. W., 92
Epstein, A. L., 10n.

Fallers, L., 169, 170
Firth, R., 53n.
Fox, R. G., 2, 31, 97, 112, 121n., 148n.
Freed, S. A., 166
Freed, R. S., 166
Furer-Haimendorf, C. von, 15, 30n., 141, 142-3

Gaborieau, M., 30n.
Gillion Gillian, K. N., 3
Ginsberg, M., 7
Gluckman, M., 168, 169, 173n.
Goodall, M., 31, 37, 55n., 241
Greenstone, J. D., 239

Harper, E. B., 91
Hazlehurst, L. W., 103
Heady, F., 8
Hitchock, J. T., 122n.
Hodgson, B. H., 53n.

Janaki, B. L., 3, 7

Joshi, B. L., 154, 157, 173n., 174n., 199n., 212, 213

Kannan, C. T., 237
Karve, I., 2, 3, 4
Kolenda, P. M., 68, 69
Kumar, S., 31, 34, 43n.
Kuper, A., 8, 170
Kuper, L., 9

Landon, P., 147n.
La Palombara, J., 52
Leach, E. R., 80, 144-5, 158
Little, K., 10n.
Lupton, T., 239
Lynch, O., 68

McDougal, C., 78n., 130, 132
McMullan, M., 239
Macfarlane, A. D., 73, 132
Mahendra, H. M. King, 184
Mair, L., 230n.
Malhotra, R. C., 32, 211, 241
Mandelbaum, D., 145
Marriott, M., 10n.
Mauss, M., 53n.
Mayer, A. C., 47, 200n., 217, 218, 230n.
Middleton, J., 4, 9
Mihaly, E. B., 132
Mines, M., 99, 250

Nicholas, R., 153
Nye, J. S., 230n., 239

Ojha, D. P., 230n.

Parkin, D. J., 10n.
Pignède, B., 122n.
Pocock, D. F., 26, 91-2, 93n., 108, 145

Ranadive, J. S., 2, 3, 4
Rao, M. S. A., 119, 237
Regmi, D. R., 17
Regmi, M. C., 17, 27, 122n., 173n.
Riggs, F. W., 8
Rose, L. E., 154, 157, 173n., 174n., 199n., 212, 213
Rosser, C., 25, 26, 30n.

Sayed, Z. A., 3, 7

Subject Index